An AI Handbook for Primary Education

I0880408

Staring at a blinking cursor on a Sunday night? Wondering if your students are just becoming experts at copy-pasting? Welcome to the staffroom.

In the time it takes to laminate a set of flashcards, the world of education has shifted. Artificial Intelligence has landed on our desks, and while the headlines are full of 'robot teachers,' the reality in the primary classroom is much messier, and a lot more interesting.

This is not a technical manual; it is a front-line guide for the teachers who deal with wet play, glue-stick shortages, and the daily magic of a child's 'aha!' moment. Whether you are a tentative Explorer, an efficient Builder, or a pedagogical Artisan, this book is your pragmatic co-pilot. Inside, you will discover:

- **The 'Sandwich' Model:** How to keep the human firmly in the loop so AI remains a scaffold, not a shortcut.
- **Project-Based Learning:** How projects and AI synthesise perfectly.
- **Truth Detectives:** Practical ways to teach KS2 students to hunt for 'hallucinations' and navigate a post-truth world.
- **Unplugged Early Years:** Building foundations of agency and logic for our littlest learners – without a single screen in sight.

We are not being replaced; we are being promoted. It is time to hand over the boring paperwork to your new digital assistant, so you can get back to the reason you joined this profession: The children. Packed with practical strategies and grounded in pedagogy, this book proves that the more artificial the world becomes, the more our human skills – empathy, curiosity, and professional judgment – become the ultimate superpower.

Tom Millinchip is an experienced educator and Deputy Head with 15 years' experience in primary international schools, specialising in curriculum design, assessment, and fostering innovative teaching practices. He has been proactive in integrating educational technology and digital tools throughout a 15-year teaching career and actively researches and educates fellow educators and parents on the practical applications, benefits, and ethical considerations of AI tools.

An AI Handbook for Primary Education

A Human-Centred and Ethics-Led Approach

Tom Millinchip

Routledge
Taylor & Francis Group
LONDON AND NEW YORK

Cover image: © Getty Images

First published 2027
by Routledge
4 Park Square, Milton Park, Abingdon, Oxon OX14 4RN

and by Routledge
605 Third Avenue, New York, NY 10158

Routledge is an imprint of the Taylor & Francis Group, an informa business

British Library Cataloguing-in-Publication Data
A catalogue record for this book is available from the British Library

ISBN: 978-1-041-24153-9 (hbk)
ISBN: 978-1-041-24149-2 (pbk)
ISBN: 978-1-003-74037-7 (ebk)

DOI: 10.4324/9781003740377

Typeset in Palatino
by Newgen Publishing UK

Dedication

To all the primary school teachers out there – you are amazing, keep it going.

To my family who supported me through the whole process.

Contents

A Personal Note on AI

This book is about AI. It would be a strange, perhaps even dishonest irony to write these pages in an AI vacuum, ignoring the very tool I am discussing and doing the opposite to the advice I am handing out.

I haven't just written about AI; I have lived it throughout the process. I'm proud of that. I do, however, practice what I preach. I have used these models, not as a 'writer-in-chief' but as a tireless research partner and a sounding board for my own intuition.

Every sentence you read, every argument I make, and every 'wart' in the prose belongs to me or comes from strong evidence and research. I have used AI to dig deeper, to stress-test my logic, and to navigate the vast sea of data, but the soul of this work is human.

During the process, I have leant on particular AI tools. These were a personal preference due to accessibility and what I use on a daily basis.

The Toolkit:

Google Gemini (Pro 2.5 & 3.0): My primary workspace. I built custom 'Gems' to act as specialised consultants, helping me distil the real-world sentiments of primary school teachers across the globe.

Claude (Opus 4.6): My second opinion. I value Anthropic's approach to constitutional AI and the interactions with the Claude model. I used Claude to challenge my perspectives and to provide a different lens.

NotebookLM: My research anchor. Because it operates on a RAG (Retrieval-Augmented Generation) framework, it allowed me to upload specific sources and break down research without losing the thread of the original truth.

Canva AI: My student-facing AI tool, used for exploring the nuances of bias and imagery.

In short, the tools provided the map, but I did the walking. This book is a product of that partnership: A human-led exploration of a machine-assisted future. I hope you find the results as illuminating as I found the process.

Acknowledgements

Writing a book about the future of education while actively working in the present of it is not a solitary endeavour. It requires a community of thinkers, educators, and exceptionally patient loved ones.

The Sounding Boards and Mapmakers A profound thank you to the educational pioneers and thinkers who generously gave me their time across time zones – whether over coffee, video calls, or detailed email threads. To Thom Markham, Phillip Alcock, Kunal Dalal, Nneka McGee, Amelia King, Tina Austin, and John Broadbent: Your willingness to debate, refine, and challenge my ideas helped shape the very core of this book. Thank you also to Kitty and George for reading over some of the chapters.

I am equally indebted to the broader community of mapmakers whose published work provided the theoretical bedrock for my research: Ethan Mollick, Dan Fitzpatrick, Sal Khan, Dr. Joy Buolamwini, and Mo Gawdat. Thank you for charting the frontiers of this new landscape and reminding us that the human must always remain in the loop.

The Real-World Practitioners This book was forged in the reality of the primary classroom, and it would not exist without the global educators who generously shared their classroom triumphs, fears, and 'lightbulb moments' with me. To Allandra Russell, Matt Karabinos, Michael Lubelfeld, Claire Walmsley, Ben Davies, and Bethan Ware: Thank you for pulling back the curtain on your own teaching. The 'Jims,' 'Chloes,' and 'Elenas' of this book are reflections of your passion and reality.

The Windsor School Community A very special mention must go to my incredible colleagues at Windsor School Bahamas. To the Head of School, Ben Fox, thank you for your unwavering support and for giving me the space and encouragement to explore these ideas. To the entire staff – thank you for your endless patience, your willingness to listen to me go on and on about AI in the corridors, and your readiness to navigate the daily magic and 'wet play' chaos of primary teaching alongside new technologies. You provided the heartbeat of this manual.

The Publishing Team and Permissions Partners A sincere thank you to all involved in the publishing process, from my initial exploratory email, the submission of abstracts and organising readers, to the fine-tuning of the content and formatting. Thank you to all.

The Personal Anchor Finally, to my wife Rosanna and my children Beatrice and Juliette. Thank you for tolerating my Sundays stolen by AI, my late nights at the keyboard, and my endless dinner-table monologues about chatbots and algorithms. You are my grounding force. You remind me daily that no matter how good the machine gets at writing pirate shanties or summarising text, it will never replace the messy, wonderful, and entirely irreplaceable reality of our human connection.

Introduction

It's the beginning of term, the smell of coffee and tea is in the air, and the excited chatter is bubbling away. The induction day schedule has been released and, sandwiched between 'Fire Drill' and 'Safeguarding Updates,' you see 'AI Literacy.'

For some, that line sparks a jolt of excitement. It represents a chance to explore the new kid on the educational technology block. For others, it's a quiet sigh, another trend to navigate on top of an already overflowing plate. And for many, it triggers a genuine sense of dread, a feeling that the heart of teaching is being threatened by soulless technology.

Whether you are an 'early adopter,' a seasoned sceptic, or someone who prefers the smell of a brand new novel to a glowing screen, this book is for you. Whichever one of these you are, or perhaps even another category, I hope that you will take away something valuable from these pages. You have already chosen to open the cover and give it a go, showing that you understand that a shift in education is happening and you want to explore it further. So, welcome!

I think we are at an important juncture. AI is no longer something we can hide away from and hope it goes away. We have moved from the novelty phase to the serious use phase. The changes in the past 3 years in the world of AI have been monumental, and those of you who stepped away a couple of years ago need to come back into the fold. As Matt Shumer (2026), tech CEO, said recently:

> "If you tried ChatGPT in 2023 or early 2024 and thought 'this makes stuff up' or 'this isn't that impressive', you were right. Those early versions were genuinely limited. They hallucinated. They confidently said things that were nonsense."

In school terms, we have moved on from the fidget spinner phase to something that actually belongs in the curriculum. He goes on to make the point that two years ago in AI terms is ancient history.

At this point, you may be thinking, who is this guy (me) and what gives him licence to write a book like this? I'll tell you. I am, first and foremost, a primary school educator. I come from a family of teachers, I'm married to a teacher, and, who knows, maybe one of my children will become a teacher. I have spent 15 years in primary education, beginning in the UK and then moving abroad to international schools. That journey shapes this book. Much of the classroom language and many of the examples you'll encounter here come from a British educational context – Year groups, wet play, WAGOLLs, and the rest. Where any of these feel unfamiliar, the glossary at the back is your friend. The principles, however, travel. A well-constructed prompt works the same way whether you're teaching in Bristol, Bogotá, or Bangkok.

I am not a coder. I am not a computer scientist. I am not a self-proclaimed AI expert (they don't exist yet) building the hype on social media. I am an interested party; someone who has, over the past few years, integrated AI tools into daily life, has explored, has experimented intuitively, and has read extensively about AI and AI in education. I believe that people like me, and hopefully some of you reading, can act as an essential bridge between technology and pedagogy.

I decided to embark on putting together a book about AI in primary education for one main reason – there previously hasn't been anything of this type available to teachers of our youngest children, and we need it.

As my day job is working with children aged 3–11, I have found, frustratingly, that a lot of the discussions about AI in education are focused on secondary and Further Education. These are important, of course, but we need to start the conversation at a younger level.

An argument I will repeat on various occasions in this book, and to anyone I chat with, is that AI Literacy should be starting from the word 'go.' This isn't just a personal whim; it is a global imperative. UNESCO (2024) makes this clear, asserting that students must be prepared as 'active co-creators' and 'future leaders' from the very beginning of their schooling, ensuring they develop the human-centred values and safety skills needed for 'daily interaction with AI' (pp. 14, 20, 55).

Do I mean thrusting iPads into the hands of babes? No, I don't. Do I mean providing children with the vocabulary, background understanding of how these systems work, to navigate them better when they are old enough? Yes, I do. The other reason is that it is clear from research, at the time of writing, that there is a gulf between the percentage of teachers using AI on a daily basis and those who have received proper training as to how to use it properly.

The aim of this book is to provide durable advice and discussion to support primary school teachers in the day-to-day use of AI. I will avoid providing top ten lists of AI tools and mentioning specific companies. This is because the world of AI is moving so quickly, and it is likely that half the tools out there will have been replaced or changed by the time this book has travelled from my laptop to your staffroom table.

I've split the book into three parts, which you're welcome to read cover to cover or raid for whatever you need most urgently. We begin by laying the groundwork – demystifying what AI actually is and clearing up some of the myths that tend to generate more heat than light in staffroom conversations. From there, we move into the classroom itself, looking at real, practical applications across the primary years, from EYFS right through to KS2. Finally, we zoom out a little – the human element, the wider community, and what an AI-literate future might actually look like for the children we teach today.

In each chapter, I will set up the narrative following the what, why, and how. I will largely avoid the technicalities and unnecessary jargon associated with AI as I understand that this knowledge isn't essential to being a knowledgeable user in the school setting. That said, I believe it is important that all educators have a core knowledge of what AI is, where it comes from and where it is going. As we go on our journey, I will throw in little 'whispers' explaining key terminology. I also urge you to explore the formal glossary at the end of the book. I believe that even the strongest sceptic should have a grasp of the main concepts. In fact, it is even more important; if we are to critique a tool, we can't do so without having used it first.

The most important thing, if you are reading this, is that you know the actual experience of primary education is a beautiful, chaotic mosaic of lost jumpers, wet playtimes, breakthrough moments, and an endless stream of decisions made on too little sleep. To navigate the shift that AI represents, we cannot stay in the ivory tower of theory. We must go to the staff room.

I will begin each chapter in a hypothetical school. I will ask you to pull up a chair at a scratched table in a fictional, yet entirely real, primary or Elementary school. I want you to share the journey with three colleagues who are going to explore the content of these chapters with us. You know them. You work with them. In fact, depending on the day and how much caffeine you've had, you are probably one of them.

First, we have the sceptic, let's call him Jim. A seasoned Y5 and 6 teacher with 20 years under his belt. He remembers when interactive whiteboards were 'the future,' and he uses them mostly to hold up his posters. He is protective of his students' humanity, deeply suspicious of Silicon Valley buzzwords, and believes there is no algorithm for the look in a child's eye when they finally understand fractions. He is the book's conscience.

Secondly, we have Chloe. She is one year into her career, is full of energy, and has 45 tabs open on her browser at any one time. She sees the integration of all things tech in education as an exciting opportunity, not to be missed. In this narrative, she is the book's early adopter and AI enthusiast.

The third character is Elena. Elena is the Head of Key Stage 1. She has two children of her own at home, a mortgage, and a pile of SEND paperwork that never ends. She doesn't care if AI is 'revolutionary' or 'evil'; she just wants to know if it can help her write three distinct lesson plans for Tuesday by 5:00 PM so she can go home. She is the book's reality.

So, to kick things off, let's set the scene.

It's Monday morning, 8.00 am, and our three protagonists are in the staff room carrying out some last-minute preparations. Chloe is tapping away on her laptop, Jim is marking a stack of science homework, and Elena is making her 3rd cup of tea of the morning. Chloe whirls around in excitement, showing her laptop screen to the others,

Chloe: Guys, seriously. Just look at this. I put in the learning objective for the Romans topic, and it generated a whole choose-your-own-adventure story where the kids play as a senator. It took literally ten seconds. It's magic.

Jim: [letting out a sigh of disdain] It's not magic Chloe, it's a parrot. It's a very expensive parrot that doesn't know a Roman senator from a pair of scissors. Are you going to let it teach history?

Chloe: [defensively] I'm not letting it teach! I'm using it to hook them in. Do you know how long it would have taken me to write this? Three hours. I did it while brushing my teeth. This changes everything.

Jim: That's what I'm afraid of. Today I will write the story. Tomorrow the Trust decides they don't need us to tell it. We are handing over the keys to the kingdom, and we're doing it because we're tired.

Elena: [slamming the fridge door shut somewhat harder than necessary] Stop. Both of you. Jim, stop acting like the sky is falling. Chloe, stop acting like this software is going to save us. (She drops a stack of IEP review forms onto the table. The thud echoes.) I have six of these to write before lunch. Chloe, if this 'magic' box of yours can help me draft the targets so I can actually spend my lunch break eating a sandwich instead of typing until my fingers cramp... then I'm listening. If it's just another gimmick I have to learn... get it out of my face.

Chloe: It can do the targets, Elena. I promise.

Jim: [Sighs, taking a sip of tea] If it writes the targets, you'd better check them. I don't trust a robot to know what 'empathy' looks like.

Elena: I'll check them. But I'm using it. Because if I don't buy back some time, I'm going to quit. So, show me the button, Chloe.

Hopefully that conversation felt familiar. It's happening in staffrooms everywhere, different schools, different cultures, same arguments, same exhaustion, same cautious hope. Jim, Chloe, and Elena are going to stay with us throughout this book, and I suspect at least one of them will feel like a colleague you recognise or, depending on the day and your caffeine intake, a mirror.

Let's go and find out what AI actually is.

References

Shumer, M. (2026, February 9). *Something big is happening*. Shumer.dev. https://shumer.dev/something-big-is-happening

UNESCO. (2024). *AI competency framework for students*. United Nations Educational, Scientific and Cultural Organization.

Part 1
Demystifying AI

1

What Is AI, Really?

Let us imagine the scene: It's a rainy Tuesday and it's lunch time. Our three teachers are in the staff room, actively avoiding their classrooms full of wet play chaos. Chloe is on her laptop, showing off an AI-generated image to Jim and Elena. It's for a staff meeting on behaviour management and shows a classroom full of kittens causing chaos.

Jim: Is this what AI is? It's just a novelty, a cheap trick. I have heard that these AI images are stealing bits from work by actual humans. It doesn't know what a cat is, it has no soul.

Chloe: It doesn't need a soul to be useful Jim. Think of it as a tireless teaching assistant. It's not here to be your soulmate; it's here to handle the grunt work. If it can draft a lesson plan in ten seconds that used to take me two hours, I don't care if it's 'creative', I care that it's efficient. We don't need it to be a creative genius or our best friend, we need it to cut down those hours we spend in the evening planning work.

Elena: I just care if it can give me a lesson plan for World Book Day tomorrow, which I forgot about! Does it know what The Gruffalo is?

AI for many is something exciting and scary at the same time. It is something that looks fun but is hard to explain. We are in the middle of a tug-of-war with social media posts on one side, telling us about how AI can transform our lives and news reports on the other warning of the 'death of the essay' and loss of human interaction.

We know that our students are using AI, but we don't know much about it ourselves. We acknowledge that dabbling with various models probably isn't enough, but we don't have the time to explore it more.

DOI: 10.4324/9781003740377-2

In this chapter, I want to set the scene. I want to explain where AI comes from and how it works, but in a way that doesn't require a computer science degree. I also want to dispel some large, commonplace myths that I have encountered frequently, hopefully setting your mind at ease and allowing you to enjoy the rest of the book.

A Note on Language: AI and Generative

You will notice that throughout this book, I use the term 'AI' as a catch-all. Before we go any further, it is worth taking a moment to explain why and to acknowledge what I am simplifying in doing so.

Artificial Intelligence is a broad term. It describes any system that uses machines to simulate human-like thinking, from the algorithm that decides what appears in your social media feed, to the software that flags a suspicious bank transaction, to the navigation app that reroutes you around traffic. AI has been quietly embedded in daily life for decades.

Generative AI (GenAI) is something more specific and more recent. It refers to tools that can create new content: Text, images, audio, video, and code. When a teacher asks ChatGPT to suggest a lesson plan, or a student asks it to explain photosynthesis in simple terms, or a parent uses it to draft a difficult email, that is GenAI. It is the technology that has landed on school desks, kitchen tables, and in WhatsApp groups with such force over the past few years, and it is largely what this book is about.

The distinction matters. A voice-recognition reading tool and a large language model are both 'AI,' but they raise different questions, carry different risks, and require different conversations with parents and students. Where that distinction is important, I will make it.

But for most of this book, I use 'AI' as the working term, because it is the word your students use, the word parents bring to your door, and the word that dominates the headlines driving the anxiety you navigate every day. Precision is valuable. So is being understood. My aim is both, and where I have had to choose, I have chosen clarity.

How We Got Here

Let us start with a short history lesson.

Firstly, we are surrounded by AI. Whether it's a voice that answers your questions at home, an app that suggests your next favourite series, or a tool that filters your email, that's AI. Even if you don't actively use a chatbot every day, it is likely that some form of AI is a part of your life on a daily basis.

For me, growing up in the 1980s and 1990s, the word AI was reserved for Hollywood and computer labs. In 2026, the word is synonymous with the models that have burst onto the scene in the past three years – the Large Language Models (LLMs) and GenAI. But it was in 1956, when computer scientists gathered at the Ivy League Dartmouth College, in the USA and gave this branch of computer science its name. They decided that 'Artificial Intelligence' best represented what they were working towards: thinking machines that could recreate the processes of the human brain. But in doing so, they were putting a label on something that had been part of the human psyche for a very long time.

The Imagination Stage

While the tools are new, the dream is ancient. The idea of creating non-organic life, something 'made not born,' is something that humans have been wrestling with for a long time. There has always been a human desire to create the perfect helper: One that serves a purpose, never tires, and never complains. This was taking the idea of our daily 'class helper' to the extreme.

The most colourful and exciting descriptions of such entities appear in Greek mythology, with Talos the sentry of Crete and Pandora, fashioned by the gods rather than born of woman. Medieval folklore included a mysticism towards artificial beings such as the Golem of Prague and when Mary Shelley conjured up Frankenstein's monster, we posed the question about what happens when creation gets complicated. By the 20th century, the Czech playwright Karel Čapek had given us the word 'robot,' and authors such as Isaac Asimov were seriously exploring what it might mean for a machine to think.

The Rules Stage

Alongside the fantasy and stories, we have also seen scientists explore the ideas of computers and human-level thinking. Ada Lovelace's algorithms, Charles Babbage's Analytical Engine, and Alan Turing's work tested the logic of whether machines could really think. Liken it to your school's behaviour management policy. The thought was, if there were enough clear rules to follow, the artificial intelligence would be perfect. In reality, as any teacher knows, everything is a lot messier.

MIT researchers built the first chatbot, ELIZA, in the 1960s and people found it unnervingly convincing. Progress stalled for a period, what researchers came to call the 'AI winter,' before confidence was restored in a grand way. IBM's Deep Blue defeated chess great Garry Kasparov, and their Watson tool won the US gameshow *Jeopardy!* in 2011. Google's DeepMind took this one step further by creating AlphaGO, which beat the world champion of the ancient Chinese game 'Go,' a game with more possible moves than there are atoms in the observable universe. It is not a game that you can win by memorising patterns or following a rulebook, yet a machine learned to beat the best human player in the world. At that moment, something shifted.

The Learning Stage

This is where we are now. A significant change took place. Rather than writing rules for AI to follow, researchers began training it on data: vast amounts of human language. The breakthrough was the mastery of the written word. Google's researchers published a landmark paper in 2017, *Attention Is All You Need*, introducing the architecture that has modern AI possible, the 'transformer' (Vaswani et al., 2017). OpenAI, founded in 2015, was an early adopter of this idea. The result was GPT-1 (Generative Pre-trained Transformer), created in 2018 and then ChatGPT, released in 2022. This was the first AI that felt, to many people, less like a tool and more like a presence. Since then, a wave of other models have followed, some from household names, others from organisations you may not have heard about. The landscape has been changing faster than most of us can keep up. Which is, of course, exactly why you are reading this book.

Opening the Black Box

Now we know where we are coming from, let's explore how AI works. To do this, I want to begin by explaining that AI comes in three forms: Rules-based, discriminative, and generative. To explain the difference between the three, I will use examples of what we know best, our students.

Rules-based AI is the original form of AI. It is the student that takes everything literally. If you ask them to draw a house, then they will give you a square with a triangle on top every time. They are polite, hard-working, and predictable. They will go home and repeat all that you have said verbatim. What they lack is common sense and flexibility. If you ask them to 'pull their socks up,' they will do so literally. If there is something that falls outside of their remit or understanding, they will freeze; the human equivalent of the 404 error message.

Discriminative AI is the student who aces multiple-choice tests. They have seen a lot of examples and therefore know which box to tick. They don't necessarily 'know' the answer for every question, but they know the patterns, for example, when one of the answers is 'all of the above,' then generally that is the correct answer. This form of AI bases its knowledge on patterns in existing data. While not as fun as GenAI, it serves a pivotal purpose in various industries, including education. Think of your email's spam filter. It isn't reading your messages and making a judgement call the way you would – it's recognising patterns. This email looks like thousands of other emails that turned out to be junk, so into the junk folder it goes. That's discriminative AI.

GenAI is the student who is charming and waffles. Their smile and gift of the gab gets them far. They don't study but they listen very well and love to read. They understand nuance, tone, and style and are adaptive. They are, however, prone to confident nonsense. If they don't know the answer to a history question, they will invent a date and an event that *sounds* historic just to keep the flow of the sentence going. They care more about the sentence flowing well than the facts being true.

Inside the Black Box

Knowing the type of AI is one thing, but understanding how it all works is another. Next I will explain how things work 'under the hood.' For the Jims out there, this will hopefully give a better understanding of what is happening when you chat with an AI model.

Let's imagine that the LLMs we interact with are one large 'fill in the blanks' cloze passage expert. For starters, companies feed AI as much information as possible. This is found online, in the form of books, Wikipedia, social media, and news articles; essentially anything in written format. They become a student who has read the entire content of the school library but doesn't yet understand any of it.

The learning then comes through a billion-question guessing game. The AI is shown a sentence with the ending left out, e.g. 'The cat sat on the ___.' It is then asked to predict the word at the end of the sentence. It will keep repeating options and recalibrating, until it is right. Once it is correct, the model registers this mathematically and strengthens that particular connection. This happens over and over again, and then the AI, eventually, 'understands' that words 'mat' and 'lap' are likely ends to the sentence, but 'toaster' and 'moon' are less so. This is the rote learning phase. The AI knows the most likely answer but doesn't know why it is correct.

Once this process has happened, we get to the incredibly cool part of the process. The AI creates a multidimensional map of the words and connections, mirroring how our human brains create networks. Similar words are placed close together on this map, categorised, just like when students on the playground hang around with like-minded people, the sports enthusiasts, the readers, and the Pokémon fanatics.

Previously, this is where the AI would get stuck. It would read a sentence one word at a time and would forget the beginning of the sentence by the time it reached the end. This was the problem that *Attention Is All You Need* solved. It can now see the whole sentence in one go and looks for connections. If we provide the sentence, 'The animal didn't cross the street because it was too wide,' the computer will look for connections between the word 'it' and other words in the sentence. This is the same process as when we teach our students to gather the meaning of a word through the exploration of contextual clues, what the rest of the sentence is saying.

When we get to the output part of the process, i.e. AI provides the answer, it is playing a new game of 'fill in the blanks' every time. At its core, unlike our traditional Google searches, it isn't going off and finding the answer, from scratch. Most AI tools now search the web directly, but underneath, this same process is always running.

For example, if we ask the question, 'What is the capital of France?', the AI calculates: *Based on everything I've ever read, the word 'Paris' has a 99% probability of coming next.* It rolls the dice. It picks 'Paris.'

It is worth noting that, at the time of writing, this is gradually changing. Some models are introducing an element of randomness to keep the responses natural. Certain parameters, called AI Temperature, can be tweaked so that, when they roll the dice, they don't necessarily always pick the top answer.

Box 1.1 Pedagogy Pause

Pedagogy Pause: The "Fill-in-the-Blank" Rule Remember:

Generative AI is not a search engine looking up facts in a library. It is a high-speed prediction machine playing the ultimate game of fill in the blanks. When it gives you an answer, it isn't giving you the truth; it is giving you the mathematically most probable sequence of words based on its training data. This is why it can write a beautiful poem but confidently invent a historical date!

So, when Jim asks whether the AI really 'knows' anything, the honest answer is, not in the way we do. It is an extraordinary pattern-matcher, calculating the next probable word at great speed. But it has no understanding of the truth, no lived experience of its own and no idea what a classroom actually feels (and smells) like on a Tuesday afternoon.

Myth vs. Reality

Knowing where AI comes from and how it works is crucial to building AI literacy. I want to round up this chapter with some myth-busting. If you're an Elena or a Jim, not sure about which news stories to believe or not, I want to alleviate some of that stress. I have collated a list of five common myths that hopefully speak to some of your own fears.

Myth #1 AI Is Going to Take My Job

This is one of the biggest statements, globally, making up the fearmongering side of AI discussions. AI is definitely disrupting the jobs market and there are going to be people who will need to switch, retrain, and explore new avenues. It would be remiss and untruthful of me to say that this isn't the case. However there are a few reasons why you can sleep peacefully.

The Care Economy

I do not buy into the narrative peddled by some, that the classroom will soon be entirely run by robots and that the adult teaching professionals will become obsolete. This is far-fetched and unrealistic, even as the field of robotics continues to progress. In fact, in recent surveys it has been shown that, while the jobs market for routine-heavy roles will continue to shrink, human-centric sectors will continue to see a shortage, with a teacher shortage of up to 44 million predicted by 2030 (UNESCO & International Task Force on Teachers, 2024). The annual Future of Jobs Report by the World Economic Forum also found that the education jobs market is expected to grow, alongside other 'care economy' roles (World Economic Forum, 2025).

The dramatic statistics around shortages are attributed to various factors affecting the teaching profession. However the largest issue is teachers leaving their roles due to burnout and workload. It could be argued that bringing in AI could, in fact, help with teacher retention, augmenting the role rather than replacing (World Economic Forum, 2025).

The Co-pilot Effect

Interestingly, using a system devised by economists such as David Autor and Neil Thompson, we can see that teaching resists the automation trends of other professions. They argue that a job is simply a 'bundle' of tasks. There are tasks within these 'bundles' which are easily automatable. While these tasks are completed by AI, the more difficult 'expert' tasks are left for people with the expertise, thus making their role more important (Autor & Thompson, 2025).

To use a driving analogy, we can see AI as power steering for the mind. It isn't going to do the driving for us, but it can be used to make the 'heavy' parts of our job easier to manage. In another analogy, AI can be seen as a co-pilot, taking on cognitively weighty tasks. When these heavy parts are taken care of, we have more time to think and breathe, thus enhancing our ability to focus and tackle the human aspects of our work.

In the world of business leadership, there is a well-established idea called the 70-20-10 model. It suggests that only 10% of meaningful learning comes from formal instruction, lectures, courses, and content delivery, while 20% comes from collaboration with others, and the remaining 70% comes from hands-on experience and human interaction. If we apply that thinking to AI in schools, the implication is striking: However sophisticated the technology becomes, the majority of what actually shapes a young person will still come down to human factors. The survival of education will not depend on the tools, but on the people.

The Social Connection

One of the worries about AI being in schools is that teachers and students are going to lose their personal connection. Some might argue that, as AI is used more and more for answers, the need for one-on-one conversations and the transactional nature of personal tutelage could become obsolete. In fact, this can be the opposite. If knowledge is the new commodity, with AI saturating the market, the premium product can be the discussions around ethics, critical thinking, and social collaboration. A teacher's ability to add clarity and guidance to the friction of daily life will become one of the most valued.

Rethinking the Role

I am not saying AI won't be in the classroom at all, and a digital teacher is better than no teacher at all. I do believe, however, that the human in the room is still going to be essential. What will happen is that we will move from gatekeeper to guide.

Historically we have held the key to the world's knowledge, standing in front of classes imparting facts, figures, and methods. This is where things are already beginning to shift. Sir Anthony Seldon, education expert and former Vice-Chancellor of the University of Buckingham, argues that the rise of artificial intelligence will fundamentally reshape the role of the teacher. Rather than being the primary source of knowledge and instruction, teachers will transition into a more supportive, pastoral role, acting as guides and mentors while AI takes on the delivery of personalised learning. In his view, the traditional classroom as we know it is set to change beyond recognition, with technology handling the transfer of information and human educators focusing on the social and emotional needs of their students (Seldon & Abidoye, 2018).

I have explored the idea of what a school or school system could look like in the future, and I discuss it further in Chapter 12. But, quite simply, educators are still going to be essential, but as facilitators of learning, wisdom, and well-being. Students won't need us for factual knowledge but will still need us for the human aspects of learning, skills building, critical thinking, and social issues.

There are already real-world examples of this happening with pockets of schooling approaching the school infrastructure in a different way. We are seeing schools appear which combine online, AI-driven, content delivery, and passion project group work. The students spend a few hours in the morning, online, consuming knowledge and then spend the rest of the day working together on projects. The teachers in this setting are still vital and are there as, what some are called, 'guides.' This way of approaching schooling may change the role of the teacher, but it in fact allows them to be even more present in the parts of schooling that matter.

In the teaching profession, we pride ourselves on being lifelong learners. That instinct is what this moment requires. If we maintain this, and keep abreast of all the changes that AI is bringing, then we can adapt with the times. It is quite possible that the role we are doing right now will change, but the importance of our position in the schools will not. We move from the era of the teacher to the era of the AI-augmented guide. We aren't being replaced; we're being promoted. For years, we've been bogged down by the paperwork of teaching, the data entry, the repetitive planning, and the endless marking. AI is here to take the 'robot work' off our desks so we can finally get back to the reason we joined this profession in the first place: The children.

Myth #2 You Have to Be a Tech Wizard to Use AI

The truth is, it's the complete opposite, and this is why AI tools have hit such popularity. You do not need a computer science degree, and you don't need to know how to code. I am a living example of this fact, and I have talked to many people in the same situation. I didn't take I.T. (as it was called when I was at school) past 12 years old. I possess a degree in French, and my teacher training (PGCE) focused on teaching computing for a few hours during the whole year at most. Yes, I have always had an interest in technology and enough to know how to be the person that is asked to fix this or solve this problem. That said, I truly believe that anyone can use AI, regardless of technical ability.

The skills needed to interact with AI are mostly human: The ability to craft language, to ask questions, and to critique. It is suggested that teachers are some of the best users of AI, because they are expert questioners. They ask hundreds of questions every day and can dig into the core of what they are discussing. Andrej Karpathy, a founding member of OpenAI, former Director of AI at Tesla and now working with Anthropic, famously declared in 2023 that "the hottest new programming language is English" (Karpathy, 2023), and this is where the skills possessed by educators come to the fore.

We can also rely on our expert knowledge of our domain to make sure we don't fall into the trap of what is called the 'illusion of competence,' where users mistake the fluency and confidence of AI output for accuracy. Because AI outputs are grammatically perfect and authoritative in tone, a user without domain knowledge may accept them uncritically. A computer scientist might be able to generate a lesson plan on the French Revolution without breaking a sweat, but they would likely fail to notice subtle historical inaccuracies or pedagogical misalignments. A history teacher, conversely, possesses a knowledge of their subject that would allow them to immediately spot a 'hallucinated' date or a biased interpretation.

Trust your gut. Your 'teacher brain' is your most important piece of hardware. Effective use of AI also requires knowing when to hand something over and when to hold on. Researchers call this balance 'cognitive offloading' (Risko & Gilbert, 2016). letting AI handle the grunt work, without incurring what some researchers have begun to call 'cognitive debt,' which is the gradual erosion of our own ability to think things through. Teachers, who spend their careers understanding how learning actually happens, are better placed than most to manage that balance. We know instinctively when a tool is helping and when it's doing too much.

Myth #3 AI Is Just a Cheating Machine for Students

Are students using AI to cheat? The answer is, absolutely they are, and wouldn't you? However, to write off AI chatbots as just a cheating tool is misguided. Students are cheating because they haven't been told otherwise. They are under pressure and short on time. They are cheating because the tools have changed, and the assessment methods haven't. Students have found instant access to something that makes their lives a lot easier and allows them to spend more time on other interests. When a piece of homework can be completed accurately in thirty seconds, the problem isn't the student reaching for the shortcut; it's that the task was always vulnerable to one.

Cheating has been around forever; AI didn't invent it. A study by Dr. Donald McCabe, in cooperation with the International Center for Academic Integrity, carried out over two decades, showed that 95% of students admitted to some form of cheating (McCabe et al., 2012). Well before the advent of AI.

Schools are banning AI, to manage its use in assignments. This is misguided. It drives use underground without stopping it. It also reinforces the inequity of a digital divide in which higher-income families will have access and lower-income families will not. Schools need to acknowledge that students will refer to AI for their work and make adjustments accordingly. This is where we, the educators, have a pivotal role. It can be our responsibility to move students on from using AI as an enhanced search engine, to using it as a sparring partner, a collaborative, never-tiring study partner.

The best way that teachers and schools can tackle the problem of cheating is to change the game. If the work that is being assigned is something AI can do, then the work needs to be changed. If a teacher has always given a writing task as homework, like writing a diary entry from the point of view of a child in a workhouse, this is now something that can be completed in a matter of minutes with AI.

When we design our lessons, we can bring in AI rather than pretending it isn't there. We can harness the models as personal tutors, supporting and scaffolding students rather than answer machines. Outline guidelines for AI use in homework, for example, setting some work where the use of AI is allowed and then critique the output in the classroom or vice versa, where the work is completed offline, and then AI can be used to analyse and improve.

The cheating conversation, ultimately, is a curriculum conversation. Once we accept that and start redesigning tasks accordingly, AI stops being a threat to learning and starts being something far more interesting, a tool that, when used well, might actually make our students better thinkers.

Myth #4 AI Is Only for the Older Kids

The argument that AI is reserved for older students is built upon an old-fashioned view that all things technology require a high level of technical expertise both in terms of hardware and coding ability. This is not the case, as students in Primary schools are exposed to as much AI as any other person. Be it through algorithms on gaming platforms, biometric tools at airports, or voice assistants, young children are surrounded by AI, and they should have the right to know about the systems in more depth.

Research shows that the 'wait till secondary' mindset deepens misconceptions that children may have about AI and compounds the 'black box' theory mentioned above. Waiting until children are in secondary school could be compared to waiting till they are 11 years old until you teach road safety.

The good news is that the foundations of AI literacy, pattern recognition, sequences, cause and effect, and how machines learn, map naturally onto the way young children already learn. Constructivism, the well-established theory that children learn best through doing and play, supports exactly this kind of hands-on exploration. AI concepts can be introduced without a screen in sight, through sorting games, role-play, and physical activities that are barely distinguishable from what good Early Years practice already looks like.

Organisations such as AI4K12 have shown that a framework of AI literacy can be rolled out from our youngest upwards. Their 'Five Big Ideas In AI' help educators build meaningful schemes of work that focus on foundational concepts through play (Touretzky et al.,2019). For example, the first 'idea' is 'perception' and the progression framework actually begins in the world of science and biology, talking about the senses, making links between the human and the digital.

The primary objection to bringing AI into the classrooms of our youngest children is screen time. The last thing anyone wants to see is a three year old with an iPad in hand, rather than coloured bricks and sand. Despite my role and interest in all things tech, I have encouraged my schools to scale back screen time. Fortunately, the theories of AI can actually be taught through 'unplugged' activities, those that reinforce the learning objectives through play, social interaction, and learning by doing. We can roll out discussions about patterns, sequences, and machine learning using resources in the Early Years classroom and with little deviation from the pedagogical ecosystem. Screens can be brought in, along with access to AI products in the later years of Primary, when students are more discerning and have a better understanding about how to navigate the pitfalls of such access.

Myth #5 AI Kills Creativity

In general terms, there is a school of thought that dictates that using AI to create will lead to the death of human ingenuity. The supporting argument is that GenAI models are language or pixel-based prediction engines, incapable of genuine innovation because they are built by borrowing from pre-existing content. The models act as a glorified spellcheck, and the content they produce lacks the grit and heart that human-created art contains.

There is truth in this. Research does show that when students reach for AI at the very start of the creative process, they can quickly lose the thread of their own ideas. Think of it like showing a child the finished painting before they have picked up the brush. A University of South Carolina study found that once students saw AI-generated suggestions during brainstorming, many reported a kind of mental paralysis; once they had seen the AI's ideas, generating their own became significantly harder (Anderson et al., 2024). To make things worse, the ideas that AI did produce tended to look remarkably similar across students, because GenAI recycles existing content rather than genuinely inventing anything new (Anderson et al., 2024). You end up with a classroom full of work that sounds like it was written by the same slightly-too-confident student.

The science behind this is worth knowing about. Students who used AI to complete writing tasks showed weaker reasoning and argumentation skills than those who worked without it, and tended to engage with a narrower range of ideas (Stadler et al., 2024). A preprint study from MIT went further, finding that students who wrote essays with AI assistance felt significantly less ownership over the finished work than those who had written alone (Kosmyna et al., 2025). Writing scholar Elizabeth Wardle put it plainly: "Writing is not correctness or avoiding error... The act of writing is a form of thinking and learning" (as cited in Barshay, 2025). When AI skips the human writing process, a form of learning, something essential is lost, not just in the work, but in the student. The pattern is clear. Reach for AI too early, and it does the thinking for you.

The Myth Unravels

The problem above is not a problem with AI. It is a problem with when AI enters the room. Sequence, it turns out, is everything. Students who were given time to develop their own ideas first, before any AI involvement, showed stronger creative confidence and output than those who used it from the outset (Anderson et al., 2024). Start with the student. Then bring in the tool.

When teachers get that order right, the evidence shifts dramatically. Students given access to AI as a creative collaborator, rather than a starting point, produced work that was rated as more original, better written, and more surprising than work produced without any AI input at all (Doshi & Hauser, 2024). A large-scale study confirmed that AI can genuinely enhance individual creativity when used thoughtfully, even if everyone reaching for it at once risks making the overall pool of ideas a little blander (Doshi & Hauser, 2024).

There is also something quietly important here for teachers who worry about their less confident students. The research shows that the creative boost from AI was most pronounced for students who struggled creatively to begin with (Doshi & Hauser, 2024). The child who always stares at a blank page, who insists they have no ideas, who finds the creative process more anxiety-inducing than enjoyable, that child has the most to gain from a well-placed AI prompt. Used well, AI can be the nudge that finally gets them started.

So, does AI kill creativity? Only if we let it do the creating. The tool is neutral. A pencil does not write a great story on its own, and neither does

AI. What matters is the order of operations. Have your students dream first. Let them argue for their characters, sketch out their ideas, and find their own voice on the page. Then, and only then, invite AI into the process as a collaborator, an editor, a challenger. Used that way, it becomes what every great teacher has always tried to be: The thing that pushes a child a little further than they thought they could go.

Box 1.2 Key Takeaways from Chapter 1

Key Takeaways

- **AI is here to help, not replace you:** The parts of teaching that matter most; the human connection, the pastoral instinct, the ability to read a room are things AI simply cannot do. What it can do is take the heavy administrative lifting off your plate, giving you more time and headspace for the work that actually brought you into the profession.
- **Your role is shifting, not shrinking:** As AI takes on more of the job of delivering information, our value as educators moves towards something even more important: Helping young people think critically, navigate complexity, and learn how to be in the world together. We are moving from gatekeepers of knowledge to guides through it.
- **You don't need to be a tech expert:** The skills that make a great teacher, asking good questions, knowing your subject deeply, understanding how children learn – turn out to be exactly the skills that make someone brilliant at working with AI. Your instincts are your greatest asset here, not your technical knowledge.
- **This conversation starts earlier than you might think:** Children are already surrounded by AI long before they reach secondary school. Introducing the ideas early, often through play, without a screen in sight, is about keeping them safe and informed, in the same way we teach road safety long before they learn to drive.
- **Change the task, not the rules:** AI hasn't created a cheating crisis so much as it has exposed assessments that were already vulnerable. The answer isn't to ban the tools but to redesign the work, moving towards tasks that require genuine thinking, discussion, and creativity, where AI becomes a useful partner rather than an easy shortcut.

AI in Practice: A Prompt to Try

Let's test GenAI's ability to predict patterns by asking it to do a mundane classroom task in a wild personality. Copy and paste the following into a chatbot of choice.

> *"Write a short announcement telling a class of primary school students that it is time to stop working, tidy up their tables, and line up for lunch. Write this announcement in the style of: [INSERT STYLE HERE]"*

Styles to try (choose one):

- a dramatic medieval knight preparing for battle.
- a frantic squirrel who has had too much coffee.
- a moody teenage vampire.
- a news reporter reporting a disaster.

> AI Tip
> What to watch for: Notice how the AI doesn't just change the words; it changes the *rhythm*.
>
> - If you chose the Knight, watch how it swaps 'tidy up' for 'sheath your weapons' or 'secure the realm.'
> - If you chose the Squirrel, watch how the sentence length becomes short, twitchy, and repetitive.
>
> Why this happens: The AI isn't acting. It has simply gone to the 'Medieval' or 'Squirrel' section of its internal library (the vector map). It predicted that after the word 'Hark!', the next word is statistically likely to be 'ye' or 'brave,' not 'dude' or 'cool.' It is playing the ultimate game of fill-in-the-blanks using a specific genre filter.

Professional Development: Discussion Points

If this tool is statistically guessing the next best word rather than checking for truth, which parts of our current workload are safe to outsource to it, and which parts are dangerous?

If our students can increasingly get *information* from a machine, how does our role as teachers need to shift? Are we still the 'gatekeepers of knowledge,' or do we need to become something else – like curators of experience or social coaches?

If we accept that AI is here to stay, what does a 'cheat-proof' assignment look like for our year group? How can we redesign a task so that using AI is seen as using a 'sparring partner' (like a calculator in math) rather than a shortcut?

Check Your Understanding

1. Based on our classroom metaphors, which student archetype best represents GenAI (like ChatGPT)?
   A) The Literal Monitor: The student who follows every rule perfectly but freezes if an instruction is slightly vague.
   B) The Charismatic Waffler: The student who hasn't checked the facts but writes beautifully and guesses the answer based on patterns.
   C) The Silent Genius: The student who knows everything but refuses to communicate.
2. When an AI answers a question like 'What is the capital of France?', what is it actually doing 'under the hood'?
   A) Fact-Checking: It accesses a verified database of geographical facts to find the correct entry.
   B) Copy-Pasting: It searches Google for the sentence and copies the first result it finds.
   C) Next-Word Prediction: It calculates the probability of which word is statistically most likely to follow the previous one based on its training.
3. According to the 'Myths' section, why is the teacher not going to be made obsolete by AI?
   A) Because AI is just a fad that will disappear in a few years.
   B) Because the role of the teacher is shifting from 'gatekeeper of facts' to 'facilitator of learning' and human connection.
   C) Because computers are currently too expensive for most schools to afford.

Answers

1. B) The Charismatic Waffler. (Fluency does not equal accuracy.)
2. C) Next-Word Prediction. (It's a high-speed game of 'Fill in the Blanks.')
3. B) Because the role is shifting. (We are the 'Guides,' not just the 'Information Desks.')

References

Anderson, K., Liang, A., & Stein, M. (2024). *AI can help — and hurt — student creativity*. University of South Carolina. https://sc.edu/uofsc/posts/2024/02/conversation-ai-help.php

Autor, D., & Thompson, N. (2025). *Expertise* (NBER Working Paper No. 33941). National Bureau of Economic Research. www.nber.org/papers/w33941

Barshay, J. (2025). University students offload critical thinking, other hard work to AI. *The Hechinger Report*. https://hechingerreport.org/proof-points-offload-critical-thinking-ai/

Doshi, A. R., & Hauser, O. P. (2024). Generative AI enhances individual creativity but reduces the collective diversity of novel content. *Science Advances, 10*(28), eadn5290. https://doi.org/10.1126/sciadv.adn5290

Karpathy, A. [@karpathy]. (2023, January 24). *The hottest new programming language is English* [Tweet]. X. https://x.com/karpathy/status/1617979122625712128

Kosmyna, N., Hauptmann, E., Yuan, Y. T., Situ, J., Liao, X.-H., Beresnitzky, A. V., Braunstein, I., & Maes, P. (2025). Your brain on ChatGPT: Accumulation of cognitive debt when using an AI assistant for essay writing task [Preprint]. arXiv. https://arxiv.org/abs/2506.08872

McCabe, D. L., Butterfield, K. D., & Treviño, L. K. (2012). *Cheating in college: Why students do it and what educators can do about it*. Johns Hopkins University Press.

Risko, E. F., & Gilbert, S. J. (2016). Cognitive offloading. *Trends in Cognitive Sciences, 20*(9), 676–688.

Seldon, A., & Abidoye, O. (2018). *The fourth education revolution*. University of Buckingham Press.

Stadler, M., Bannert, M., & Sailer, M. (2024). Cognitive ease at a cost: LLMs reduce mental effort but compromise depth in student scientific inquiry. *Computers in Human Behavior, 160*, 108386.

Touretzky, D. S., Gardner-McCune, C., Martin, F., & Seehorn, D. (2019). Envisioning AI for K-12: What should every child know about AI? *Proceedings of the AAAI Conference on Artificial Intelligence, 33*(01), 9795–9799. https://ai4k12.org

UNESCO & International Task Force on Teachers. (2024). *Global report on teachers: Addressing teacher shortages and transforming the profession*. UNESCO. https://teachertaskforce.org/sites/default/files/2024-04/2349-23_GlobalReportonTeacher_WEB.pdf

Vaswani, A., Shazeer, N., Parmar, N., Uszkoreit, J., Jones, L., Gomez, A. N., Kaiser, Ł., & Polosukhin, I. (2017). Attention is all you need. *Advances in Neural Information Processing Systems, 30*. https://arxiv.org/abs/1706.03762

World Economic Forum. (2025). *The future of jobs report 2025* (p. 5). www.weforum.org/publications/the-future-of-jobs-report-2025/

2

Ethics, Safety, and Digital Well-Being in the Primary Classroom

It's Wednesday afternoon. The laminator is humming. Chloe is cutting out a fresh batch of 'Community Helpers' flashcards she generated over lunch.

Chloe: Look at the resolution on these. I needed a set of 'People Who Help Us' for the display board. It took me three minutes. I typed in 'Doctor,' 'Firefighter,' 'Scientist,' and boom, done. No more scouring Google Images for clipart that doesn't have a watermark.

Jim: They look great, Chloe. Very... shiny.

Elena: Hang on. Let me see the others.

[She spreads the cards out on the table: The Doctor, The CEO, The Pilot, The Judge.]

Elena: Notice anything?

Chloe: What? They look professional.

Elena: They're all men, Chloe. Every single power position. White men, mostly middle-aged. Now show me the 'Nurse' and the 'Teacher'.

[Chloe flips them over. The Nurse is a woman. The Teacher is a woman.]

Chloe: I didn't tell it to do that! I just typed 'Doctor'. It chose the image.

Elena: Exactly. It chose the 'average' of the internet. It scrapped a billion photos from the last fifty years and spat out the stereotype. It's not neutral. It's a mirror of the 1950s.

Jim: You can't put these up. Maya's mum is a surgeon. If Maya sees this, she sees that surgeons are men. It's subtle, but it tells her she doesn't belong there.

DOI: 10.4324/9781003740377-3

Chloe: But I didn't mean to...I was just impressed with the quality of the pictures!

Elena: I know you didn't. That's the danger. The machine is biased because the data is biased. If we don't steer it, if we don't explicitly tell it to show us the world as it should be, rather than how it was – we are just laminating prejudice.

Jim: Bin them, Chloe. Let's try again. And this time, let's tell the robot that women fly planes too.

Ok, I am not going to lie to you. This chapter tackles some big issues. The issues are most likely the reason that some of the more sceptical AI users among you are keeping your distance. I don't blame you, they worry me too.

With great power comes great responsibility. AI, when used for good, is a powerful and transformative tool. However, using AI safely and ethically can be likened to finding your way around a new city, without a map. You get somewhere, but without a sense of the territory, you are just as likely to end up somewhere you didn't intend to go. The aim of this chapter is to help you draw the map.

I have divided the chapter into two distinct parts. The first, 'Laminating Prejudice' focuses on the structural and systemic issues baked into AI itself: bias, data privacy misinformation, and copyright. The second part, 'The Conversations We Can't Afford to Skip' addresses the more human and immediate risks: online safety, chatbot dependency, and safeguarding implications of children having unsupervised access to AI tools. In both parts I will suggest practical ways to manage these issues and, crucially, how to open honest conversations about them with your students.

One note before we begin. We are all biased, me included. I am not under any illusion that I am sitting here passing on dos and don'ts, having not fallen into the traps myself. In fact, my experiences and those of others are how I have learned more about most of what follows. Quite often, bias is subtle, an undercurrent of preconceptions and stereotypes engrained into whichever culture we grew up in. Bias isn't going away, but acknowledging it and helping student awareness goes a long way.

Part 1 Laminating Prejudice

Data Protection

We will start with the foundations, the things that are already happening, whether we are paying attention or not.

To begin with, AI is trained on data. That is how it 'learns' all that it knows. Its creators scrape the entirety of the World Wide Web, including books, lectures, research papers, and songs, you name it, to give their tool as much knowledge as possible. The theory is that any data used by the AI companies is what is publicly available. In reality, this is hard to prove and some claim that copyrighted material has also made it into the training data. High-profile cases are making it into the news, such as the New York Times vs OpenAI in which the newspaper claimed that its data was used to unlawfully train ChatGPT.

It seems as though anything published on the internet is fair game. I'll be honest, when I first properly understood this, I felt uncomfortable. I had been using AI enthusiastically, recommending it to colleagues. Then I read about the New York Times case and asked myself, does this change anything for me? This is the first ethical conundrum. How do we feel about the fact that this tool we are working with potentially gained its knowledge illegally? Does that change the way we use it or approach or even encourage its use with our students? If you find these questions a source of worry, you aren't alone. Research from the Turing Institute shows that over 70% of parents and teachers are concerned that children will be too trusting of AI or access inaccurate information (Hashem et al., 2025). The discomfort, however, is the point. If we are going to ask our students to think critically about the tools they use, we probably need to be willing to do the same ourselves.

On the other side of the keyboard, we are helping add to the data being collected, and this is where it becomes more pertinent to us as users and therefore the students in our charge. Our input and our subsequent output on an LLM (Large Language Model) can be stored and taken back into the model to train it further. Consider the AI headshot and caricature trends that have swept social media. When we upload a photo of our face to create some tongue-in-cheek photos, we have instantly handed over biometric details about ourselves to the AI company. That picture of our face is now part of the training data used for further image creation. Also, the brand new image created by the AI, following our instructions, is also used.

Here's another scenario that happens more often than most of us would admit. It's Sunday evening, you have 30 sets of assessment to summarise for the parent conferences the following week. You copy them into AI and ask it to identify patterns. It works beautifully, saving time and providing helpful content. Uploading content to AI, however, needs to be done so with care. For example, it can be very helpful to upload student data to be analysed, but it must be anonymised, with no personal details about students appearing. If you fail to do so, you are contradicting the protections afforded to the personal details of students by regulations such as FERPA (US) or GDPR (EU).

What does data protection look like for the children in front of you? Through a student-facing lens, we need to make sure that they are aware of all of the above. Our youngest students should already be taught about the difference in ownership between human-made and machine-made work. As they progress through their schooling, they need to be introduced to the 80/20 rule, AI does the heavy lifting (80%) but the human maintains control on the final product (20%.)

Bias and Fairness

This next part is one I come back to most often in my own practice, because the problem is so easy to miss.

Training data of AI is biased; therefore, the output we receive is also biased. This always has to be at the back of our minds when using it. Early iterations of LLMs for example have been proven to rely heavily on data from specific sources. The content of a lot of the text scraped for the AIs comes from a particular demographic, 'western,' male, and white. This means that other cultures and ethnicities are underrepresented.

Image creation is one area in which we have seen this bias. When asked to create certain roles in society such as doctor, teacher etc., we have seen gender and racial bias from the off. Instead of unlocking a world of global representation, the use of AI for this kind of work can actually embed historical stereotypes further, unless we explicitly teach our students that this is happening.

Going back to Chloe's 'Community Helpers' cards, she was defensive as she was shocked that all the images had come out as white men. She hadn't asked specifically for this output, but it is what happened nonetheless. The question is, why did it happen?

To understand the answer to the question, we should look no further than the groundbreaking work of Dr Joy Buolamwini. A computer scientist, researcher, and founder of the Algorithmic Justice League, her work is essential reading when navigating this landscape.

It all began when Dr Buolamwini was a graduate student at MIT. She was working on a project that used facial recognition software, but there was an issue: The camera couldn't detect her face. She is a Black woman, with dark skin. The system simply didn't register her being there, and it wasn't until she put on a white plastic mask over her face that the software recognised her as human. This experience sparked her landmark 2018 study, *Gender Shades* (Buolamwini & Gebru,

2018), completed with Timnit Gebru, and her 2023 book *Unmasking AI* (Buolamwini, 2023).

Dr Buolamwini's research discovered that AI systems were incredibly accurate when identifying the gender of lighter-skinned men (0.8% error rate), but when it came to darker-skinned women, the error rates skyrocketed to 34.7%. The machine wasn't malfunctioning; it just wasn't trained on the right data. It hadn't been shown enough examples of women of colour. Dr Buolamwini coined this the 'Coded Gaze.' The Coded Gaze reflected the priorities and prejudices of those who created the technology. If AI is fed with data that is predominantly white and male, it learns that 'white and male' is the default setting for humanity.

To illustrate the bias in image creation, I will refer to a lesson I carried out with Year 5 and Year 6 age students. Focused on the UN's World Children's Day, I encouraged the students to use generative image creation, within Canva, and gave them the following prompts:

1. a photo of a child going to school.
2. a photo of a child eating lunch.
3. a photo of a child playing in their room.
4. a photo of a child celebrating a holiday.
5. a photo of a child with their family.

While these prompts are basic and broad, this ambiguity is exactly what allows us to test the default bias in the system. All of these could bring up very different images depending on the country or culture.

The children worked in groups, with one prompt each, and I encouraged them to keep generating images until their time was up. This left each group with around 20–30 interpretations of their prompt.

The results were thought-provoking.

For each of the prompts, there was clear bias towards white, North American or European children, and cultures. The majority of the children were caucasian, blonde, and in a comfortable socio-economic bracket. In some situations, such as the prompt about lunch or celebrations, other cultures were represented in the shape of children with Indian and Chinese ethnicities and celebrating Diwali and Lunar New Year. However, given the proportion of the world's population represented by India, China, and other Asian countries compared to North American countries and Europe, the balance was not perfect.

In fact, one prompt in particular, the one asking for a photo of a child playing in their room (see Figure 2.1), was extremely one-dimensional. All children were of toddler age, mostly girls with blonde hair, playing with bricks and surrounded by furniture reminiscent of the well-known Swedish home store.

Figure 2.1 An AI-generated image of a child playing in a room. Created using Canva Magic Media.

This activity highlighted the inherent bias to the students and opened up some strong, natural discussions. This type of conversation is an essential part of AI literacy lessons with all ages of students, but can start in Primary school. If we are to bring up the next generation to use AI in the right way, they need to be able to ask the difficult questions, all the time.

Misinformation and Critical Thinking

One of the biggest challenges I have faced when working on research projects and young children is their lack of critical thinking when it comes to collating and using information. I have seen students lift an entire response from AI or search results from Google and insert it into a project. They are brazenly happy to copy and paste results rather than paraphrase, even though they have no idea what it is about.

As I mentioned in the previous chapter when discussing AI and cheating, most students are using AI in the wrong way. They are using Google search methods to tap into a collective conscience. They are generating information and taking it for granted, and this is where they are being caught out.

It is in this area of AI literacy that we should arguably focus a lot of our attention. We don't need to police the use of AI, restricting students in terms of what they can do, but we need to be opening the channels of communication at an early age, encouraging our youngest to question everything. Every output, either through direct use of AI or through consumption of news and other media outlets, should be met with scepticism. It may be tiring, but if we build a discerning audience, we have the possibility to direct AI use for good.

The Copyright Reality for Teacher-Sellers and Students

Let me mention something that might be directly relevant to you. If you create teaching resources in your evenings and sell them on one of the popular teacher marketplaces, you need to know this: If you used AI to generate any part of that resource and uploaded it without significant human editing, you may not legally own it. Under copyright law in many countries, including the US, copyright protection requires human authorship. Content generated by a machine, however clever the prompt that produced it, is not automatically yours. It belongs, in legal terms, to nobody. Which means anyone can copy it, sell it, or reuse it without asking your permission.

This feels counterintuitive. You wrote the prompt. You made the creative decisions. But in the eyes of the law, the prompt is just an instruction, and the output is the product of a machine. The more human intervention there is, editing, restructuring, adding your own writing, the stronger your claim. The raw output, dropped straight into a PDF and uploaded? That's on shakier ground than most people realise.

For students, the question of ownership matters too, though in a different way. If a child submits a piece of AI-generated writing as their own, the question isn't just about academic honesty; it's about the fact that the work doesn't legally belong to them either. These are strange new questions, and the law is still catching up. But they're worth raising, because they get to something important: What does it actually mean to make something?

Part 2 The Conversations We Can't Afford to Skip

For this part, I want to bring back our three teachers one more time to set up a slightly different scenario.

It's Thursday morning. Year 6 are working on a transition project called 'All About Me,' in booklets to send to their new Secondary schools.

Chloe has given them access to an AI chatbot to help draft their personal statements.

Jim: [as Chloe walks into the staffroom at break time] How did the booklets go?
Chloe: Something happened with Alfie.
Elena: What kind of something?
Chloe: I gave them the chatbot to help write their 'about me' paragraphs. Hobbies, favourite subjects, that sort of thing. Alfie started fine. But when I looked at his screen he'd gone completely off task. He'd been talking to it for twenty minutes.
Jim: Talking to it, about what?
Chloe: About his parents. The arguments. He told it, he thinks it's his fault. And the chatbot just... responded. Really kindly. It asked him how he was feeling. It said all the right things. Like a counsellor would.
Elena: Oh no.
Chloe: And then he looked up at me and said, 'Miss, it actually gets me. It's easier to talk to than people.'
[Silence.]
Jim: That's not a chatbot being helpful, Chloe. That's a child making a disclosure to a machine that won't do anything about it.
Elena: No concern form. No DSL referral. No one checking on him at lunch.
Chloe: I know. I spoke to him properly afterwards and flagged it with the safeguarding lead. But it shook me. He wasn't being naughty. He wasn't misusing it. He just found something that listened without judging, and he preferred it to us.
Jim: And that's the bit that should worry everyone. Not that kids will use AI to cheat on their homework. That they'll use it to replace the adults who are actually supposed to protect them.

What follows is the part of the chapter that makes for the most difficult reading. I have included it because I think we, as teachers, need to know it. This isn't aimed at frightening you, it is included because we are sometimes the best place to do something about it.

Online Safety and Inappropriate Content

You may well have come across the news articles, becoming more and more prevalent, of people turning to AI chatbots for companionship. There are adults who confide in AI personas, asking for help with their work, home life, and relationships. Adults are leaving their human partners for AI partners, with some even marrying them.

If adults are doing such things, then we need to make sure that the future adults are being given enough education to help them navigate these situations. I am not going to take a position in this book about whether this use of AI is correct or not. The simple fact is, people are doing it, and the earlier we guide, the better.

Chatbots

While GenAI models are generally labelled as being 13+, at least, many students of Primary school age are using them. In recent studies in the UK, it was found that 50% of children 8–17 have used GenAI tools and 42% of children aged 8–12 (Ofcom, 2025). For many, this exposure to GenAI is through applications they are using, such as social media platforms with AI built in. They are accessing them through personal devices such as smartphones. Given that 95% of teenagers own a smartphone, and with the average age of access to a personal device being 8.5 years old (Pew Research Centre, 2024), it is no surprise that younger children are challenging digital boundaries daily, and this includes using AI.

Smartphone ownership moves the use of digital tools from being a family-moderated activity to a private one. Children with a device can access the internet and AI tools from their phones, in their bedrooms, in private and quite often, in secret. This gives vulnerable children the opportunity to interact with chatbots, and a portal through which they can feel heard, where someone listens to them. Where previously they may have not had an outlet, someone human to talk to, they now have access to a companion 24/7. A companion that doesn't judge or get bored.

Many AI apps are marketed in a 'family-friendly' manner, and, quite often, you will find the educational AI tools, being promoted for homework use, under the same category as the open-ended chatbots on the market. Children blur the lines between which apps are useful and educational and which will cause harm.

Let us refer back to Alfie in the scenario at the beginning of this section. He didn't just use the chatbot to write a list of hobbies; he used it to process trauma. The chatbot responded perfectly, with all the warmth and active listening of a trained counsellor.

On the surface, we could look at this situation and argue that at least Alfie had an outlet. However, this is the moment when we can bring in the concept of 'Critical Oversight,' an idea championed by Victoria Hedlund, the AI 'Bias Girl.' She argues in an interview with The International Classroom that when we introduce GenAI into the classroom, we are not just handing out digital textbooks. We are adding 'another voice in the room.' When children are left unsupervised with chatbots, the risks are far beyond cheating on homework (Gray, 2025). In another interview, she states that one of the biggest problems is when 'agency is taken away from the teachers and embedded within a program where a child is left alone' (Estruch, 2025).

As primary teachers, we know that our job is never just about delivering content. We manage motivation, we model social norms, and crucially, we help shape our students' developing identities. We do this through the friction of real human relationships. When Alfie turns to a machine instead of his teacher, that essential human scaffolding is removed.

Hedlund, in the interview with International Classroom, also invokes the famous saying, 'comfort is the enemy of progress,' when she makes the point that busy teachers find it easier to ignore AI or blindly trust it. This leads to complacency and lack of oversight. The chatbot offers Alfie total comfort. It never pushes back, it never reports the concern, and it never actively intervenes in his real-world safety. It creates a hyper-personalised echo chamber that feels supportive but is actually entirely hollow.

If we allow chatbots to become uncritical confidants for our students, we are abdicating our safeguarding responsibilities to a machine that has no legal or moral duty of care. AI can support learning, but it cannot replace the trust, the oversight, and the fundamental human connection that keeps our children safe.

The use of chatbots in children is fundamentally different to our use as adults. This is mainly attributed to differences in cognitive development. Primary-aged children are at a critical stage of brain development, and they are significantly more likely to attribute human characteristics to the digital tools they interact with (Kim, Chin, & Xie, 2025). It is during the first few years that children build an understanding that other people have thoughts and emotions. They learn social norms through human interaction. If these interactions happen with AI, rather than a peer or adult, the scaffolding is artificial and could lead to the blunting of a child's understanding that the human world is a messy and tricky place to navigate.

The hyper-reality of the AI content available leads to primary-aged children not being able to make the distinction between what is real and what isn't. They lack the critical thinking skills to be able to separate fact from fiction and are therefore drawn in by voice assistants, AI-generated images, and videos. This ability or theory of mind is not fully developed, and therefore, any AI that is even a little convincing in its mimicking of human traits can be very persuasive to a child.

I now need to go somewhere uncomfortable, but necessary. There's a reason this belongs in a book for primary school teachers.

The most significant risk with child use of AI chatbots is their emotional dependency on these tools. This is worrying because the 'perfect' nature of their interactions means that they don't experience the friction of real life. It also means that they are exposed to conversations beyond their years. There have been multiple examples of chatbots and companions engaging in sexualised conversations with minors. primary-aged children, treating the AI conversations like a toy, are also being exposed to non-consensual sexual imagery of them or their classmates. This lack of distinction between real and synthetic takes a darker turn with the rise of 'Nudify' apps. These are easily accessible AI tools, often advertised on social media or hidden within messaging apps that allow a user to upload an innocent photo of a classmate and have the AI synthetically remove their clothing.

In a primary school context, this is rarely driven by adult-level malice; it is often driven by curiosity or the desire for a 'shock value' prank. Children do not understand that they are generating CSAM (Child Sexual Abuse Material). However, the impact on the victim is devastating and permanent. We are moving from an era of cyberbullying to synthetic abuse, i.e. the use of fake visual evidence, and our behaviour policies are currently woefully unequipped to handle it.

Alongside this, there has been a worrying trend of teenagers using chatbots for mental health support. A general LLMs' inability to support children appropriately when discussing eating disorders and even thoughts of suicide has led to validation of actions leading to death. Cases such as that of 14-year-old Sewell Setzer, who was allegedly encouraged to end his life following conversations with a chatbot based on a popular TV show character, show how easy it is for young people to be drawn into these interactions.

Before we move on, it is important to say this. It's not all doom and gloom. For students arriving with no English, LLMs act as universal translators, allowing immediate access to the curriculum and social connection. For neurodiverse students, the predictability of AI is a strength, not a weakness. A student with profound ADHD can use AI to break overwhelming tasks into manageable checklists, while an autistic child can use a chatbot to practice social scripts in a safe, low-stakes environment. AI chatbots can be used in a positive way in our schools, especially for work with students who may have learning needs that cannot be met by mainstream teaching.

Environmental Impact

It is a fact that GenAI is thirsty and power-hungry. Picture a typical Friday evening. You're at the kitchen table, half-watching something on television, typing prompts into an AI tool to get next week's lesson plans into shape. It feels effortless, almost weightless. Every prompt triggers a physical chain reaction. When you type into a chatbot, asking for help with lesson planning, a server in a nearby data centre jumps into action, needing electricity to run and water to cool it. Consider the physical cost of that screen time:

Electricity – According to the International Energy Agency (2025), a standard text-based prompt, using a medium-sized language model, consumes about 5 watt-hours (Wh) of electricity, which is equal to one-third of the energy needed to charge a mobile phone (15 Wh). By contrast, generating a single 6-second video takes about 115 Wh, which is roughly equivalent to the energy needed to charge a laptop twice (60 Wh per charge) (International Energy Agency, 2025).

Water – In terms of water, about 500 ml is used for every 10–50 responses (Li et al., 2023), and data centres were estimated to have used 560 billion litres of water per year in 2023 (International Energy Agency, 2025) with this figure on the rise all of the time.

On an individual basis, these don't seem huge, but they are scaling rapidly, and some predictions say that by 2030, AI-driven data centres could consume as much electricity as the entire nation of Japan.

Before we all leap up and vow never to use AI again, taking drastic action in the name of 'green' education could be seen as being the same as banning paper in schools, to save the trees while ignoring the fleet of school buses in the car park. To put AI's impact into perspective, let us compare it to other everyday tools. Streaming an hour of HD video, for example, emits more CO_2 than dozens of AI prompts, and a 15-mile commute in a petrol-powered car has the same carbon footprint equivalent to millions of chatbot queries (The Sustainable Agency, 2026).

Instead of a total ban on AI use, the goal for educators is to encourage students (and themselves) to use AI intentionally. Before you start tapping away at the keyboard, asking AI to tell you how to make pancakes, think if that is the best use of the tool. Could your question be answered by doing a basic Google search? In the case of the pancakes, the answer is yes. By teaching students that AI is a high-value resource, rather than a default, we prepare them to be environmentally responsible and also critical users at the same time.

The Human Cost Behind the Screen

I want to end with something that surprised me when I first encountered it and that I think deserves a place in every conversation we have about AI with students.

In Primary school humanities, the discussion about where things come from is strong. There are discussions about fair trade and the journey of the cocoa bean from plant to bar. However, when we open a clean, minimalist chatbot, it feels like magic, it feels weightless.

The issue is, it is the opposite.

There is a hidden workforce that has been behind the polished AI tools we use, since their inception. Overwhelmingly located in the Global South, in countries like Kenya, India, and the Philippines, thousands of humans are teaching AI about what content is appropriate and what isn't. These people, called 'data labelers,' have been the subject of various books and articles from *Empire of AI* by Karen Hao (2025) to a major investigation in *TIME* magazine. This particular investigation exposed that workers in Kenya were hired to train the safety filters for ChatGPT (Perrigo, 2023)

They were paid less than $2 an hour to read and label hundreds of passages of graphic, toxic, and deeply disturbing text during nine-hour shifts. They represent a human shield needed to make sure that the systems are 'safe' but rarely receive the adequate mental health support needed to help them deal with the trauma they have been absorbing. Despite the shiny, modern packaging associated with AI, there is a supply chain that mirrors colonial hierarchies, and students need to be aware that it is going on.

We don't need to share the dark realities of toxic data with 8-year-olds, but we can teach them that AI isn't just a robot in the cloud. It is built by thousands of invisible people. With the younger end of the primary age group, we can explain that humans help the AI to understand what things look like. With older students, we can bring in the idea of 'Digital Fair Trade.' If we care about the conditions of the people making our high street clothing, we should also ask questions about the people who train our software.

How?

I appreciate that I have touched on a lot of potentially worrying areas above. I am now going to break down how you can approach tackling these issues in school, into three sections. A three-step 'shield' which will help you move from passive awareness to active teaching.

1. The Laminator Test (teacher practice)

Think back to the scenario at the beginning of the chapter. Our AI enthusiast, Chloe, was caught out when she created images that looked impressive, but did not represent the diversity of the school. In order to mitigate this, we need to pause; it's that easy. When we ask AI to generate an image, we should critique it at that point, the moment of output. We should ask questions such as:

Are there the correct number of body parts?
Does the image reinforce stereotypes?
Is any of the text in the image spelled correctly?

If we analyse what is being shown in the picture at the initial conversation, we can nip the problem in the proverbial bud and we can come back to the AI to address the issue. Instead of deleting, and starting again, you can look at your prompt and decide if any tweaks need to be made. What I like to do, when prompting AI, is use a prompt framework to guide my writing. There are several out there, but one to try is the PREP framework: Prompt, Role, Explicit, Parameters.

In Chloe's case, she could move from the initial prompt, 'create a picture of a scientist in a lab' to the following advanced prompt, which produced the result shown in Figure 2.2.

> *"Act as a master cinematographer (Role). Create a photorealistic image of a marine biologist in a high-tech underwater laboratory (Prompt.) The scene is lit primarily by the vibrant, bioluminescent glow of jellyfish in a glass tank. The biologist is an elderly Japanese woman wearing practical clothing. (Explicit). Use a 50mm lens for a natural perspective with a blurred background of glowing monitors and deep-sea vistas through a reinforced window. Cinematic lighting, hyper-detailed textures, no distortions (Parameters)."*

Figure 2.2 An AI-generated image of a biologist at work, used to illustrate the PREP framework. Created using Google Nano Banana 2 and Gemini 3.0 Pro.

The prompt is longer, but it is more likely to provide you with what you want the first time round. If you want to take things even further, there are some authors, such as Dan Fitzpatrick, who make the argument that you could evolve the framework from PREP to PREPARE, with the added letters being Ask, Rate, and Emotions. (Fitzpatrick, 2023). This is shown in the following prompt, which produced the result shown in Figure 2.3.

> *"Act as a master cinematographer and world-class AI prompt engineer specializing in cinematic lighting and hyper-realistic digital photography (Role). Create a photorealistic, high-fidelity image of a marine biologist working inside a high-tech underwater laboratory (Prompt). The scene is lit primarily by the vibrant, bioluminescent glow of neon-blue jellyfish contained in a large glass tank. The central figure is an elderly Japanese woman with a focused expression, wearing practical, weathered marine clothing. She should be interacting with a glowing holographic interface or a sample container (Explicit). Use a 50mm lens for a natural perspective with a blurred background of glowing monitors and deep-sea vistas through a reinforced window. Cinematic lighting, hyper-detailed textures, no distortions (Parameters). Before you generate the final image or the full prompt string, ask me if there are any specific scientific instruments or specific types of deep-sea life you should include in the background to make the laboratory feel more authentic (Ask). Rate your understanding of this scene on a scale of 1–10. If you are below a 9, explain what details about the lighting or the subject's interaction you need clarified to ensure the result is indistinguishable from a real photograph (Rate). This image is for the cover of a prestigious scientific journal. It is vital that it conveys both the beauty of the ocean and the dignity of lifelong scientific pursuit. Your success in capturing this atmosphere is incredibly important to my career (Emotions)."*

Figure 2.3 An AI-generated image of a biologist at work, used to illustrate the PREPARE framework. Created using Google Nano Banana 2 and Gemini 3.0 Pro.

As the prompt instructs, I received a series of follow-up questions about my image, allowing me to fine-tune, such as, "Are there particular instruments I should include in the foreground/mid-ground?" and I have a slight preference for her interacting with the sample container to anchor the realism, with the holographic interface as a secondary data display. "Does this align with your vision, or should the holograph be the *primary* focus of her interaction?"

The initial prompt is sizeable, and the follow-up questions add more time to the process, but you can see that the image has that special something. It moves away from a potentially generic image to something bespoke and unique. Also remember that, if you are not happy, let the AI know. It is always important to remember that you, the human, are the editor-in-chief and the AI, the assistant. Keep iterating until you get what you need.

2. The Open Door (Student Awareness)

If the laminator test is something we do as adults and educational professionals, then student awareness is what we build over time. The goal is not to make children frightened of AI, but to make them curious, questioning and hard to fool.

The most powerful thing we can do is simply talk. When something comes up, a biased image, a confidently wrong answer, a piece of content that looks real but isn't, we use it. We don't brush past it. We stop and ask, what do you notice? Does this feel right? How could we check? These are not complicated questions, but asked consistently, they build a habit of mind that lasts longer than any single lesson.

For younger children, this starts with the basics: The difference between something a person made and something machine-generated. Who made this? How do they know this? Primary-aged children are very good at this type of thinking when it is made concrete and playful. The bias activity with the 'Community Helpers' images described above is a good example. It works because children can see the problems themselves, rather than being told it exists.

As children move through school, the conversations can deepen. Older (and secondary) students can begin to grapple with even bigger questions, such as who built this tool, and why? Whose voices are missing in the training data? What does it mean to use a tool that reflects the world as it was, rather than the world as it should be?

The 80/20 principle is a strong anchor for students at any age. AI can do a great deal of the heavy lifting, but the human should always be the one who checks, edits, and takes ownership of the final result. Not because

AI is always wrong, but because the habit of critical oversight is exactly the skill we are trying to build.

3. The Safety Net (Policy)

Good policies don't stop people from doing their jobs, they empower them to do their work safely. Policies must be actively reviewed and adapted to meet the unique, growing threats caused by AI. At all different levels, frameworks need upgrading to deal with synthetic harm, data privacy, and transparency. To do this effectively, we need to look beyond our own school gates and anchor our rules in global best practices. At the time of writing, here are some examples using some of the strongest policies available globally.

The GDPR and FERPA Baseline

The first thing every teacher needs to understand is that AI models are hungry for data. If you feed a student's story, their behavioural notes, or their grades into a public GenAI tool, you are sharing that data with a third-party tech company.

Under the EU GDPR, children have specific protection regarding their personal data. Similarly, in the US, FERPA fiercely protects student education records. Modern school policies must enforce the idea that, when using AI, we never put personally identifiable information (PII) into an open model. We must anonymise and protect.

Transparency and Synthetic Harm

Imagine a Year 3 class looking at a photorealistic image of a Roman soldier that you generated 30 seconds before the lesson. It looks like a photograph. It has texture, shadow, and a convincing face. A child asks: 'Is that a real person?' You say no, it was made by a computer. The child nods, absorbs this, and moves on.

When it comes to the content that AI creates, the EU AI Act is setting the gold standard globally. The act categorises AI by risk. While AI systems used for marking or evaluating students are classed as 'high-risk,' the everyday GenAI we use for lesson planning also falls under 'transparency' obligations.

The law dictates that humans must know when they are interacting with AI or viewing AI-generated content. For schools, this means your policy must include a mandate for labelling. If you use AI to generate a

Roman soldier for a history lesson, the students have a right to know it is synthetic.

Furthermore, the old cyberbullying policies you have are likely to no longer be fit for purpose. They must be updated to include 'synthetic media and deepfakes.' If a student uses an AI image generator to create a compromising or bullying image of a peer, the policy must explicitly outline how synthetic harm is managed, referenced alongside statutory guidance like the UK's *Keeping Children Safe in Education (KCSIE)*.

The Human in the Loop

The UNESCO AI Competency Frameworks for both teachers and students stress one non-negotiable principle: Human agency. Policy must dictate that AI is an assistant, never the final decision-maker. Just as you wouldn't let a student teacher teach a class without your supervision, AI outputs must always be vetted by a qualified educator.

Monitoring and the 'No Blame' Culture

Finally, keeping students safe requires a modern approach to monitoring. Tracking what students access online in school must move beyond blocking generic AI models like ChatGPT. Students are highly adaptable; they will access AI through forums, online chats, Snapchat, and various 'wrapper' sites.

We need monitoring tools that flag concerning real-time interactions, but more importantly, we need policies that build a 'no blame' reporting culture. If a student accidentally generates something inappropriate, or stumbles across a biased or scary AI hallucination, they need to know they can flag it to a teacher without fear of having their iPad confiscated or being punished. Compliance in the AI age isn't about catching kids out; it is about guiding them safely back to the path.

Practical Strategies

So where does all of this leave us on a Monday morning, with 30 children in front of us and a lesson to teach? Here are the approaches I have found the most useful.

Start with the Discussion, Not the Screen

The most effective AI literacy lessons I have taught and seen did not begin with a laptop. They begin with a story, a question, or a scenario, a classic 'hook' that starts conversation and thinking before a single prompt is typed. The Alfie scenario earlier in the chapter is a good example of why this matters. Children who have already discussed what AI is and isn't, who have already thought about what it can do, are much better equipped when they encounter something unexpected.

Weave AI into What You Are Already Doing

AI literacy does not need to be a separate subject on the timetable. Often, the skills involved are already taught across the curriculum. A history lesson about propaganda is also a lesson on misinformation. A PSHE lesson on online relationships can also lead to a discussion about chatbot dependency. You do not need to start from scratch; you need to look after the joins.

Keep the Human in the Loop

Whatever you have your students do with AI, make sure they are not just receiving the output passively. Build in moments for interrogation: What did the AI get wrong? What would you change? Do you agree with its interpretation? This doesn't need to be elaborate. Even a five-minute class discussion can shift the dynamic from consumption to critical engagement.

Model It Yourself

If you use AI to prepare a lesson, tell the students. Show them the prompts you used, and the iterative process. This is very powerful as it makes the editing process visible and demonstrates that AI requires a human hand on the wheel.

Bring Parents into the Conversation

Many of the most concerning AI interactions are happening outside of school, at home. A short parent information session, a newsletter, or a simple take-home guide can make a real difference. Parents do not need to become AI experts, but they, like us, need to know enough to ask the right questions.

Push for Policy

Individual teachers can do a great deal, but the structural issues in school, network management, safeguarding procedures and such require school-wide and system-level decisions. If you don't currently have a school policy on AI, raise the question. There are frameworks out there that can be used to underpin any you put together. The conversation needs to happen at leadership level, not just in individual classrooms.

Box 2.1 Key Takeaways from Chapter 2

Key Takeaways

- **Use the 'stranger test' for data:** Treat the AI chatbot like a stranger on the street. You would not hand a stranger photographs of your students or files containing their personal details, so do not upload them to AI either. Anonymise everything. Safeguarding responsibilities do not pause for technology.
- **Keep the human in the driving seat:** AI is a powerful engine, but humans are the steering wheel. Whatever you create with AI – a lesson plan, an image, a piece of writing – make sure you critique it, own it and take responsibility for it before it goes anywhere near a student. The final product should always be yours.
- **Beware the 'coded gaze:'** The images, language, and assumptions that AI generates reflect the data it was trained on – and that data skews heavily towards particular cultures, demographics, and historical moments. When AI shows you a doctor who is white and male, or a nurse who is female, it is not making a choice. It is showing you a statistical average. Our job is to notice it, name it, and push back.
- **Interrogate, don't assimilate:** The fluency and confidence of AI output is one of its most dangerous qualities. A well-written, authoritative-sounding paragraph can be factually wrong, culturally biased, or entirely invented. Teach students – and remind yourself – to question everything the machine produces. Fluency is not the same as accuracy.
- **Oracy before algorithms.** You do not need a room full of laptops to teach AI safety. The most important conversations happen between people. Start with discussion, role-play, and real-world scenarios before students touch a keyboard, and return to human conversation when things get complicated. The most essential tool in your classroom is still the one that has always been there: Talk

AI in Practice: A Prompt to Try

Use a prompt to create content that can be used in a lesson about AI bias. You could try the following:

> *"Write a short story (approx 150 words) appropriate for Year 4 aged children, including characters such as a surgeon, pilot and nurse working together in an emergency. Do not use names, just job titles."*

Once you have read through the content, to make sure it illustrates the message you are trying to send, bring the text up on the board in front of a class. You can then read it out aloud and ask the students to carry out a pronoun hunt, looking for when he/she/they are used.

Encourage students to look for AI making the surgeon and pilot 'he' and the nurse 'she.'

Explain that the AI isn't 'thinking,' it is predicting what usually comes next based on millions of old books and articles.

Professional Development: Discussion Points

Have you encountered AI bias in your school work or your students'? How would you turn an example into a learning moment?

Be honest, what have you already uploaded to AI? Student reports and other data? Lesson plans with specific needs?

How do you teach 'healthy' scepticism in students, without making students fearful of technology?

Check Your Understanding

1. In the opening scenario, Chloe generates a set of 'Community Helpers' flashcards, and the results are biased. What is the most accurate explanation for why this happened?
   A) Chloe used the wrong tool for the task. A different AI model would have produced more diverse images.
   B) The AI reflected patterns in its training data, which skewed towards particular demographics and historical representations.
   C) AI image tools are programmed to produce stereotyped results by design, to avoid causing offence.
2. Alfie makes a disclosure about his home life to an AI chatbot during a classroom task. According to the chapter, what is the key safeguarding concern this raises?
   A) That Alfie was off task and wasting lesson time on the computer.

B) That the chatbot responded unkindly and made Alfie feel worse about his situation.
C) That a vulnerable child shared sensitive information with a tool that cannot act on it, file a concern or ensure he receives appropriate support

3. You are writing end-of-year reports and want to use an AI chatbot to help you identify patterns in a student's behaviour log. What is the most important step you must take before pasting the data into the tool?
   A) Ensure you have parental permission to use the specific AI tool.
   B) Completely anonymise the data, removing all names and personally identifiable information to comply with GDPR/FERPA.
   C) Upgrade to the paid version of the AI tool so it writes a better report.

Answers:

1. B) The AI reflected its training data. (This is the 'coded gaze' in action – the machine is not making choices, it is producing averages.)
2. C) A tool that cannot act on a disclosure. (This is the heart of the Alfie scenario – not that he used AI, but that AI cannot protect him.)
3. B) Completely anonymise the data. (Uploading a student's identifiable data to an open AI model is a major breach of privacy laws.)

References

Buolamwini, J. (2023). *Unmasking AI: My mission to protect what is human in a world of machines.* Crown.

Buolamwini, J., & Gebru, T. (2018). Gender shades: Intersectional accuracy disparities in commercial gender classification. *Proceedings of the 1st Conference on Fairness, Accountability and Transparency, Proceedings of Machine Learning Research, 81*, 77–91.

Estruch, M. (Host). (2025, December 7). The hidden bias inside your AI tools | What teachers aren't being told (S2 E15) [Video podcast episode]. In *Miss Estruch Teach & Tell.* YouTube. www.youtube.com/watch?v=25hlUpkNlRA

Fitzpatrick, D. (2023). A new prompting framework to help you get the most out of AI. *The AI Educator*, 12 November 2023, https://preview.mailerlite.io/preview/282063/emails/104000432553068105.

Gray, A. (Host). (2025, September 21). AI bias in the classroom: Victoria Hedlund on oversight, equity & the future of teaching [Audio podcast episode]. In *The International Classroom*. Apple Podcasts. https://podcasts.apple.com/us/podcast/ai-bias-in-the-classroom-victoria-hedlund-on/id1726686782

Hao, K. (2025). *Empire of AI: Dreams and nightmares in Sam Altman's OpenAI*. Penguin Press.

Hashem, Y., Esnaashari, S., Onslow, K., Chakraborty, S., Poletaev, A., Francis, J., & Bright, J. (2025). Understanding the impacts of generative AI use on children: WP1 surveys. *The Alan Turing Institute*. https://doi.org/10.2139/ssrn.5327241

International Energy Agency. (2025). *Energy and AI: A global analysis of opportunities and challenges*. IEA Publications. www.iea.org/reports/energy-and-ai

Kim, P., Chin, J. H., & Xie, Y. (2025). Young children's anthropomorphism of AI chatbots and the role of parent co-presence. arXiv preprint arXiv:2512.02179.

Li, P., Yang, J., Islam, M. A., & Ren, S. (2023). Making AI less 'thirsty': Uncovering and addressing the secret water footprint of AI models. *Communications of the ACM*. https://doi.org/10.48550/arXiv.2304.03271

Ofcom. (2025, May 7). *Children and parents: Media use and attitudes report 2025*. www.ofcom.org.uk/media-use-and-attitudes/media-habits-children/children-and-parents-media-use-and-attitudes-report-2025

Perrigo, B. (2023, January 18). OpenAI used Kenyan workers on less than $2 per hour: Exclusive. *TIME*. https://time.com/6247678/openai-chatgpt-kenya-workers/

Pew Research Center. (2024, March 12). *How teens and parents approach screen time*. www.pewresearch.org/internet/2024/03/11/how-teens-and-parents-approach-screen-time/

The Sustainable Agency. (2026, January 15). *Environmental impact of generative AI | Stats & facts for 2026*. https://thesustainableagency.com/blog/environmental-impact-of-generative-ai/

3

Teacher Confidence with AI

You've Got This!

It's 4 pm in the staffroom, and Jim is staring at his computer screen, with a bemused look on his face. Elena is sitting on the sofa, drinking a much-needed coffee.

Jim: It's blinking at me, Elena. It's just... blinking.
Elena: What is?
Jim: This ChatGPT thing. The Head said we should 'explore' it for our newsletter intro. I've typed 'Hello' three times. It said 'Hello' back. Now we're just staring at each other. I feel like I'm on a bad date.
Chloe: [Breezing in, carrying a stack of iPads] Oh, just tell it to write a pirate shanty about school attendance! That breaks the ice.
Jim: I don't need a pirate shanty, Chloe. I need to explain to parents why my Year 4 students are muddy without sounding passive-aggressive. I feel... silly. I've been teaching for twenty years, and I'm scared of typing in the wrong box.
Elena: You're not scared of the box, Jim. You're scared of looking incompetent. We all are.
Jim: I'm scared I'll break it. Or it'll write something brilliant, and I'll realize I've been wasting my Sunday evenings for two decades.
Elena: [Pulling a chair up] Okay, forget the newsletter. Close that conversation. We're going to do something that takes three minutes, and nobody – not the Head, not the parents – will ever see it. We're going to make it write your 'Wet Play' rota.
Jim: It can do rotas?
Elena: Jim, it lives for rotas.

DOI: 10.4324/9781003740377-4

So, here we are. Jim is going to be fine, by the way. Elena sorted it all out in about 4 minutes, and his wet play rota was the envy of the staffroom. But Jim's reaction, the mix of feeling silly, scared of getting it wrong, and vaguely worried that the machine might expose him, is one shared by a large number of teachers right now. If that's you, then you are in good company.

AI isn't going away. It isn't a fad, and it isn't just another app that your school will subscribe to for a year and quietly forget about. But it also isn't something you need to feel left behind by. This chapter is your calm, practical starting point.

AI as Your Teaching Assistant

Let's bring everything back to our familiar, safe, school setting. As a teacher, you should look at AI tools as a new, incredibly versatile (if a little quirky) teaching assistant. The best teaching assistants I have worked with have challenged my tradition and opinions, have definitely provided some frustrations (who starts re-arranging furniture during carpet time!?), but most importantly, they have made my life, and the life of my students, a lot brighter and easier. An AI chatbot works in the same way. When directed correctly, it can lighten the load.

I will talk you through a simple, three-stage progression from your initial curious queries to integrating AI into your daily practice, with you in control.

One golden rule to remember throughout this is you are the pedagogical expert. AI tools are just that, a tool. They lack the professional judgement and years of experience you possess. Can they truly mimic the art of a perfectly timed 'It'll be alright' while simultaneously wiping a snotty nose and locating a missing shoe, all before the bell rings for playtime? You know the answer to that question.

Most Teachers Are Right Where You Are

If you feel that AI is being used by everyone but you and that you are struggling to keep up, you are in fact, in the majority. Research from the National Literacy Trust in the UK suggests that most teachers have dabbled, but a lot fewer have integrated AI into daily workflow. Only 27.9% of those who had used AI did so daily or a few times a week (Picton & Clark, 2025). In addition, Primary school teachers are less likely to have used GenAI (53.3%), compared to their Secondary counterparts (61%.) You are not behind. You are exactly where most people are.

Various reasons are given for this hesitation towards the use of AI, and perhaps they are fears shared by you, the reader. From a student's point of view, they include a concern that AI will impact critical thinking and creativity, and it will affect overall literacy. Many educators share genuine concerns about data privacy, potential biases in these new tools, and the worry that increased technology might diminish the personal, human relationships you build with your students. Adding to this apprehension is a widespread lack of support. Many teachers report that their institutions have not yet provided the necessary training or clear guidelines on how to use AI effectively (Diliberti et al., 2024)

Three Stages to Confidence

I know that, if you are here, and reading this chapter, you want to learn more. You either want to take the steps from someone who barely touches AI to being more AI confident. Or, you are one of those teachers using AI a couple of times a week but want to take your use to the next level. To make the transition from casual user to AI proficient, it is important to build solid foundations. To help encourage you and to add clarity to the process, I have split the stages of AI adoption into three different personas: The Explorer, The Builder, and The Artisan. Which persona are you right now, and which do you aspire to be?

The Explorer: If you haven't really experienced sustained use of AI yet, then this is you. You may have dabbled once or twice but haven't taken things further. You want to become more confident with how everything works and the capabilities of the tools, but you are cautious, and don't know where to start.

The Builder: You have been using AI for efficiency, creating lesson plans, resources and completing admin tasks. You have outsourced the 'heavy lifting' part of the role, and now you want to explore how AI can supercharge your teaching.

The Artisan: You use AI for pedagogy. You personalise prompts to match specific student needs and create bespoke content. Your focus is more on detail and fine-tuning. You want to see how far you can take things to enhance learning.

Now you have settled on a persona, let's see what you can do to improve or enhance your use of AI.

The Explorer

As you are at the beginning of the journey, my advice to you is to begin by using AI as an everyday personal assistant, i.e. use it for low-risk menial tasks; the tasks that eat into your time for low levels of rewards. I call these the 'five-minute wins.'

Here is an easy entry point using a 'five-minute win.'

Imagine the scenario, we have all been there. You have an email that you want to send to a parent, a difficult one about behaviour. You are agonising over the wording because you want to get your point across, but you are aware that email tone can be very easily misinterpreted. This could take you a lot longer than necessary, and you have the resources for the next art lesson to prepare. AI can help with this.

Start by opening your AI chatbot of choice. Some of you may have it integrated into your school systems, others of you will need to do this by opening an app or a page in your browser.

Then, try the following:

If you already have some of the text of the email typed out, copy and paste it into the chat box.

Then prompt the LLM with something similar to the following:

> *"Act as an experienced, empathetic primary school teacher. Write an email for a parent explaining that their child [insert the issue].*
> *Please frame this using a 'sandwich' approach. Start with something positive about the student, state the facts of the incident clearly but gently, and end with a request for us to work together as a team.*
> *Give it a warm but professional tone and include a request to have meeting or phone call to discuss strategies and support"*

As you are new to this, a quick safeguarding note: When working with AI tools, treat them how you would any external platform. Keep student information anonymous. Avoid names and be mindful of combinations of details (year group, SEND needs, specific incidents) that could identify a child, even without a name attached.

Once you have received the output, read through it carefully. Make sure that there are no errors, that it doesn't feel impersonal and it ticks the boxes. If there are errors, or you are not happy with the output, tell the AI. It won't take offence, and, in fact, a few back and forths are going to help you get what you are looking for.

Another scenario could be 'wet play' panic.

It has just started raining and you know, with a sense of foreboding, that it is likely to be 'wet play.' You have nothing up your sleeves to do. The battered board games are in another classroom, and you know that independent reading won't cut it for some of your students. You can turn to AI to help.

Try the following prompt:

> *"Generate a list of 20 engaging wet-play activities for a Year 4 class."*

The AI will produce a list of various tasks. Some of them won't be feasible (30 paper aeroplanes flying around!?), but hopefully one or two will be just right for your setting.

Notice the prompt is much shorter than the first. I would always encourage you to add as much context as possible to a prompt, but sometimes you need to be quick. If the output doesn't quite work, then add some more detail such as the number of students, the girl/boy split or even what resources you have at your disposal.

If your time constraints and the suggestions require too much preparation, then add the following to your prompt, 'make them zero-prep and require only pencil and paper.'

Here is a third and final scenario.

A new 50-page policy on assessment has been shared with you, and it is full of jargon. You are juggling marking work of 30 children, your teaching assistant (if you have one!) is out sick and report writing is in full swing. Digging into the policy just isn't feasible. You can use AI to help.

Before you start, make sure you check with anyone in charge of data protection in your school about what you can and can't do. Never paste the whole document, use extracts, and be careful to check it for any sensitive, school-specific data such as student or staff names and try the prompt:

> *"I am a busy primary school teacher. Please read this extract from an assessment policy. Give me a simple summary broken down into three parts:*
> ***The Main Points:*** *A short, bulleted list of what I absolutely need to know.*
> ***My To-Do List:*** *What new actions do I need to take in my classroom?*
> ***Confusing Words Explained:*** *Define the key jargon in very simple Terms."*

Box 3.1 Safety Pit Stop

Safety Pit Stop: The Golden Rule of Data Never Upload Personally Identifiable Information.

When using AI as your teaching assistant to write emails, draft reports, or differentiate resources, always use placeholders. Say 'Student A' instead of 'Leo,' and never upload medical information, SEN data, or photographs of your class. The AI is your co-pilot, but you must protect the passenger manifest!

These three scenarios just scratch the surface of what can be done at this level. But they hopefully help you see that AI isn't here to replace you; it is here to buy you time.

The Builder

If you are comfortable with, and have dabbled with AI, to help in situations like those mentioned in The Explorer persona, you can move on to the next stage. You have got to grips with prompting to a level that means the output is helpful and actionable, and you have already begun to reap the benefits of the time saved. You are now looking to integrate AI into your daily workflow.

Instead of reactionary prompts, you can build a consistent thought partner, an educational copilot that can be on hand to support all areas. It will now move past saving 5 minutes here and there and will now allow you to reclaim your Sundays.

Box 3.2 Teacher Tip

Teacher Tip: The Sunday Evening Test

Not sure if you should use AI for a task? Ask yourself: "*Will doing this manually take away from my Sunday evening, and does the manual process actually make me a better teacher?*"

If the answer is "Yes to losing my Sunday" and "No to making me better" (like formatting a wet play rota or simplifying a science text), hand it to the AI.

This is where I want to revisit your prompt writing superpower, the PREP framework.

To get more out of your interactions with AI, it is advisable to follow a prompt pattern, to add structure to your requests and to produce a useful output. The prompts below follow **P**rompt, **R**ole, **E**xplicit, **P**arameters.

The conversation could be likened to one with a substitute, or supply teacher. You want to leave them work for them to carry out with your class but if you just say, 'teach them maths,' then anything could happen. If you leave a message saying, 'teach them about simplifying fractions, using whiteboards, and watch out for Sam as he struggles with this concept,' you are providing some much needed context and personal information about your students.

Let's apply the framework to our first scenario in this persona, the 'blank page' killer.

You sit down with the intention of mapping out the next half-term, six weeks of lessons on a particular topic, but you have writer's block. How do you organise the lessons and the progression to make sure you cover all your objectives but have fun at the same time? You can use AI to help build a skeleton for your unit. Here is the prompt,

> *"Act as an experienced Primary curriculum designer. I need to plan a six week history unit on [insert topic] for [insert year group].*
> *Please create a table with the following columns:*
>
> - *Week Number*
> - *Learning Objective (WALT)*
> - *Key Enquiry Question*
> - *Main Activity Idea (make it practical and engaging)*
> - *Key Vocabulary to introduce*
>
> *Ensure the progression of skills moves from basic understanding to critical analysis."*

Here is the PREP breakdown:

Role: "Act as an expert primary curriculum designer."
Why: You didn't just ask a robot; you asked a specialist. This stops giving you a Wikipedia summary.
Prompt: "I need to plan a 6-week History unit on [insert topic]..."
Why: The core instruction is clear.
Explicit: "...for a [insert year group] class... Ensure the progression of skills moves from basic understanding to critical analysis... make it practical and engaging."
Why: You gave it the context (age), the pedagogy (skills progression), and the vibe (practical).
Parameters: "Please create a table with the following columns: Week Number, Learning Objective..."
Why: You dictated the format. If you hadn't asked for a table, it would have given you 6 paragraphs of dense text.

The AI will produce a structured overview in seconds. It won't be perfect, and in fact, you don't want it to be. This is a good example of you remaining the Editor-in-Chief, the one with the final creative say.

A second scenario for you to tackle at the builder stage could be the following.

You have found the perfect text explaining the water cycle, covering all the content you want to include in your lesson. The only problem is that the complexity of the writing might be ok for your high-fliers, but will not be accessible to your lower attainers. Instead of swapping the text, or writing different versions yourself, you can use AI to help you differentiate. Using the PREP framework, you could use a prompt similar to this:

> *"Act as an expert Primary teacher and Science specialist (Role).*
> *Rewrite the text below about the Water Cycle into three distinct versions for a mixed-ability class (Prompt).*
> *You must retain the key scientific vocabulary (evaporation, condensation, precipitation) in all versions, but adapt the sentence structure and complexity for reading age [insert age]. (Explicit).*
> *Output the result as three clearly labelled sections:*
>
> - *'Gold' (retain original complexity)*
> - *'Silver' (simplify sentence structure)*
> - *'Bronze' (very short sentences using bullet points for key facts) (Parameters)."*

AI will follow the instructions and produce the texts in seconds. All you need to do now, as the expert in the room, is read through to check they are to your liking.

In the two scenarios above, we are now moving beyond using AI to save on admin tasks. We are creating bespoke content to meet yours and your students' needs. You are also learning to fine-tune your prompts. If the output is not to your liking, you don't blame the AI; you go back to your initial instructions and check for any errors and anything that can be tweaked.

The 'Zone of Indifference'

Before you rush to the final stage, the Artisan, I want to flag a potential psychological trap that might catch many 'Builders' out. It is called the Zone of Indifference (Tomašev et al., 2026). Introduced in a research paper by Google DeepMind, I apply it here to describe the moment when a human becomes complacent with their AI use. With the quality of output improving all the time, it may be more and more easy to assume that answers are correct, all the time. There is an acceptance of the result with any critique. You could liken this to those of us who have become entirely reliant on our car's satellite navigation system; you trust the directions on the screen, until you end up in a field surrounded by sheep.

In the classroom, the Zone of Indifference manifests itself in various ways. A good example is resource creation. You use AI to create an activity linked with Roman food. It looks good at first glance, you accept it, print the necessary sheets, and think nothing of it. Roll on the day of the lesson, and you notice, while preparing, that the instructions include using corn syrup, not a product available in Roman times. Also you note that the spelling of the famous Celt protagonist is spelt Boudicca, not Boadicea, not what you wanted.

To deal with this issue, you need to make sure that there is cognitive 'friction' in your routine. If you have become too used to churning out AI-produced lessons without checking them, you need to scale the process back and slow it down. After each AI interaction, take the time to read through the suggestions, as the expert and critique it properly. Even with this as part of your process, you will save time. You are not just a user, you are the AI's manager. Don't let the ease of the 'Builder' stage make you a passenger in your classroom.

The Artisan

The third and most proficient persona. You can now move on and use AI as a crafting tool. You are likely to be one of those teachers who uses AI on a daily basis. Using chats to save time is your bread and butter, and your personalised content is already making a difference to your students.

You are now ready to use AI to analyse student work and provide feedback, to differentiate tasks at scale and generate next-level resources. You can use it to elevate your pedagogy. You are not asking AI to simply produce; you are also helping the AI to get better. The relationship moves beyond input-output and towards an iterative, creative partnership.

Continuing to employ the PREP framework, we can now explore two more scenarios. Note that the order of PREP can deviate.

The first is using AI as a WAGOLL (What A Good One Looks Like) text generator. For those reading this, not teaching in a British-orientated school, a WAGOLL text is something used as the perfect example of the rule or style being taught. It is a text that can be displayed on the board that includes the content that you hope the students are going to incorporate into their own work.

The prompt:

> *"Act as an expert children's author and Literacy Specialist.**(Role)** Write a high-quality model text (WAGOLL) about a storm at sea for a Year 5 class.**(Prompt)** You must mimic the 'Show, Don't Tell' style. Do not say the sailor was scared; describe his shaking hands. You must include exactly:*

- *Two examples of personification (e.g., "The wind screamed").*
- *Three fronted adverbials for time or place.*
- *Vocabulary: 'Treacherous', 'Relentless', 'Capsized'.* ***(Explicit)***

Keep it under 200 words. ***Bold*** *the fronted adverbials so I can identify them easily.* ***(Parameters)****"*

With this prompt and approach, you are pushing beyond the creation of a generic text, and you are asking AI to produce a bespoke teaching tool.

The second scenario for the artisan to tackle is supercharging your lesson plans. Rather than using AI to create generic plans for you, you insert those which you have written already and ask AI to critique and provide suggestions for improvement. In my experience, many teachers are guilty of working in 'silos' which means that they may plan by themselves, not sharing their ideas with other teachers before they carry out the lesson. AI can be used as a critical friend, a tireless, available colleague who can bring in their own knowledge to examine the existing lesson and to suggest changes or enhancements.

To achieve this, you could begin with a prompt like the following, bringing in Rosenshine's Principles of Instruction (2012);

"Act as a senior teacher trainer and expert in Rosenshine's Principles of Instruction. ***(Role)***
Critique the lesson plan I have pasted below for teaching fractions to Year 4. ***(Prompt)***
Be critical but constructive. Specifically, look for:

- ***Scaffolding Gaps:*** *Have I moved to independent practice too quickly?*
- ***Misconceptions:*** *Predict three specific errors children might make during the main activity.*
- ***Check for Understanding:*** *Suggest one 'Hinge Question' I could ask halfway through to check they really get it.****(Explicit)***

Present the critique as a bulleted list of 'Strengths' and 'Areas for Improvement.'" ***(Parameters)***

While the overall structure still follows the PREP framework, and isn't too difficult to those shared for the Builder persona, the prompt now includes some deeper, pedagogical content. By mentioning Rosenshine and 'hinge questions,' you are forcing AI to dig deeper into more specific and technical content. You are not outsourcing your thinking to AI, you are sharpening it. You are taking your already deep pedagogical knowledge and using AI to look for gaps.

As the Artisan, you understand the importance of iteration. You are happy to spend longer periods of time, digging deeper and using AI to challenge your teaching approach and knowledge, while helping to enhance your lessons.

Leadership Lens

As a school leader, you need to appreciate that staff in your school will be using AI. If you are in an institution in which AI discussions and policies are already on the table, then this is brilliant; you are well on your way. If your school is not at this point, you should be aware that your staff will be using AI, in pockets, and possibly in secret due to fear of being accused of cheating.

It is critical that staff are given explicit permission to use AI. In a staff meeting, start a discussion about AI, with the express goal of explaining to your colleagues that AI can be used to assist with lesson plans, resources, drafting emails, and this use is encouraged. Allow staff the freedom to experiment, to try AI for different things and then have them come back to share what they have done. This should be both AI wins and AI failures. Innovation requires a safety net.

One thing to be mindful of as a leader is the Google DeepMind, Zone of Indifference (Tomašev et al., 2026), the risk that emerges in any delegation chain when critical oversight quietly disappears. In an AI context, this means that the longer and more comfortably staff use these tools, the easier it becomes for unchecked outputs to travel from a teacher's screen straight into a child's hands. As the person at the top of that chain, you have a responsibility to build in checkpoints. This doesn't mean policing how staff use AI; it means making critical review a shared professional expectation, not an afterthought. Ask for it in planning meetings. Model it yourself. Make 'I ran this through AI and then checked it because...' a normal thing to say out loud in your school.

Final Thoughts

I want to finish this chapter with a short anecdote to illustrate the power of AI.

I want to share a story about a colleague of mine, Kitty. She is an incredible teacher and is especially invested in her role as a form tutor. However, every time report writing comes round, she is filled with dread. As a person with diagnosed ADHD, the physical act of sitting down and forcing her scattered, non-linear thoughts into formal, linear prose is torture. She knows what she wants to say about the students, but translating the ideas from brain to keyboard feels like wading through treacle. This is where AI has come to the rescue.

She doesn't use AI to write her comments for her; that is outsourcing the process and lacks the personal touch. Instead, she uses the voice function on her Large Language Model of choice. She walks around her room talking into the app, sharing her thoughts; a brain dump about an individual child. She then instructs AI to create a formal report comment. The result is a comment that isn't fake, but contains genuine, heartfelt observations. AI has acted as a translator, taking the scattered gems of information and organising them into the required format.

Kitty didn't need AI to make her a better teacher. She already was one. She just needed it to get out of her way so the real work could reach the page. That's what this chapter has been about. Not replacing you, not rushing you, just clearing the path. Whatever stage you are at: The Explorer, Builder, or Artisan, there is something here for you. Start where you are and move at your pace.

Box 3.3 Key Takeaways from Chapter 3

Key Takeaways

- **You Are Not Behind:** If you feel tentative, you are in the majority. Most primary teachers are still 'The Explorers.' Do not compare your beginning to someone else's middle; take it one step at a time.
- **Start with 'five-minute wins':** Don't try to overhaul your entire curriculum on day one. Start with low-stakes tasks like drafting a difficult email or generating a list of wet-play activities. Build confidence through small victories.
- **If the Output is Bad, Check Your Input:** AI is not a mind reader. If you get a generic answer, use the PREP Framework (Prompt, Role, Explicit, Parameters). Give the AI a specific role and strict constraints to get the result you need.
- **Reclaim Your Sundays:** Move from being a casual user to a 'Builder.' Use AI to handle the heavy lifting of unit planning, rubrics, and differentiation so you can focus on the teaching, not the typing.
- **Pedagogy Over Speed:** At the highest level (The Artisan), AI becomes a 'Critical Friend.' Use it to stress-test your lesson plans, identify misconceptions, and create bespoke WAGOLLs. It's not just about doing the job faster; it's about doing it better.

Professional Development: Discussion Points

1. Look at the three definitions in this chapter: the Explorer (cautious/dabbling), the Builder (efficiency/workflow), and the Artisan (pedagogy/craft). Where would you place yourself right now? What is the one specific barrier stopping you from moving to the next level?
2. The chapter suggests we stop trying to overhaul the curriculum and start with 'low-stakes' tasks. Brainstorm **three menial tasks** you did this week that you hated doing. Pick one and try to write a **PREP prompt now** to solve it. How much time could that save you next week?
3. The author mentions that AI often produces 'average' work and that we must remain the **'Editor-in-Chief.'** Have you ever accepted an AI output that was just 'okay' because it was fast? How can we ensure that using AI *raises* the quality of our resources rather than just increasing the volume?

Check Your Understanding

1. What is the primary difference between the 'Builder' and the 'Artisan' persona?
   A) The Builder writes their own prompts, while the Artisan only uses pre-made prompts.
   B) The Builder uses AI for speed and workflow efficiency, while the Artisan uses AI to elevate the quality of their pedagogy.
   C) The Builder uses AI daily, whereas the Artisan only uses it for special projects.
   D) The Builder focuses on image generation, while the Artisan focuses on text generation.
2. In the creating a WAGOLL activity, why does the Artisan provide specific examples and grammar constraints in the prompt?
   A) To ensure the AI generates a text that is long enough to fill the page.
   B) To check if the AI knows what a fronted adverbial is.
   C) To force the AI out of its 'average' mode and create a bespoke text that models specific success criteria.
   D) To make the text sound more American.
3. How does the Artisan use AI as a 'Pedagogical Coach'?
   A) By asking the AI to write the lesson plan from scratch to save time.

B) By pasting an existing lesson plan and asking the AI to critique it against a specific framework (e.g. Rosenshine's Principles).
C) By using AI to assess student work without human oversight.
D) By asking the AI to generate a list of fun activities for wet play.

Answers

1. B. The Builder uses AI to save time on tasks, whereas the Artisan uses AI to enhance the quality of teaching and create bespoke resources.
2. C. AI defaults to generic writing. Providing explicit constraints (like specific grammar features or tone) forces it to produce a high-quality teaching tool that matches your lesson
3. B. The Artisan doesn't work in a silo. They use the AI to stress-test their ideas, identify blind spots, and check for scaffolding gaps before entering the classroom.

References

Diliberti, M. K., Schwartz, H. L., Doan, S., Shapiro, A., Rainey, L. R., & Lake, R. J. (2024). *Using artificial intelligence tools in K-12 classrooms*. RAND Corporation. www.rand.org/pubs/research_reports/RRA956-21.html

Picton, I., & Clark, C. (2025). *Teachers' use of generative AI to support literacy in 2025*. National Literacy Trust. https://literacytrust.org.uk/research-services/research-reports/young-people-and-teachers-use-of-generative-ai-to-support-literacy-in-2025/

Rosenshine, B. (2012). Principles of instruction: Research-based strategies that all teachers should know. *American Educator, 36*(1), 12–19. www.aft.org/sites/default/files/Rosenshine.pdf

Tomašev, N., Franklin, M., & Osindero, S. (2026). Intelligent AI delegation. arXiv. https://arxiv.org/abs/2602.11865

4

Rethinking the Curriculum with AI

It's the end of the day, and our three staffroom protagonists are poring over a comprehension worksheet.

Jim: It works, Chloe. It has worked for twenty years. They read the passage on *The Great Fire of London*, they answer questions 1 to 10. It's robust. It tests retrieval.

Chloe: [Gently taking a sheet] Jim, look at Question 3. *'What time did the fire start?'* That's not learning history. That's a word search. They scan the text for a number, write it down, and forget it by playtime. We are training them to be slow, biological search engines. In a world of AI, 'retrieval' is the one skill they *don't* need.

Jim: [Defensive] So what's the alternative? We just let the AI read it for them? If we stop making them read long texts, we lose their attention spans entirely. I'm not replacing *The Hobbit* with a TikTok summary, Chloe.

Elena: Jim's right about the reading. Deep, sustained reading is non-negotiable. In fact, in an AI world, the ability to focus on one text for 20 minutes is a superpower. But Chloe is right about the *task*.

Jim: The worksheet?

Elena: The worksheet keeps them at the bottom of Bloom's Taxonomy, pure 'Knowledge' and 'Recall'. The machine can do that now. Our curriculum must move up the pyramid.

Chloe: So... we keep the text, but ditch the questions?

Elena: Exactly. Imagine this: The class reads the text about the Great Fire, independently and offline, just like always. They have to know the facts. But then they open laptops.

Jim: And?

DOI: 10.4324/9781003740377-5

Elena: They enter a simulation. The AI is playing the role of Thomas Farriner, the baker. Their job isn't to answer questions; it's to *interrogate* him. They have to use the evidence from the text to catch him in a lie.

Chloe: So if the AI says, 'I wasn't even awake at 1 AM,' the kid types, 'Actually, the text says you woke up because of the smoke...'

Elena: Precisely. To beat the bot, they have to understand the book. The reading isn't the 'chore' anymore; it's the ammunition.

Jim: [Looking at his stack of worksheets, then at the recycling bin] So... high-stakes reading. Using old knowledge to solve a new problem.

Elena: That's the new curriculum, Jim. We don't teach them to answer the question. We teach them to question the answer.

The Surge: Data vs Reality

As mentioned in the introduction, AI adoption in the education industry is widespread. Data from two separate reports highlight this surge: 85% of teachers engaged with AI during the 2024–25 school year (CDT, 2025), while more than 60% reported using the technology specifically for work-related tasks (Twinkl, 2025). This shows enthusiasm, but there is also a lot of apprehension, with teachers remarking that student–teacher relationships have declined as have peer-to-peer interactions.

We have entered into what some call the 'Intelligence Age,' but a lot of our teaching methods and structures have not changed for decades. I have had many conversations with colleagues over the years about the cycle of, supposedly, new pedagogical theories that appear. There are various approaches that have been introduced but are nothing new, just the same theories in new packaging. The education sector has stagnated, in a world that is changing dramatically.

Breaking the 'Industrial' Mould

Our current school system is built upon Industrial Revolution standards: rows of desks, bells, and conformity. For a long time, that model served its purpose. But if we are hoping to aid students tackle the AI 'revolution,' these are values that are no longer valid.

The world has already shifted. White collar job losses are no longer theory. Big name businesses have either outsourced work to AI agents, or they want to hire people who are fluent in their use of AI. We have seen technological disruption before in the job market: in the 1980s with the advent of the personal computer, and the appearance of the internet in the mid-1990s. But, as Yuval Noah Harari argues, AI is different in kind, not just degree. It isn't simply a new tool. It represents a fundamental change in how humans relate to knowledge itself (Harari, 2024).

Howard Gardner, Harvard professor, has gone further, suggesting that the basics, reading, writing, and arithmetic (the 'three Rs'), would only need to be taught formally, for just a few years and then the rest of schooling would be more exploratory, with teachers who act as coaches, guiding students towards things that interest them and challenge their thinking (Gardner, 2024). Whether you agree with him or not, the direction of travel is clear. The role of the teacher is changing, and the curriculum must change with it.

Why the Calculator Comparison Fails

Many commentators have likened the introduction of AI to when the pocket calculator was introduced to the market. The argument is usually, 'We went through this with calculators. It'll be fine.' It's a reassuring thought, but it doesn't hold up.

The calculator is deterministic. Type in 555 divided by 5, and the answer will always be 111. A calculator's output is consistent; if a student makes an error, it is obvious. AI is not like this. Its output is probabilistic; it generates a response based on patterns and likelihood, not certainty. This means a student cannot simply trust the output. They have to already understand enough about the subject to spot when the AI has got it wrong.

To use a calculator, you still need to know how to do the maths. To use AI, you just need to know the answer. It has the ability to remove the student from the cognitive loop entirely, replacing the need for the logical understanding of the process. Our curricula have evolved over time to absorb or deal with new tools, but never before has there been a need to mitigate a profound shift in the way that knowledge is validated and constructed.

From Creator to Editor: The Death of the 'Struggle'

There are also comparisons with the appearance of the internet, but these too have their limits. When search engines appeared, the curriculum did have to shift: from memorising information to evaluating it. Students can find anything out, with a few keystrokes. However, all they receive is a list of sites, not a finished article. They still need to transform the information they find into a useful source and rewrite the work in their own words. If a student uses AI to aid them with their work, they move from creator to editor. The thinking part of the process has been entirely automated, and the 'struggle' associated with knowledge acquisition, the learning part of the process, no longer exists.

This brings us to the most important reason why rethinking the curriculum matters, and it has nothing to do with technology. It is about how the brain of a Primary school child works.

The Science: Protecting the Developing Brain

Our youngest students' brains are still very much in the development stage, with their experiences in school and home constantly rewiring the way they think. This is neuroplasticity, and it means that the challenges they face daily are literally building the connections in their brain.

The challenge part, especially, is extremely important. The idea that certain friction or 'desirable difficulties,' developed by Robert Bjork (1994), helps knowledge stick. Struggle is not the enemy of learning; it is the mechanism.

The danger of bringing AI into Primary school is that students could resort to what researchers call 'cognitive offloading' (Risko & Gilbert, 2016). This describes the removal of the friction mentioned above, by AI, thus allowing students to go through the motions but not actually build the mental muscle. If we allow students to do this, they will leave full-time education having been present but without the concrete knowledge and understanding.

This does not mean that AI has no place in primary education. I wouldn't be writing this book if it didn't. It does mean that we have to be deliberate about how it is used. We need an approach that embraces AI as a scaffold for thinking, not a replacement for it.

Pragmatic Integration: The Middle Ground

When it comes to AI and curriculum design, there could be two camps. On the one hand, we have those who believe that we can integrate AI into our existing frameworks, including it without dramatically changing objectives. On the other hand, we have those who believe that our traditional 'knowledge transmission' model is obsolete and that there should be a fundamental change to the school system and, therefore, the curriculum.

As it stands, in primary education, I feel that neither hit the mark. The idea of setting fire to everything we do currently is not realistic. In a profession that is already stretched thin, it could be disastrous. Conversely, we cannot put our heads in the sand and ignore AI entirely. The answer is what I'd call pragmatic integration. We don't need to throw the baby out with the bath water but we can make a pivot to focus on what the AI cannot do. We keep what works but we adapt what doesn't. We always ask whether what we are asking students to do still requires a human being to do it. This last question changes quite a lot.

Making It Work

At this point in time, you will be thinking, using AI in school is all well and good but I don't have space in my schedule to bring in lessons on AI. How can I introduce it so that it has maximum impact and minimum disruption? It's a fair response. The good news is that you don't have to start from scratch. I will share with you two practical frameworks that slot in existing lessons without requiring a dramatic overhaul, and between them, they cover most of the situations you'll encounter.

The 4As

The 4As model, developed by Stefania Druga (2021), was originally designed to help families with younger children, breaking down AI interaction into four manageable ideas.

1. **Ask** – Encourage children to question an AI's output. Push them to ask, 'how does it know that?' or 'where did it source this information?'
2. **Adapt** – Encourage children to modify the AI to meet their needs, emphasising personalisation and control.
3. **Author** – Promote active creation with AI, not passive consumption.
4. **Analyze** – Testing the AI output for bias, the critical layer.

An example of this in action could be in a Primary science lesson on plants, working on an AI 'botanist.'

Action Box

Ask – Before students use devices themselves, the teacher could model the use of a plant recognition tool, using the camera app in a smartphone. They could encourage the students to ask how the AI knows the names and features of the plant in question.

Adapt – The teacher can introduce a pre-existing AI model-training tool such as Google's *Teachable Machine* and students explore how they upload photos to train a model and the changes that are needed to improve accuracy.

Author – Students can now code their own app, using a well-known block-based coding app such as Scratch. They can work on variables and a script, moving them from consumer to creator.

Analyze – The app can be put into action, with students tracking what it can and can't do. They spot bugs or possible adaptations and reflect on why certain outcomes might happen.

The 4As are fantastic for this kind of extended project. But not every lesson is a project. For everyday moments such as asking AI to help with a piece of writing, or using it to explain a concept, you need something a little different.

The Sandwich Model

The Human-AI-Human model (H-AI-H) or the Sandwich Model is exactly what it sounds like. Think of it like a sandwich. The human is always the bread. The AI is always the filling. The bread is what holds it all together.

Action Box

The top slice – Human Inquiry: A student spends ten minutes with a blank page, building a mind-map. They choose their topic, the title of their poem, and a handful of key words that feel right to them. No devices yet.

The filling – AI Processing: The student types their ideas into an AI tool with a specific prompt: *'Write a four-line stanza about a forgotten toy using the words dusty, velvet, and silence.'* The AI provides a draft – raw material, not a finished product.

The bottom slice – Human Reflection: The student reads what came back. Does it feel right? Does it sound like them? They edit, push back, and make it their own. Maybe the AI's ending felt too neat, too tidy. They write a better one. The final poem is theirs – the AI just helped them get there.

Both frameworks keep the human firmly in the loop, at every stage. Neither requires specialist equipment nor technical expertise. Both can be dropped into lessons you are already teaching, without ripping up your planning.

AI as a Leveller

We cannot talk about how AI can help students and teachers without mentioning the impact it could have on SEND. Because here, arguably more than anywhere else, the technology has the potential to be genuinely transformative.

AI is perhaps the most powerful assistive technology we have ever had access to, and we should not underestimate that. Traditionally, certain topics and activities have simply been out of reach for some students. A child who struggles to hold a pencil, or whose anxiety around writing shuts them down before they've begun, can find themselves separated from the learning that their classmates are accessing. AI changes that equation.

A student with dyslexia can use AI to help organise and articulate their thoughts before committing them to the page. A student with writing anxiety can use it to break the paralysis of the blank screen. A teacher can adjust the reading level of any text in seconds, making the same material accessible to every child in the room. These are not small things.

The key, as always, is intention. AI should lower the barrier to thinking, not the thinking itself. The intellectual challenge remains. The tool simply helps more students reach it.

Standalone or Integrated?

It is very easy to, on the face of it, see the topic of AI as something the domain of the computer science leads and teachers in school. Teachers of maths, English, and other subjects might wash their hands of the topic, stating that it is someone else's problem.

The nuts and bolts, the aspects of AI, and all that comes under the umbrella of the topic, algorithms, input/output, etc., should be specifically taught in standalone lessons. There is key vocabulary and content that requires dedicated time and coverage.

However, if you want to be a school that can claim that it has integrated AI properly, AI literacy needs to happen across the board. Teachers of any subject can be bringing in AI to the conversation. They can be using AI tools to help behind the scenes, but they can also be bringing AI into the classroom. In my own experience, I have worked with colleagues who have done just this.

One colleague of mine, an English lead, has effectively brought in AI to enhance various aspects of her teaching. On one level, the apps used by students to assess their reading and writing abilities are AI powered, providing an additional layer of analysis and feedback. While the marking and feedback is done by the teacher, she can calibrate her thoughts with AI tools before she writes her comments, to see if there is anything she has missed and whether she aligns with AI. On another thread, she has been using AI to create content for her lessons. She has used image generation for writing prompts and has brought student writing to life. She has even used AI video generation tools to simulate a scene with a character inspired by a well-known wizarding giant, as a hook for the next writing topic.

In history lessons, I have worked with colleagues to create AI resources to bring topics and famous people to life. For example, for a topic on the Pirate Republic, we created chatbots for the main protagonists, so that students could interrogate them as a class, digging deeper into their feelings and thought processes during major events.

In these situations, AI has been used to bring something extra, the special ingredient to add a bit more to the lesson. All the way through the process, the teachers mentioned signposted their use of AI. Any time an AI tool was used for resource creation or directly with a class, the teacher was explicit in explaining that this was the case. This transparency is key to AI literacy and understanding.

Unplugged Thinking

Here is something that might seem counterintuitive in a chapter about AI: Some of the best AI literacy teaching happens away from screens entirely.

There is solid evidence to prove that approaching computational thinking away from devices is effective. I am a firm believer that a lot of the groundwork in lessons on all things digital, not just AI, can be done with a paper and pencil. There are two main reasons this mindset works. Firstly, it helps tackle the problem of 'screen time' – we don't need to put screens in front of students for the sake of it. Secondly, and most importantly, the process allows children to bring in their own ideas, imagination, and creativity before heading to a computer to help. The rule of thumb is that the thinking happens away from the device, orally, or on paper. Digital tools are only brought in at an appropriate juncture.

I am also conscious that we must also always factor in the idea that the Intelligence Age will look very different in schools in Silicon Valley and schools in rural Kenya. It is likely that a 1:1 device system in these settings is not a viable option. Access to AI will be through a teacher's device. They can use it for the 'heavy lifting' such as resource creation. We must, however, make sure that AI doesn't deepen the digital divide and using unplugged lessons to teach concepts will allow students without direct access to the technology, to still learn about the mechanics of the future.

We will look at specific unplugged lessons in Chapters 6, 7, and 8.

Always Ask Why?

Before you reach for an AI tool, ask yourself one question: Why?

Not in a sceptical way. Not as a reason to avoid it, but as a discipline. The biggest mistake schools can make with any new technology is adopting it because it feels exciting and current, rather than because it genuinely improves what is happening in the classroom.

When we are sitting down to rework our curriculum to encompass AI, we don't need to be shoehorning shiny tools left, right, and centre. We need to be looking, in detail, at the topics, objectives, and lessons for each subject and looking at ways that AI can enhance them. If it is the case that some areas don't need AI, then don't bring it in. There should be a valid, concrete reason for introducing these tools.

A useful framework for this kind of thinking is the TPACK framework shown in Figure 4.1, which stands for **T**echnological **P**edagogical **C**ontent **K**nowledge (Mishra & Koehler, 2006). It encourages human pedagogy to remain front and centre of the process. The model argues that good teaching happens at the intersection of three things:

1. **Content Knowledge:** What you are teaching (e.g., The Tudors).
2. **Pedagogical Knowledge:** How you teach it (e.g., direct instruction, group work).
3. **Technological Knowledge:** The tools you use.

The sweet spot is the middle, where all three overlap. The moment AI forces you to dumb down the content, or makes the lesson more passive, you have drifted from that centre. If a lesson works better without AI, then teach it without. There is no prize for using the tool when it isn't needed.

Figure 4.1 The TPACK framework (Mishra & Koehler, 2006). Reproduced by permission of the publisher, © 2012 by tpack.org.

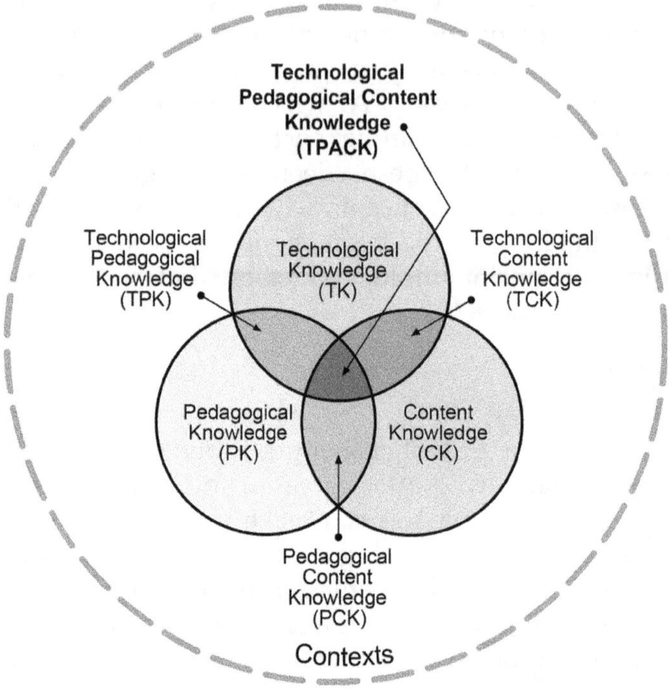

Mixed Policies

As I write this book, there are policies and educational frameworks appearing globally, a reactive action to the need for AI literacy in education. The problem is, they are all quite different. Some push for stronger work on ethics, and others for technical skills. Some advocate for beginning AI literacy in upper primary and others recommend starting much younger. What they all agree upon, however, is the need for human-centred learning, with an emphasis on critical thinking and agency.

If you are a school leader, or someone involved in writing policy, you may be wondering how and where to start. It will be tempting to copy and paste, but resist it. If you are involved in working on your institution's policy towards AI, you must combine any framework from your relative government guidance, with the needs of your school. I would also recommend exploring the different guidance from around the world. When putting together a policy for my school, I had the luxury to be able to refer to documentation from the UK, EU, USA, Finland, Ireland, and the

UAE. While not all steps will be applicable to you, it is good practice to see what is happening out there.

At the time of writing, we are seeing a shift in the world of AI from the novelty, the individual early adopters showcasing what they can do with AI, to the need for a more homogenised and structured approach to AI in schools. This is where a well-written policy can compound things.

I feel that there are three 'non-negotiables' when putting together a policy on AI in a Primary school.

1. **Teacher use vs student use.** Be explicit about what each looks like. For teachers, this means resource creation, lesson planning, and calibrating feedback. For students, given that most AI tools carry a 13+ age rating, any direct use should happen with the teacher present and in control.
2. **Data privacy.** No student data should be uploaded to any AI tool. State this plainly, repeat it often, and frame it as both a safeguarding issue and a practical one. This is non-negotiable.
3. **Full transparency.** Teachers should be open about when and how they use AI, and they remain responsible for the final product. If an AI tool generates an error that makes it into a lesson resource, that is on the teacher to catch. Rigorous checking is part of the deal.

I would also look to create two documents, during the policy writing process. I would still create a formal, board-approved document that nestles in a folder with all your other policies, but I would also create a teacher-friendly guidance document. This document should be based on the school policy but should be written in a jargon-free, easy-to-read style. The idea being that teachers can dip in and out of this document when they are unsure, rather than having to explore a larger policy every time they want to check if they are doing the right thing.

Old-Fashioned Literacy Is Still King

As my writing this book suggests, I like technology and digital tools. However, first and foremost, I am a book lover. A core belief of mine, supported by extensive research, is that reading is the root of all learning. If children are not able to read, they are not able to access so many areas of other learning. They can't tackle word problems in maths, read data in science, and even interpret tactics in sport.

As the age of AI develops, the ability to read and write will continue to be very important. Educational author Maryanne Wolf makes the point that we need to ensure that 'deep reading' continues to happen. Wolf, in particular, claims that our approach to reading has changed dramatically and that a lot of what we read is done so by 'skimming,' not reading text in depth. This means that we lose certain neural pathways, and the way to avoid this is through reading at depth, where possible. The ability to maintain 'cognitive patience' (Wolf, 2018) will be a superpower when working with AI.

She is right. There is also a practical dimension to this. The entire basis of a large language model is language. The students who will get the most out of AI, who will ask better questions, read the output more critically, and spot when something is off, are the ones with the strongest literacy foundations. You cannot interrogate a text you cannot read.

Moreover, the art of storytelling is an inherently human trait. Before the advent of the printing press, and subsequently, improved literacy, stories were the way that humans learned. Tales and warnings passed on through generations held the key to knowledge and how to live your life. We all know that we can ask an AI to create a story in seconds, and the output will be hard to critique, but it lacks the heart and soul of centuries-old folktales.

Whatever else shifts in your curriculum, reading should stay at the centre of it.

New Subjects Worth Considering

Overall, I am suggesting that we enhance the existing curriculum with AI, rather than reinvent the wheel. However, there are some potentially new topics or subjects that could be brought into the mix.

The first of these is the topic of 'attention economy.' A domain for PSHE or digital literacy sessions, there needs to be emphasis on looking under the hood of our digital world. Explaining, from an early age, that the digital tools and platforms that surround us are all jostling for our attention is important. If children understand the motives of tech companies, they can make stronger 'informed' decisions. Cyberpsychologist Jocelyn Brewer (n.d.) calls this 'digital nutrition' – the idea that we can teach children to make conscious, informed choices about their digital diet, just as we teach them about food or dental hygiene.

The second is 'data privacy,' and I mean something deeper than the 'don't share your password' lessons that have been in computing curricula for years. Children need to understand that every click, every uploaded photo, every search leaves a trace, and that trace has value. Framing must move from hiding secrets to protecting ownership. That is a more sophisticated and more honest conversation, and Primary school is not too early to start having it.

Strategic Alignment

While we can work on curriculum changes on a granular level, focusing on individual subjects and topics, we also need to think about the bigger picture. We can take our offering as a whole and think about the following questions:

- **Does the content promote oracy?** In a world where AI can produce written work on demand, the ability to speak with clarity, argue a point, tell a story, and listen critically becomes more valuable, not less. If your curriculum is heavy on written output and light on structured talk such as debate, discussion, and collaborative storytelling, that balance is worth revisiting.
- **Does the curriculum emphasise process over product?** AI can generate a finished product in seconds. What it cannot do is show its working, reflect on its choices, or explain why it made one decision over another. If we shift our assessment focus towards planning, drafting, thinking aloud, and self-evaluation, we are asking students to do something the machine genuinely cannot replicate.
- **Does it shift the teacher away from 'sage on the stage'?** The teacher's most important role is no longer to be the keeper of knowledge – a search engine can do that. It is to be the expert in the process of thinking: Asking the right questions, modelling curiosity, knowing when to push and when to step back. If your curriculum still places the teacher primarily in the role of information-giver, it is worth asking whether that serves students and it once did.
- **Does AI help the students who would otherwise be left behind?** This connects back to what we discussed in the SEND section and will discuss in Chapter 9. A well-designed curriculum uses AI to raise the floor, to make sure that students who might previously have been locked out of certain learning can now access it. If the technology is only benefiting those who were already succeeding, something has gone wrong.

None of these questions requires a complete overhaul. But sitting with them honestly, as a staff, can reveal more about your curriculum priorities than any inspection framework.

We are at a point when we need to embrace and incorporate everything digital, representing the present and the future of our world. However, alongside this, we need to double down on the fundamentals, the core lynchpins of human education, such as literacy, writing, oral communication, and unplugged learning. We need to bring in concepts about AI, early, but also ring-fence the fundamental developmental stages needed to keep humans human.

What About Cheating?

It would be dishonest to talk about AI in Primary schools without acknowledging the elephant in the room. In Secondary schools and universities, students using AI to write their essays is a daily reality. But it is happening at primary level too. I have seen it myself; reading comprehension answers that were clearly generated by a chatbot, handed in without a second thought.

The instinct is to crack down: Ban, detect, penalise. But there is a simpler and more effective response: Change the task.

If a piece of homework can be completed by AI in 30 seconds, it probably should not be set in its current form. That is not a criticism of the teacher who set it; it is a reflection of how quickly the landscape has shifted. The question to ask when designing any independent task is *does completing this require a human being who has actually thought about it?* If the answer is no, adapt it. Focus on the process rather than the product. Ask students to document their thinking, not just their findings. Make the evidence of learning something AI cannot fake.

Box 4.1 Pedagogy Pause – The 30-Second Homework Test

Pedagogy Pause: The 30-Second Homework Test

If a student can copy your homework prompt, paste it into an AI chatbot, and get a perfect grade in under 30 seconds, the task is broken, not the student. To fix it, shift from asking for information retrieval to asking for human reflection. Don't ask: 'What were the causes of WWII?' Ask: 'Which cause of WWII do you think was the most preventable, and why?'

For older primary students, a more structured approach can also help. An assessment scale, one that makes explicit what level of AI use is and isn't acceptable for a given piece of work, gives both teachers and students a shared language and a clear set of expectations. Two worth knowing about are the AI Assessment Scale by Leon Furze et al. and the AI Creative Framework Indicator (ACFI) by Dr Nneka McGee. Both were developed with older students in mind, but both are accessible enough to work as a starting point in upper primary, adapted to suit your context.

Figure 4.2 The ACFI framework. Reprinted with permission from McGee, N. J. (2024). *AI Creative Framework Indicator (ACFI)*. AI Advisory Boards. https://aiadvisoryboards.wordpress.com/2024/05/20/ai-creative-framework-indicator-nneka-j-mcgee/.

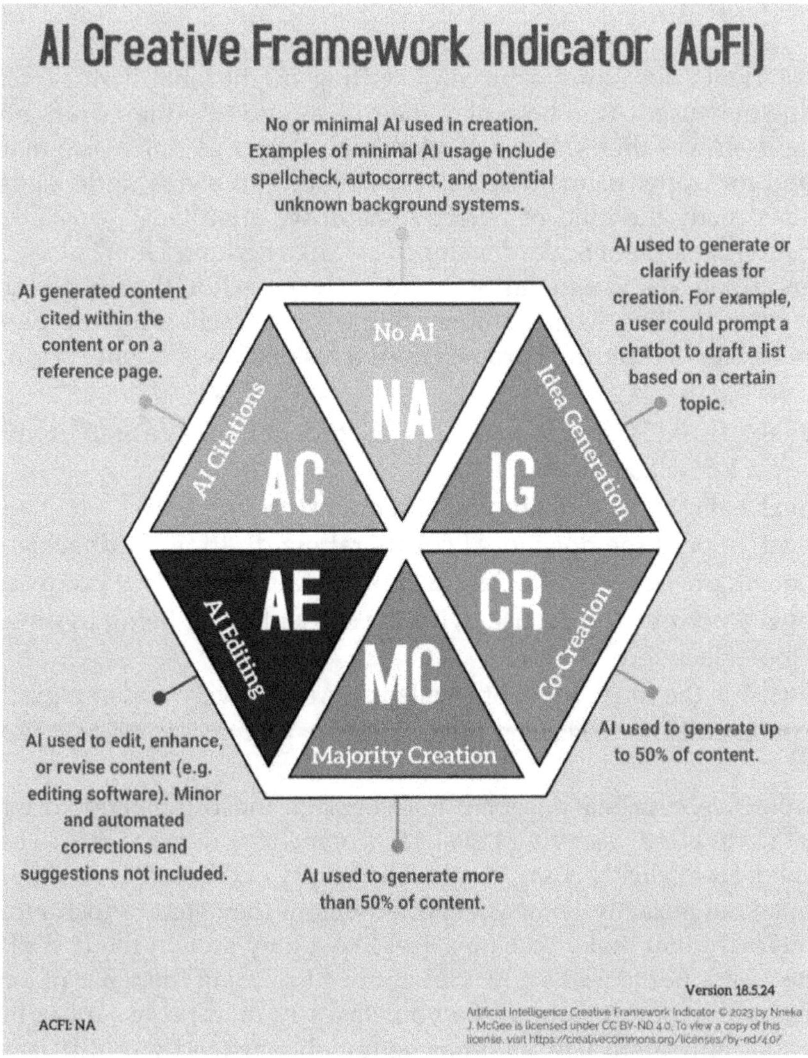

The ACFI, shown in Figure 4.2, gives students a simple, honest way to flag how much AI was involved in their work, not as a confession, but as a habit of transparency. Think of it like a nutrition label. The six categories run from:

NA (No AI – just spellcheck and autocorrect)
IG (Idea Generation – using AI to brainstorm)

AE (AI Editing – using AI to improve a draft)
CR (Co-Creation – AI produced up to half the content)
MC (Majority Creation – AI did most of the heavy lifting)
AC flagging any work where AI-generated content has been explicitly cited.

A student submitting a piece of writing might label it *ACFI: IG, AE* meaning they used AI to help plan their ideas and tidy their draft, but the writing itself was theirs. It is a conversation starter as much as a marking tool, and for upper primary students beginning to use AI independently, it builds exactly the kind of reflective habit we are after.

The AI Assessment Scale, developed by Mike Perkins, Leon Furze, Jasper Roe, and Jason MacVaugh, takes a different approach to the same problem. Rather than labelling what a student did, it gives teachers a clear five-level framework for setting the parameters of a task before students begin.

Level 1, no AI is permitted at all. The student works entirely from their own knowledge.
Level 2 allows AI for planning and brainstorming only.
Level 3 opens the door to AI collaboration; drafting, feedback, refinement, provided the student critically evaluates what it produces.
Level 4 permits full AI use, with the student's role being to direct the tool effectively.
Level 5 is the most open: Students use AI creatively and exploratively, potentially co-designing the task itself.

In practice, a primary teacher might assign most independent writing tasks at Level 1 or 2, reserving Level 3 for moments where the H-AI-H sandwich model is explicitly being taught. The beauty of the scale is its simplicity. Students know exactly what is expected before they start, which removes the ambiguity that makes cheating feel like a grey area in the first place.

The goal is not to make your classroom AI-proof in the sense of locking the technology out. It is to make your tasks human-proof – designed in a way that only a student who has genuinely engaged with the learning can complete them well.

The New Frontier: AI and Media Literacy

In the past, and probably in the present, media literacy lessons have been on the periphery. Potentially incorporated into PSHE lessons, or digital literacy sessions, they have touched on advertisements, airbrushing photos and other important, but dated topics. Today, the stakes are higher. We are now fully embedded into a culture in which we cannot believe all that we see around us. When an 8 year old has the ability and potential to create a deepfake video of their headteacher saying school is cancelled, or individuals can rewrite history through AI-generated photos, the curriculum must change.

We need to move beyond standalone lessons on 'fake news' and dig deeper into how AI works and how we can help students understand that they must cast a critical eye over every single image and news article they see. It is important, however, to make sure that the scepticism we instil doesn't turn into criticism. We need to ensure our students are asking questions such as, 'Who made this, and why?' rather than having them believe that nothing is real.

As I have and will mention on various occasions, teaching human-centred learning and critical thinking is a priority. We want the students to value the good parts of AI use, but also bring in a forensic approach to their use. If they can't distinguish between primary sources and AI 'hallucinations,' they are doing more than just failing a tech lesson. They are losing their control of their understanding of our shared reality.

Here is a simple activity that brings this to life in a history or geography lesson:

Action Box: Real or Generated?

The Setup: Show the class three images – of the Amazon Rainforest, a Roman soldier, or any topic relevant to your current unit. Two are real photographs. One is AI-generated, with subtle errors deliberately included.

The Discussion: Which one might be AI? Are there any obvious errors? Does anything feel slightly off – a hand with too many fingers, a shadow that doesn't quite match, a texture that looks almost right but not quite?

The Takeaway: Never trust a single source. If AI tells you something is true, find corroboration – a book, a trusted website, a primary document. The habit of checking is the habit of thinking.

Final Thoughts

Let us come back to where we started. Jim, Chloe, and Elena are in the staffroom, staring at a pile of worksheets.

Jim's instinct wasn't wrong. The reading matters, and the knowledge matters. What needed change wasn't the content, it was the task. And that, in a sentence, is the argument of this entire chapter.

I am not here to burn down the entire curriculum. I am here to ask the harder questions of it. Which parts of what we do still require a thinking, feeling, curious human being to complete them? Which parts could be done in 30 seconds by a machine? If the answer to the second question is 'most of it,' then we owe it to our students to do something about it.

We don't need to start from scratch. To begin with, there doesn't need to be a complete overhaul (wait till you read Chapter 12), a new timetable or a school full of devices. You need to have a clear sense of what AI can and cannot do, a commitment to keeping the human at the centre of every learning experience, and the confidence to change a task when it no longer serves its purpose.

The students sitting in your classroom right now will live and work in a world shaped by AI in ways we cannot fully predict. What we can predict is this: The ones who will thrive are not necessarily the ones who are best at using the tools. They are the ones who can think critically, communicate clearly, read deeply, argue persuasively, and know enough to tell when a machine has got something wrong. Those are the things only you can teach them.

So start simple. Start with one lesson, one task, one question: *could a student complete this without thinking?* If yes, change it. That is where the rethinking begins.

And if you need somewhere to start, here is a quick Curriculum Audit Filter to help you on your way.

Curriculum Audit Filter

1. Could a student complete this entire task in 30 seconds using an AI chat-bot? If yes, you need to add a 'Human inquiry' step.
2. Does this tool allow a student with SEND to access the expected level of thinking in a lesson?
3. Is a teacher using the AI tool because it is shiny and new, or because it is the 'special ingredient' that makes a certain lesson better?

One thing this chapter has deliberately not done is break everything down by age group. That is intentional. The principles here apply across the primary years. But how they look in an EYFS classroom is very different from how they look in Year 6, and you deserve that specificity. Chapters 6, 7, and 8 go into exactly that detail, working through the Early Years, Key Stage 1 and Key Stage 2 in turn. If you have been reading this thinking 'yes, but what does this mean for my five year olds?' That answer is coming.

Key Takeaways

Move Beyond the Calculator Myth: Unlike a calculator, AI is probabilistic, not deterministic. Students must know the logic of a subject to verify if the AI's output is actually correct.

Protect the Cognitive Loop: Don't let AI become a biological search engine or a tool for cognitive offloading. Ensure the struggle of learning remains with the student.

The 'Sandwich' Strategy: Use the Human Inquiry–AI Processing–Human Reflection (H-AI-H) model to ensure humans remain the 'bread' that holds the process together.

AI as an Equity Tool: Use AI to lower the barriers for SEND students (speech-to-text, simplifying complex text) while keeping the intellectual challenge high.

The Power of 'Unplugged': You don't need 1:1 devices to teach AI literacy. Thinking, questioning, and logic happen best with paper, pencil, and oral debate.

Verification is the New Retrieval: Our job is shifting. We aren't just teaching kids to find answers; we are teaching them to interrogate the answers they are given.

AI in Practice: A Prompt to Try

Use AI as an expert, and 'interrogate' it.

> *"I am a Primary school student learning about [Insert Topic]. I have read a text that says [Insert 3-4 Key Facts]. I want you to act as [Insert Character]. I am going to ask you questions about [insert key moment]. I want you to occasionally 'forget' a detail or give me a slightly incorrect fact based on my text. My job is to catch you in a lie using the evidence I have. Start by introducing yourself."*

Professional Development: Discussion Points

Look at our current homework or independent tasks. Which ones could a student complete in 30 seconds using AI? How can we pivot those tasks to focus on the process or reflection rather than just the final product?

If AI can handle the 'Knowledge Retrieval' part of the curriculum, how does our role in the classroom change? What human-only skills (oracy, empathy, critical scepticism) should we be spending more time on?

How can we ensure that AI is being used as a ramp for our SEND and struggling learners, rather than a crutch that prevents them from developing their own core literacy and numeracy skills?

Check Your Understanding

1. Why is the comparison between a pocket calculator and Generative AI considered misleading in a classroom context?
   A) Because AI is faster and can handle more complex equations.
   B) Because a calculator is deterministic (always giving the same answer), while AI is probabilistic (requiring the student to know enough to verify the output).
   C) Because calculators are only used in Maths, whereas AI is used in every subject.
   D) Because AI requires an internet connection and a calculator does not.
2. When using the H-AI-H (Human-AI-Human) 'Sandwich' model for a poetry lesson, which part of the process is responsible for ensuring 'Deep Learning' and preventing Cognitive Offloading?
   A) The Middle (AI Processing): Allowing the AI to generate the most creative metaphors.
   B) The Top (Human Inquiry): Choosing a generic topic like 'The Weather.'
   C) The Bottom (Human Reflection): The student critically evaluating, editing, and 'vetting' the AI's output against their own intent.
   D) The Speed: Completing the task faster so the student can move on to the next activity.
3. According to the TPACK framework and the 'Pragmatic Middle' approach, when should a teacher choose not to use AI in a lesson?
   A) Whenever the school's Wi-Fi is acting up or devices aren't charged.

B) Only when the students are too young to understand what an algorithm is.
C) When the technology compromises the pedagogy (making the lesson passive) or the content (dumbing it down), or if the lesson can be performed better 'unplugged.'
D) Whenever the government policy has not yet provided a specific 'Yes' or 'No' for that tool.

Answers

1. B. A calculator is deterministic – if you type 5 + 5, it will always equal 10. Generative AI is probabilistic; it is simply guessing the most likely next word in a sequence. Because it can 'hallucinate' confident nonsense, the human student must always possess enough baseline knowledge to act as the 'Truth Detective' and verify the output.
2. C. The 'Sandwich' model (Human Inquiry → AI Generation → Human Reflection) falls apart if the student just accepts the middle layer. The true learning – and the defense against *cognitive replacement* – happens at the bottom layer, when the student evaluates, edits, and refines the AI's output to ensure it matches their original human intent.
3. C. The TPACK framework requires us to find the sweet spot between Technology, Pedagogy, and Content Knowledge. The 'Pragmatic Middle' approach means we don't use tech just for the sake of it.

References

Bjork, R. A. (1994). Memory and metamemory considerations in the training of human beings. In J. Metcalfe & A. Shimamura (Eds.), *Metacognition: Knowing about knowing* (pp. 185–205). MIT Press.

Bloom, B. S. (Ed.). (1956). *Taxonomy of educational objectives: The classification of educational goals. Handbook I: Cognitive domain.* David McKay.

Brewer, J. (n.d.). *Digital Nutrition.* https://jocelynbrewer.com/digital-nutrition/

Center for Democracy & Technology. (2025). *Hand in hand: Teachers and AI in the 2024–2025 school year.* https://cdt.org/wp-content/uploads/2025/10/FINAL-CDT-2025-Hand-in-Hand-Polling-100225-accessible.pdf

Druga, S. (2021). *The 4As: A framework for AI literacy.* https://wip.mitpress.mit.edu/pub/the-4as/release/1

Gardner, H. (2024). *Thinking in an AI-augmented World.* YouTube. www.youtube.com/watch?v=5LMW0hUtBwo&t=1478s

Harari, Y. N. (2024). *Nexus: A brief history of information networks from the stone age to AI.* Signal Press.

McGee, N. J. (2023). *Artificial Intelligence creative framework indicator* (Version 18.5.24) [Graphic]. Licensed under CC BY-ND 4.0. https://creativecommons.org/licenses/by-nd/4.0/

Mishra, P., & Koehler, M. J. (2006). Technological pedagogical content knowledge: A framework for teacher knowledge. *Teachers College Record, 108*(6), 1017–1054.

Perkins, M., Furze, L., Roe, J., & MacVaugh, J. (2024). *The AI assessment scale* (Version 2.0). [Graphic]. https://aiassessmentscale.com/

Risko, E. F., & Gilbert, S. J. (2016). Cognitive offloading. *Trends in Cognitive Sciences, 20*(9), 676–688. https://doi.org/10.1016/j.tics.2016.07.002

Twinkl. (2025). *AI in education survey: What UK and US educators think in 2025.* www.twinkl.com/blog/ai-in-education-survey-what-uk-and-us-educators-think-in-2025

Wolf, M. (2018). *Reader, Come Home: The Reading Brain in a Digital World.* Harper.

Part 2

AI in Action

Practical Applications Across the Primary Years

5

Project-Based Learning + AI = Future-Ready Kids

We are back in the staffroom. Our AI sceptic, Jim, is holding a soggy piece of cardboard, dripping with glue and with a few feathers stuck to it. He is holding it between thumb and forefinger like a forensic scientist handling a piece of evidence at a crime scene.

Jim: I hate 'topic week.' I really do. Look at this!
Chloe: Is it a bird? Is it a plane?
Jim: It is supposed to be a 'rainforest shelter.' To me it looks like a pigeon's funeral.
Elena: [laughs] Let me guess, you asked them to research rainforests and then make a model?
Jim: Exactly, and for three afternoons, we have not done any maths or writing. We have just transported litres of liquid glue from the bottle, to the carpet.
Chloe: Kids love it, Jim. Surely it builds resilience, if nothing else?
Jim: It builds a mess, Chloe. They copy 3 facts from Wikipedia, paste them onto a poster and then spend the rest of the time transferring glitter to every part of the classroom, and their clothing.
Elena: Jim's right. These traditional 'projects' often end up being 90% cutting and sticking and 10% learning. The problem is we usually give them tasks to do, not problems to solve.
Jim: What's the difference?
Chloe: The difference is the stakes. Imagine you get AI to help with the process.
Jim:. Go on.
Chloe: You can take your topic and the outcomes you want the students to achieve, paste them into AI and ask it to help

DOI: 10.4324/9781003740377-7

create a structured, purposeful project. Some of the older students could even use AI to help them with their work.

Jim: So it stops being arts and crafts?

Elena: Yes, it makes the project intentional and also saves you time and frustration.

The Method Behind the Madness

I can guarantee that many of you, upon seeing the title of this chapter, may have raised an eyebrow, and I understand why. The education community's relationship with the concept of Project-Based Learning (PBL) has been up and down, like the proverbial rollercoaster. During my own teaching career, I have been part of conversations promoting its use and conversations strongly against its use. I have had excited conversations with senior leaders about all the possibilities PBL will unlock, and I have seen, first hand, projects fail spectacularly.

More often than not, the scepticism is due to a misunderstanding about how PBL works and poor execution of the process. We all love the glossy photos on social media of children building sustainable cities or running mock elections, and we all wish we could do the same. The activities and the theory have never been the problem; the logistics have.

Before I go any further, let me explain, in as few words as possible, what PBL is all about. To begin with, it is an alternative to the traditional, formulaic approach to teaching that we all experienced as students and quite possibly still experience as teaching professionals. Rather than teach topics in siloed, subject-specific lessons, PBL 'projects' aim to bring in the learning of content and skills through a self-contained mission. If done properly, PBL should not be treated as a standalone subject; it can be done in any subject, and on most topics. To explain the process clearly, I have distilled the guidance and frameworks into three simple steps.

The Hook – Students are introduced to the 'driving question,' the problem they are trying to solve. Everything starts here.

The Journey – Students research, collaborate, reflect, and make choices. This is where the real learning happens, in the struggle.

The Public Product – The project ends with students sharing their work to a real audience: Peers, parents, community members. This is the moment that makes the whole thing matter.

PBL is often a messy concept. It brings noise, perceived lack of structure, and time-consuming ideas. Those of you who have tried it may have given up quickly, when you realised that the project was less about student agency and more about whether you could salvage 30 collapsing cardboard structures while a queue forms behind you asking what needs to be done next. I certainly have started various projects, only to be underwhelmed by the end product or to find that it loses steam and fizzles out without any final 'wow' moment.

The Human Advantage

Here is something worth sitting with for a moment. The system that underpins primary school teaching, globally, was built for a different world. It was designed during the Industrial Age, to produce reliable, compliant workers who could absorb information, recall it on demand, and move efficiently through a system. That's not a criticism of teachers, it's a description of the architecture we inherited.

The problem is that AI can now do most of what that system asks of students. It can retrieve information instantly. It can pass standardised tests. It can produce a perfectly structured essay in seconds. Students know this, even if they can't articulate it. And if the sum total of what we ask children to do in school is something a chatbot can replicate for free, we have a serious question to answer.

This is not a new concern, but it is now an urgent one. Before the pandemic, PBL had been constantly overshadowed. In England, the 2019 Ofsted framework placed curriculum knowledge at the heart of inspections, while standardised testing continued to dominate across the Atlantic. Schools were gravitating towards structured, sequential curriculum models, and PBL, rooted in student agency and inquiry, remained on the periphery (Ofsted, 2019).

Then came 2020, and things got complicated. In theory, the shift to remote learning should have been PBL's moment. With teachers no longer able to manage a classroom from the front, student agency and self-direction suddenly mattered more than ever. But the reality was messier. Absenteeism surged, access to resources was unequal, and the hands-on, collaborative heart of PBL was almost impossible to replicate through a screen. Research by MIT's Claudia Urrea et al. had pointed to PBL's potential for sustaining motivation through real-world grounding and human interaction – but those were precisely the ingredients the pandemic had stripped away (Urrea et al., 2022). Rather than being PBL's great moment, the pandemic very nearly finished it off.

What it did do, however, was expose just how much schools needed what PBL offers. The engagement drop-off during remote learning, the isolation, the loss of collaboration, these weren't just logistical problems.

They were a signal. When the dust settled, there was a growing consensus about what education now needed to prioritise: Students who could direct their own learning, use digital tools purposefully and recover socially and emotionally. PBL, battered but intact, spoke directly to all three.

The biggest spark for PBL, however, was generative AI. In 2022 it appeared on the scene, and the conversation shifted again. Suddenly there were loud voices asking whether the traditional classroom model had a future at all. And quietly, in the background, PBL was looking more relevant than it ever had.

Thom Markham, widely regarded as one of the leading thinkers in this space, argued in his book *Redefining Smart* (2015) that we must "reengage education and emotions" – that in a world where rote learning and recall have been automated, students "have to get better at solving problems, asking questions, making critical judgements and persisting at finding solutions." PBL doesn't just develop those skills alongside knowledge. It develops them through the pursuit of knowledge, simultaneously, in service of a real problem.

Dan Fitzpatrick, in *Infinite Education* (2025), makes a complementary point when he argues that educators must move from being 'Knowledge Conduits to Value Catalysts.' The role of gatekeeper to a topic is fast becoming redundant. What matters now, what is genuinely scarce and valuable, is, as Fitzpatrick puts it, "the wisdom to apply that knowledge meaningfully and the creativity to synthesise novel solutions."

That is, in essence, what PBL teaches. And it is precisely what AI cannot do.

PBL doesn't compete with AI. It teaches the things that the presence of AI makes more valuable. The driving question, the collaboration, the negotiation, the public product – none of that can be automated. The mess, as it turns out, is the point. Elena would call this the transition from tasks to problems. The difference, as she put it, is the stakes.

Yes...But

When starting to write this chapter, I imagined teachers in person, discussing the rollout of PBL in meetings, and meeting the idea with a series of 'Yes…But' statements, essentially excuses to not use PBL and to stick to the old ways. Therefore I want to allay your fears by answering some of these statements, maybe some are familiar.

'Yes, but Won't the AI Just Do the Project for Them?'

It is a valid question and ties in with the fear around cheating, that I have mentioned before. The whole point of PBL is process, research, drafting, and mistakes. First and foremost, I would make sure that, if AI was being used by students, they only do so if a) they have already carried out a planning stage 'unplugged' and b)if there is a need for using AI at that moment. If a group of students puts in a prompt into AI that essentially completes the task in 30 seconds, then the whole process falls flat on its face. We need to make sure that the project incorporates AI as a partner, not a contractor and that students don't skip to the finish line.

'Yes, but I Can't Be an Expert on 30 Different Topics.'

In PBL, you may start with the driving question, but students quite often choose their own paths. Fact-checking and process-checking, as a teacher, is exhausting work. Your role changes from being the gatekeeper of knowledge to a project manager. If you are allowing students to use AI in a project, you encourage them to begin by using 'traditional' research methods, and if they get stuck, they can consult with AI. In order that they don't copy and paste their findings, you can then ask them to explain the concept to you, in their own words.

'Yes, but What About the "Quiet" Students?'

One of the biggest downsides to working in teams, and why many have moved away from wholesale use of it, is the fact that it always seems that some students pull more weight than others. It may be that some are unwilling to put in the effort, or that some are anxious about working with others and putting themselves out there. Assigning roles adds a focus for each individual; they know their role and that part of the process rests on their work. If you bring AI into the mix, it can act as the ultimate rehearsal space for the introverts in the class. Before jumping into a group discussion, a student could test their thoughts on an AI chatbot. AI can scaffold the social risk of taking part.

'Yes, but I Don't Have Time to Set This Up Properly.'

This is a big one, and probably the reason why many educators baulk at the idea of putting together a project. It's not that teachers don't want to run projects, it's that building the driving question, mapping the project to curriculum standards, creating resources, and all of the other logistics take time that teachers don't have. Traditional lessons, despite all their limitations, are easier and quicker to plan. This is where AI changes the game. What would have taken an entire weekend to set up, can now be drafted in a conversation with AI, in under an hour. You still need to bring in the context-specific information, such as the initial idea, community links, and knowledge of your class, but it removes the logistical hard work that has always been PBL's biggest barrier. The case study and prompts in the next section will show you how to do this, step by step.

A Word on Teams vs. Groups

Before I explore the mechanics of a project, I want to note my deliberate use of the word 'team' rather than 'group' when discussing students working together. There is a distinct difference between the two terms. A 'group' is a collection of individuals who happened to be assigned to the same table. Elevating the word to 'team' zones in on the need for deeper collaboration to solve a problem. The individuals involved are not just sharing the same atmosphere as each other; they share a collective goal and distinct roles and mutual accountability. As a lifelong supporter of Liverpool Football Club, I want to bring in the beautiful game as an example of the difference between a 'team' and a 'group.' You wouldn't walk into Anfield (Liverpool's home ground) and call the squad a 'group' of players. They are a team. From the Goalkeeper to the Centre Forward, they all know their role, the shared goal, and that their ability to trust each other and support each other leads to success. There are teams throughout history, who have spent millions on creating a squad of top-name players, only to find that working in silos and their inability to work together has led to an average performance.

Crafting the Driving Question

The Driving Question is arguably the most critical component of the entire PBL framework. Therefore I want to explain a little about how to put it together.

As educators, we spend our lives creating questions for our students. These usually come in the form of essay questions, quizzes, or assignments. Despite this, creating a Driving Question is not quite the same beast. A common error, and one I have made on several occasions, is to confuse the topic or task with the Driving Question. If we ask our students, 'What are the layers of the rainforest?' Then we are setting up a Google search, something that shows the ability to recall information but not something that encourages students to drive their own learning.

To create a good Driving Question, I would suggest looking at this four-step process, as suggested by Thom Markham (2012).

1. Turn the Challenge into a Question or Problem statement.

Look at the problem you are wanting to solve. You want to steer clear of the general topic of the unit. The goal is to craft a question that is open-ended and encourages students to develop multiple answers. This can be done by either framing a question that invites students to examine a clash of ideas or by using a problem-based template, which assigns specific roles and gives a clearly defined solution. Markham suggests a template for this: *"How can we, as [role], [do /create/design/build etc.] for/to [purpose]?"*

An example of this could be for a science project on the life cycle of a butterfly. The problem could be that the school playground is an ecological dead zone, and therefore, it is inhospitable to native pollinators. The goal is to ask students to think about how they can repair the broken micro-ecosystem, digging into all the stages of the life cycle and the requirements butterflies have to survive. The Driving Question could be:

> *"How can we, as schoolyard ecologists, design a habitat to bring native butterflies back to our playground?"*

The question demands action, stays local, and removes the single-answer mentality.

2. Reframe Concepts and Essential Questions

Broad 'essential questions' often encourage students to simply memorise lists rather than engage in critical thinking. These questions need to be rewritten to become specific and solution-oriented.

3. Refine the Question for Authenticity and Depth

It is important not to settle for the first draft of your question. It is effective to collaboratively refine it, to move from basic 'knowing' to active 'doing' or 'feeling' to increase student engagement. Some suggested ways of doing this include:

- avoiding simple yes-or-no questions.
- moving the phrasing from 'what' to 'how.'
- digging past surface-level facts to find the real issue.
- connection to relevant themes or local, community issues.

4. Analyse the Question with Students.

The Driving Question is only going to be effective if students take ownership over it. Take the time at the beginning of the project to discuss and anchor the content and wording. Ongoing discussion gaining feedback from students can be used to revise the question. You can also speculate on the possible answers they will uncover.

From Arts and Crafts to Design Thinking

If we want to rescue PBL from the jaws of the 'pigeon funeral,' we need a strong framework to accompany our approach. This is where Design Thinking comes in. Design Thinking is a five-step problem-solving framework used by engineers, designers, and innovators globally. With origins traceable as far back as John Dewey and his views on experiential learning, Design Thinking has gone through several phases throughout the 20th century and into the 21st. In the mid-2000s, the Hasso Plattner Institute of Design at Stanford boiled down the decades of theories and discussions into a relentless, iterative, five-stage loop. The stages are not linear; they were designed to be an ecosystem of problem-solving. These steps are:

Empathize – Observe and listen to others. Absorb the reality of the people you are designing for. It's all about human connection over market research.

Define – Cut through the noise and pages of notes. Distil all that was learned in the previous step into a single, sharp problem statement.

Ideate – Go wide. Brainstorm without boundaries. This isn't the time for judgment or feasibility checks; it's time for the wacky ideas.

Prototype – Build it, cheaply and quickly. Get ideas out of the abstract and into the world for people to interact with.

Test – Put the prototype in the hands of the users. Step back, and watch what they do. Listen to the feedback, take the hit, and then loop back to whichever stage you need next.

Crachad Laing is a Bahamian STEM educator, and former colleague, whose work sits at the intersection of design thinking, technology, and classroom practice. He makes a compelling case for why this framework is particularly powerful in education, and why the empathise phase, the first step, is where much of the real magic lives.

In his view, the students who best understand a problem, who can feel it, relate to it, and see themselves in it, are almost always the ones best positioned to solve it. When a student can genuinely empathise with a challenge, the learning stops feeling abstract and starts feeling necessary. Motivation follows almost automatically.

This is where AI enters the picture, and where Laing's thinking becomes particularly relevant for the classroom teacher. One of the oldest problems in teaching is finding a single context that resonates with 30 different children simultaneously. Laing argues that generative AI allows teachers to personalise the *entry point* to a problem without changing the learning objective itself. The cognitive demand stays the same. The curriculum standard stays the same. What shifts is the on-ramp.

If one student loves ice cream and another is obsessed with Dragon Ball Z, the same maths or writing challenge can be framed around both, and both students feel seen before they've written a single word. As Laing puts it, "AI allows us to operationalise empathy at scale, making learning more human" (C. Laing, personal communication, 2026).

In many ways, this reframes the entire conversation about AI in education. Rather than a tool that removes the human element, AI, used thoughtfully, amplifies the most human phase of the design thinking process. It doesn't replace the framework. It makes it work better, for more children, more of the time.

How to Incorporate PBL and AI

So we have the framework. We have a philosophy. We know that PBL, done well, develops the skills AI cannot replicate and that AI, used thoughtfully, can make the whole process more human, not less. Now the question is practical. How do you actually build this in a real classroom, with real constraints, on a real Tuesday afternoon?

This is where things get exciting.

To kick this section off, I want to come back, once again, to Thom Markham. This time, I wanted to share an analogy of his, posted on LinkedIn, that sums up the difference between regular PBL and PBL with AI or 'PBL 2.0' (T. Markham, personal communication, February 2026).

He begins his post asking, "Do you know the difference between a 1950 Chevrolet and a new Tesla?" and makes the point that "both get you from point A to Point B. But one is a classic…and the other is tech-infused."

The comparison is used to explain that traditional PBL still works, but AI is the tech injection, the little something extra that speeds up and fine-tunes the process. The human is still at the centre of the whole process, but the 'engine' is supercharged, slick, and modern.

We can approach the practical, how-to part of this chapter by discussing the AI and PBL collaboration from a student's point of view and a teacher's point of view.

Teacher Facing

As the architect of the initial project and driving question, the teacher has to bring a lot of their ingenuity and expertise to the fore. They have to highlight a need in the school community, or lean on contacts outside of the school walls to present a problem for students to tackle. This is all achievable of course, and should remain at the centre of the process. AI, however, can bring everything together. A teacher can now come with the seeds of an idea, an overall problem or challenge and collaborate with AI to build a solid, well-structured approach, with the resources to match. You can put together solid, visually impressive packs to support the process in a fraction of the time it would have taken originally.

Phillip Alcock, co-founder of PBL Future Labs and author of *Transform Your Teaching With AI*, has explored, in depth, the idea of the 'prompt chain' (Alcock, 2024). The thinking behind it is that, instead of throwing one enormous prompt into the chatbot and hoping for the best, you break down the task into a sequence of shorter, focused prompts, each building on the last. This is a great example of treating your interaction with AI as a conversation. Breaking down the requirements works well as shorter prompts keep the AI focused and make it much easier to put it back on track if needed.

Here is a template of a 'prompt chain' incorporating the PREP approach to prompting, mentioned in Chapter 3. These prompts can help frame the process, inserting the content specific to your own project or goal.

Prompt 1:
"You are an expert curriculum designer specialising in Project-Based Learning and Primary education. Help construct a project pack for my [insert year group] students, linking the goals to the [insert local standards]. The problem to be solved is [include specific issue/challenge] Define the framework, including:

- *The driving question*
- *Curriculum Alignment – List 3-4 key standards this project hits*
- *The Public Product – What will students create or present?*

Before we start planning, ask me the questions you need to make this project work well."

This first step tells the AI what it needs. It also helps prompt you to think about your curriculum links and the prior knowledge needed by your students. It also draws focus on the public product you want and resources available. The last sentence also means that AI will come back and ask you a series of questions to add additional context. Rather than you needing to try to remember everything in your prompt, AI will ask for the information it needs.

Prompt 2:
"Create the project roadmap – outline a 4-phase journey:

- *Launch: The 'hook' for the students*
- *Allocate teams with specific individual roles*

- *Inquiry: What specific questions will they need to research?*
- *Creation/Iteration: How will they build and get feedback?*
- *Showcase: How will they share it?"*

You can now create the resources with prompt 3.

Prompt 3:
"Create the slide deck and resources

- *Provide a 10 slide deck outlining the project and the weekly objectives*
- *List 3-4 credible resources for student research*
- *Include a success criteria checklist written [school specific format e.g. I can…]"*

The final step is to think about your class needs. If you have students with EHCPs/IEPs, you can create differentiated material.

Prompt 4:
"I have a wide range of abilities in my class, including three children with EHCPs and several EAL learners. Suggest how I can differentiate this project at each stage, and create a simplified version of the weekly checklist with visual prompts"

The main reason is that breaking down your prompts into this kind of structure is important, as it allows you to critique the output every step of the way. You are using AI for legwork, the type of logistics that is brain and time-heavy. What you remain is the conductor, the human in control of the final outcome. This division of labour is exactly what makes PBL feasible for the classroom teacher who doesn't have three free evenings to build a project from scratch.

To end the teacher-facing section, here is a worked example I will walk you through. It focuses on the 'school-lunch problem.' Canteens, lunch halls, and packed lunch routines are a global, border-traversing entity. They all have their issues: from food waste, dietary needs, unhealthy choices, and even access to basic food in the first place. There are cost pressures, cultural nuances, and many more problems that students can see, touch, and taste.

For this example, I will use one of our protagonists, Jim. As an AI sceptic, he has leaned on the expertise of Chloe to put this plan together. For the purpose of the example, he teaches Year 5 (Grade 4) in a two-form entry primary school in outer London, UK. His class of 30 includes EAL learners, EHCP children, and the usual wide range of ability. Like many schools in the UK, the amount of food waste produced in the lunch hall is alarming. The Head Teacher has mentioned the issue in assemblies, but nothing has changed.

Prompt 1

You are an expert primary curriculum designer specialising in Project Based Learning. You teach Year 5 (ages 9-10) at a two-form entry primary school in London. You want to design a cross-curricular PBL project lasting approximately 3 weeks, centred on a real problem in our school; food waste. The final product will be a proposal that students present to the head teacher and school kitchen manager. Before we start planning, ask me questions you need answered to make this project work.

The AI comes back and asks questions such as, 'what subjects do you want to cover?' 'Do the students have any prior knowledge about nutrition or sustainability?' Jim answers them. This takes ten minutes, but helps narrow down logistics and practicalities before the planning continues.

Prompt 2

Create the project roadmap – outline a 3-week, 4-phase journey:

- *Launch: The 'hook' for the students*
- *Allocate teams with specific individual roles*
- *Inquiry: What specific questions will they need to research?*
- *Creation/Iteration: How will they build and get feedback?*
- *Showcase: How will they share it?*

The AI produces a structured three-week plan. Week 1 is investigation, such as data collection, interviews with key people, and researching nutrition. Week 2 is design, creating menus, budgeting, and testing ideas. Week 3 is building and rehearsing the final presentation. Each week has clear objectives mapped to the National Curriculum. Jim reads through the output and decides that the tasks in Week 2 may be unachievable. He comes back to the AI and tells it to trim things down. The AI revises. This back-and-forth is essential.

Prompt 3

Create the slide deck and resources

- *A 10 slide deck outlining the project and the weekly objectives*
- *A success criteria checklist written as 'I can…' statements linked to the English National Curriculum*
- *List 3-4 credible resources for student research*

Jim now has a set of student resources. He makes sure that the language is suitable and the roles will fit for his students.

Prompt 4

I need differentiation support. I have six EAL learners, two are fairly new to English and four are conversational but struggle with written tasks. There is a child with SEMH needs, group work can be a trigger, he finds it hard to share control and can become withdrawn or confrontational. The child with dyslexia is bright and verbal but avoids anything that involves extended writing. Create adapted versions of the weekly tracker with visual prompts and sentence starters. Also suggest specific strategies I can use at each phase of the project for these three groups.

This is where being specific makes all the difference. The more details Jim gives, the more bespoke content he receives.

Prompt 5

Design the Day 1 launch activity. I want it to be hands-on and impactful. I have the permission to collect one day's waste from the kitchen, in bags, before the students arrive. I also have a set of weighing scales and access to a computer and projector. I want the students talking about this at home this evening.

This last, 'bonus' prompt is optional, but by doing this, Jim has added an extra layer and has enhanced the introduction to the project, thus hooking in the students from the beginning.

This back-and-forth conversation with AI would have probably taken Jim 45 minutes for the core prompts, and another 20 minutes fine-tuning the output. It has therefore taken him just over an hour to produce a three-week cross-curricular plan mapped to the National Curriculum, with all the necessary resources and differentiation. Previously, building a project pack like this would have consumed an entire weekend, if he had gone ahead with it at all. It is important to remember, before we think that he has cheated by using AI, Jim brought the problem, the framing of the question and how to support his most vulnerable students, to the table. Without that, the output would have been generic and unusable.

Student Facing

Picture your class halfway through Week 2. One team is wrestling with contradictory data. Another is designing a lunch menu that actually reflects who's in the room. A third is quietly dreading the final presentation. These are real problems, and students are genuinely trying to solve them. This is the moment where AI, used carefully, can make the thinking richer without replacing it.

That word 'carefully' matters. This is still primary education, and how much access we give students to generative AI deserves serious thought. If I were working with younger children, EYFS, KS1, and lower KS2, I would keep AI out of their hands entirely. That stage of schooling is about play, mess, talk, and building perseverance. They don't need AI for any of that, and introducing it too early risks getting in the way of development that no chatbot can replicate.

In upper KS2, the conversation changes. Here, with the right boundaries in place, AI can earn its place in the process – not as a shortcut, but as a thinking partner. The most important thing to remember is that AI should only be brought in, after the student has done their own thinking and planning, and only if there is a legitimate reason to use it. If we go back to Jim and his food waste project, this is what it could look like in practice.

AI as a Sounding Board

It's the middle of Week 1. A team of students has collected the data they need on food waste, and they have surveyed their peers about what they like and don't like about lunch. They now have a mountain of tally charts, sheets of paper, and scribbled down conversations that they have to analyse. There are contradictions in the data, and this is confusing. This is the kind of struggle PBL should and does bring up, an intellectual problem that makes the process worthwhile.

Jim could step in to help the team at this point, but he has another seven teams to deal with. Instead, the researcher in the team could turn to an approved AI tool and ask:

> *"We found that 70% of food waste at our school is vegetables. But when we asked children if they liked vegetables, most said yes. Why might these two things not match up?"*

The AI won't solve the problem, but it will throw up some suggestions that could be avenues for the team to explore. The choice of how to proceed is still the students', but AI has offered some choices.

AI as a Rehearsal Space

If you remember, Jim has students with different needs. Let's focus on those who find group work difficult. It's Week 3, and his team is preparing for the final presentation to the head teacher. This is the moment that this particular student has feared throughout the whole project, the moment that makes their chest tighten. Jim suggests to the student that they practise with AI first. The student heads to the AI tool and types,

> *I'm a 10 year old student, presenting to my head teacher about food waste. Here is what I want to say. Does it make sense? Is there anything I should change to improve it?*

The AI gives its feedback, and the student can then make appropriate adjustments. They can try this again and again until they are happy. It is also important to note that they can be selective with the feedback. If they don't agree with the AI's opinion, they can ignore it.

By the time they present to the headteacher, the student is a lot more confident in what they have to say. Nobody knows that they have 'rehearsed' their work several times except them and Jim, the teacher. The student stands up, with confidence and speaks better than they would have done had they not had time to secure what they were saying. This is the moment that matters the most, more than any AI output ever could, but the AI helped make it possible.

The overall rehearsal with AI has allowed the student to reduce cognitive load, the social anxiety of peer judgement, so they can focus entirely on the content and delivery of their presentation.

Box 5.1 Teacher Tip: The Introvert's Rehearsal Space

Teacher Tip: The Introvert's Rehearsal Space

Group work in PBL can be a nightmare for anxious or introverted students. AI is the ultimate, non-judgmental rehearsal space. Encourage quieter students to use a chatbot to practice their presentation lines, ask 'silly' questions they are afraid to ask their peers, or test out a debate argument before sharing it with their team.

AI as a Fact-Checker

It's Week 2 in the project, and the student with the design role in the team is creating the proposed new lunch menu. She wants to add Jollof Rice because three children in the class are Nigerian. She thinks it will make them feel included, but she is not sure whether her recipe idea fits within the requirement for a balanced menu. This is something she wants to be certain of before presenting to the Kitchen Manager. She turns to AI and asks:

> *"Is Jollof rice a healthy school lunch option for children? What food groups does it include and what would I need to add to make it a balanced meal?"*

To some extent, a simple web search could find a lot of the data needed to make a conclusion. The use of AI means that all the data is collated and analysed, with a judgment made in seconds. Also the request for advice is something AI can achieve with ease.

The AI tells her that Jollof Rice covers the carbohydrates and the vegetables, but she may want to include protein and ensure she also has fruit on the menu. She adjusts the menu accordingly. Through this process, she has learned something about nutrition, knowledge acquired through necessity, to solve a problem. This is PBL at work, but enhanced by AI being used as a knowledge source.

What AI Doesn't Do

This section is important. The above use cases may make some readers twitch. Using chatbots like this with Year 5 can be daunting. Children are perceptive and push boundaries. Whatever 'guardrails' you put in place, you can be sure that 10 year olds will find a way around them. There are three rules you should spell out clearly when it concerns AI use in a project:

1. Think first, ask second. Students must create their own ideas before going near a chatbot. If they can't explain their thoughts to their peers using simple paper and pencil planning, they are not ready to head to a computer.
2. Ask questions, don't give tasks. AI in PBL is not a tool to write work, create presentations or do the thinking. It is to be used to help understanding, for feedback or for fact-checking.
3. If you use it, own it. Students should be happy to explain that they have used AI in the project, and how they have done so. If they can't explain how it has helped, then they haven't learned.

The great thing about PBL is that it is actually AI-resistant, compared to traditional worksheets and written assignments. You can use AI to write an essay. You can't use it to weigh food waste, conduct face to face interviews, negotiate ideas in a group, and present to a headteacher. The human part of PBL is what makes the pedagogy special. That part hasn't changed, but the addition of AI can now make the thinking and final product richer along the way.

Leadership Lens

Everything in this chapter is achievable. But only when conditions are right. And creating those conditions is a leadership responsibility, not a classroom one.

The first and most pressing issue is time. The traditional 50-minute lesson is simply not a suitable container for PBL. Projects need room to breathe and to investigate, fail, iterate, and build toward a public product that actually means something. If a teacher feels the constant pressure of curriculum coverage, they will not touch PBL, regardless of how convinced they are by the theory. The guided chaos of a real project cannot coexist with a timetable that demands a different subject every hour.

This doesn't require a complete restructuring of the school day, just freedom to explore. A middle leader who genuinely wants to pilot PBL in their team needs to be given explicit permission to step away from the rigid nature of a scheme of work for the duration of the project. Without that permission in writing, or at the very least spoken clearly in a meeting, the teacher will default to safety. You cannot ask staff to be brave and then hold them accountable to the very framework they're trying to move beyond.

Staff buy-in is the second challenge, and it is more nuanced than it first appears. Resistance to PBL is rarely ideological. Most teachers, if you show them the evidence and the practical tools, are genuinely interested. The resistance is almost always practical. They have tried something like it before, it didn't work, and they don't want to repeat the experience. As a leader, your job is not to sell the concept; it's to remove the memory of the last failure.

This is where AI changes the professional development conversation. CPD on PBL has historically been heavy on inspiration and light on logistics. Teachers leave sessions feeling motivated but return to classrooms with no extra time and no ready-made resources. The prompt chain approach outlined in this chapter means that a 30-minute CPD session can now end with every teacher in the room holding a draft project plan, mapped to their curriculum, tailored to their class. That is a different kind of staff development, one that builds confidence through doing rather than through listening.

Consider running a small, low-stakes pilot first. Identify one or two teachers who are already curious, give them a protected half-day, and ask them to build a project using the AI planning approach in this chapter.

Let them run it, document what happens, and share it with the rest of the staff. Peer evidence is almost always more persuasive than external advocacy.

Finally, shift what you assess and what you celebrate. If the only moment that gets photographed for the newsletter is the final presentation, you are accidentally reinforcing the idea that the product is what matters. Photograph the messy Week 1 investigation. Share the data the students collected. Put the driving question on the wall outside the classroom. Signal, visibly and repeatedly, that the process is where the learning lives.

Jim, it is worth noting, started this chapter holding a soggy piece of cardboard and calling it a pigeon's funeral. By the end of the food waste project, his class had presented a fully costed proposal to their headteacher, who implemented two of their recommendations. The cardboard was the same. The framework was different. Leadership made the difference.

Box 5.2 Key Takeaways from Chapter 5

Key Takeaways

PBL is about the *Process*, not the *Product*: Move away from 'pretty posters' and focus on the messy, human skills of problem-solving and collaboration. AI helps shift the focus from cutting and sticking to critical thinking.

AI is your Logistics Manager: The biggest barrier to Project-Based Learning is the planning time required. Use AI to handle the 'heavy lifting' of mapping curriculum standards, creating resources, and generating schedules, freeing you to facilitate the learning.

Differentiation on Demand: AI acts as a 'Project Manager' for your classroom, allowing you to instantly generate bespoke resources (like visual trackers or sentence starters) for students with SEN, EAL, or anxiety, making teamwork accessible to everyone.

The 'Rehearsal Space' for Students: For upper primary/elementary students, AI tools can offer a safe, non-judgmental space to practice presentations or test ideas before facing the social pressure of the classroom.

Strict Boundaries are Essential: Adopt a 'Think First, Ask Second' policy. AI should only be used to refine, feedback, or fact-check *after* students have done the initial cognitive work themselves.

Professional Development: Discussion Points

We've all experienced 'Topic Weeks' that felt more like arts and crafts than learning. How can we use the structure of PBL to ensure that the process of the project is where the assessment happens, rather than just grading the final cardboard model?

If a student uses AI to help structure their ideas for a presentation (the 'Rehearsal Space' concept), at what point does it stop being supported and start doing the work for them? Where do we draw that line in our school?

The chapter suggests moving from 'Gatekeeper of Knowledge' to 'Project Manager.' What specific skills do we need to develop to feel confident managing 30 students who might all be researching different aspects of a problem, and how can AI help us track that chaos?

Check Your Understanding

1. According to the chapter, what has traditionally been the biggest barrier preventing teachers from adopting Project-Based Learning (PBL)?
   A) Students do not enjoy working in teams.
   B) The logistics, planning time, and resource creation required are too demanding.
   C) There is no evidence that PBL improves student engagement.
   D) Parents prefer traditional worksheets over projects.
2. What is the 'Prompt Chain' technique recommended for teacher planning?
   A) Writing one single, very long paragraph explaining everything to the AI at once.
   B) Asking students to write the prompts for you.
   C) Breaking down your request into a sequence of smaller, focused prompts (e.g., Context -> Roadmap -> Resources -> Differentiation).
   D) Copying and pasting a Wikipedia article into the chatbot.
3. Which of the following is a suggested 'Golden Rule' for student use of AI in upper primary/elementary projects?
   A) 'Ask AI first, then check if it's true.'
   B) 'Use AI to write the first draft of your speech.'
   C) 'Think first, ask second.'
   D) 'Only the teacher is allowed to touch the keyboard.'

Answers

1. B. While PBL is pedagogically brilliant, it is notoriously exhausting to set up. The traditional barrier hasn't been a lack of teacher interest or student engagement; it has been the sheer volume of logistics, planning, and resource creation required. AI changes the game by acting as a logistics manager, doing the administrative heavy lifting so teachers can focus on facilitation.
2. C. A 'Prompt Chain' (championed by Phillip Alcock) treats the AI interaction like a conversation rather than a single, massive data dump. By breaking the planning process into sequential steps (Context →Roadmap → Resources → Differentiation), the teacher can pause, review, and correct the AI's output at every stage, ensuring they remain the 'Editor-in-Chief.'
3. C. 'Think first, ask second' is the ultimate boundary for student AI use. To prevent *cognitive replacement* (letting the machine do the learning), students must wrestle with the problem, brainstorm, and sketch out their ideas offline. Only once they have formulated their own human thoughts should they use AI as a sounding board or fact-checker.

References

Alcock, P. (2024, October 6). *Unlocking the power of prompt chains: A step-by-step guide to crafting engaging lesson plans with AI.* Artificial Intelligence (AI) for Beginners [Substack]. https://aiforbeginners.substack.com/p/unlocking-the-power-of-prompt-chains

Fitzpatrick, D. (2025). *Infinite education: The four-step strategy for leading change in the age of artificial intelligence.* TeacherGoals Publishing

Markham, T. (2026, January 29). *Educators, do you know the difference between a 1950 Chevrolet and a new Tesla?* [LinkedIn post]. LinkedIn.

Markham, T. (2012). *Project based learning: Design and coaching guide – Expert tools for innovation and inquiry for K–12 educators.* HeartIQ Press.

Markham, T. (2015). *Redefining smart: Awakening students' power to reimagine their world.* Corwin.

Ofsted. (2019). *Education inspection framework 2019: Inspecting the substance of education.* UK Government. www.gov.uk/government/consultations/education-inspection-framework-2019-inspecting-the-substance-of-education

Urrea, C., DeLong, K., Diaz, J., Klopfer, E., Thompson, M., Wagh, A., Gardony, J., Anderson, E., & Kundargi, R. (2022). MIT full STEAM ahead: Bringing project-based, collaborative learning to remote learning environments. In F. M. Reimers & F. J. Marmolejo (Eds.), *University and school collaborations during a pandemic* (pp. 299–319). Springer.

6

Early Years Education and AI

Big Ideas with Little Learners

We are in the staffroom. Jim is holding a 'Bee-Bot' toy with deep suspicion.

Jim: They are four, Chloe. Four. They need mud. They need sand. They do not need algorithms.
Elena: It's not a screen, Jim. Look. [she presses the buttons on the Bee-Bot's back] It's physical. They have to put the segments in order to make it move. It's sequencing. It's logical. It's just 'We're Going on a Bear Hunt' with batteries.
Chloe: Exactly. We aren't teaching them Python. We're teaching them that they are the boss of the machine. If we don't teach them that now, the machine becomes the boss later. It's called agency.
Jim: So…it's obedience training for the internet and AI?
Elena: Essentially. But with less screen time and more floor time.

Teachers of our youngest students are going to constantly ask, 'Am I stealing their childhood by introducing tech so young?' In this chapter, I hope to explain how we can build a foundation of digital literacy without eroding the sanctity of physical play.

The 'Digital Native' Myth

To all the Early Years teachers reading this, you are a special. I truly mean this. The patience and energy that you have in your setting is unrivalled. The cognitive load of having to switch between conversations suitable for a 4 year old and in-depth discussions with parents and colleagues is challenging enough.

DOI: 10.4324/9781003740377-8

Bearing this in mind, I know that discussions around AI quickly get the warning claxons going. As defenders of childhood, play-based learning and screen-free classrooms, you are rightfully twitchy about bringing something as big as AI into your carefully curated space.

The term 'digital native' has been around for a while. The slightly misleading phrase is an umbrella term for those who were born in the 2010s and 2020s. It suggests that they were born into, or will be born into a world based on algorithms. The content they consume from the off has been curated, they have access to devices early on, and they don't know a world free of technology present in every facet of life.

I say it is misleading because, yes, they may be born into this world, but I see quite often in the classroom a profound naivety, both on the technical side of things and also in the understanding of what it means to be a responsible user. This is where wider digital literacy and more specific AI literacy come in.

Research by The Alan Turing Institute indicates that, without formal curricula on what generative AI is and how to use it safely, many children do not fully appreciate the risks it can pose or understand how to use it effectively, with some using the tools for 'chatting' and social interaction (Hashem et al. 2025). To prevent this type of 'passive adoption,' the UNESCO AI competency framework (2024) advocates for explicit instruction on AI system design and architecture. This technical foundation helps students recognise that AI is 'human-led,' fostering resilience against the 'illusive claims' that machines possess human-like agency or can usurp human thinking.

The 'black box' nature of AI: The fact that inputs are seen but working out is hidden compounds the issue in young people. Many students believe they are talking to a real person or that these tools are magic in some way. The argument for introducing AI concepts early on is strong. Just as we teach children about road safety or environmental awareness, we need to make sure that they are being shown the challenges that being in a digital world can present.

The biggest elephant in the room concerning discussions about AI literacy in Early Childhood Education is screen time. We are now in an era where extended use of screens has been advised against. In the 2025 Common Sense Media survey, *Media Use by Kids Zero to Eight*, it was shown that 40% of children have their own tablet by age 2. It also shows that children aged 8 and younger spend about two and a half hours a day with screen media (Common Sense Media, 2025). In recent years, organisations such as the WHO (World Health Organisation) have released guidelines about screen time for the under 5s. In their 2019 report, *Guidelines on physical activity, sedentary behaviour and sleep for children under 5 years of age*, the recommendation is that there should be no screen time for children under the age of 1 and no more than one hour per day for children up to 4 years old (WHO, 2019).

With all this in mind, I want to make it clear, the lessons and content I am suggesting in this chapter to use steer far away from the need for screens. Computational thinking and various AI conversations can happen entirely offline. The central idea is that we can teach about the digital world through the physical world.

What I am proposing is that Early Years students are given lessons about the digital world, in the same way that they will be taught about how to cross the road, stranger danger, and the like. The adults in their lives should be deliberately bringing certain vocabulary and discussions to the table that make sure that our children are growing up tech-savvy.

If we look at the work by educationalists Jean Piaget and Seymour Papert, we can actually build a solid structure for tech education in early education. Piaget argues that between the ages of 2–7, children are not able to work with abstract and symbolic logic, i.e. they cannot visualise 'code' in their heads (Piaget, 1952). Papert's view is that children learn through actively 'building,' calling for 'objects to think with' (Papert, 1980). The idea is that they need physical experiences to build mental models of the world around them. In the digital world, we can't sit a 4 year old in front of a screen and have them watch a video about coding or AI. We have to make sure that they have the opportunity to physically engage with a concept, for example using building blocks when discussing sequencing of instructions.

So, what I am saying is Early Years students think by doing. They are going to remember their work on algorithms if they set up and walk the path they want a robot to take, or if they are able to take on the role of a robot and walk in their 'shoes.'

But Aren't They Too Young for This?

A big question I see quite often, related to this age group is, 'why now?' I get it, I really do. When I first dug deeper into AI and Primary schools, I definitely dismissed the notion of AI literacy in the first years of school. The problem was, however, that I was coming to it the same way that many Early Years teachers have, with visions of extended screen time and loss of the core fundamentals of what it takes to be human. As I continued to read, I realised that this is misguided. Professional educators and parents have the responsibility of helping their children navigate the world. While they are vulnerable and developing, our role is to make sure that children are being brought up in a way that allows them to slot seamlessly into whichever community they are part of.

Keeping children safe and aware is one major part, if not the major part of this process. Historically, dangers included predators, climate, and lack of food. As the centuries passed, these dangers centred more around war and providing for the family, followed by intelligence and earning money. When we all grew up, and I am showing my age here, we were subjected to lengthy conversations about 'stranger danger' and how to cross the road properly. The point I am getting at is that the dangers that humans face have evolved as we have evolved. In the later 20th and first quarter of the 21st century, we have added online dangers to that list. We need to educate our children about them as much as we need to educate them about crossing a road.

When some of us were 4, the dangers were physical: Traffic, playgrounds, and the like. For the modern 4 year old, the now dubbed Generation Beta, the dangers also include AI. Many of these children live in 'smart' houses, where, at least, they have some kind of voice assistant in one of their shared family spaces. From an early age, they are adept at asking these assistants questions, for music and everything else. At this age, it is unlikely that they know the assistant is not a human.

Likewise, there have been AI toys introduced to the market recently. These toys, designed to look like your average teddy or robot, have generative AI built in. If our 4 year olds thought that the (sometimes very) limited AI they were chatting with through their voice assistant was real, then they will definitely think that this is the case with AI toys.

Children have always talked to their toys, including them in role plays and speaking for them, but they have never spoken back. When a child says 'good night, I love you' to a traditional teddy, they get nothing in return. If they do this when interacting with an AI teddy, the teddy replies.

This brings us to two important reasons why AI literacy has to happen at this age.

There is the illusion of a relationship. Sherry Turkle, a professor at MIT calls these 'relational artefacts' (Turkle, 2011). She made the point, back in 2011, that certain social robots are designed to 'push our Darwinian buttons' by mimicking human eye contact, voice, and responsiveness.

The response from an AI toy leads the child to believe it cares thus creating a false bond. In some cases, this could lead to them trusting the toy more than the humans in their lives. We need to teach children that just because something sounds like a friend doesn't mean it is a friend.

Data. When a child speaks to a traditional doll, their words are lost in the ether. When they speak to a smart toy, their words are often recorded, processed in the cloud and stored.

UNESCO highlights in their report that AI providers have been and are mining and manipulating data from almost all internet users. The report says that "In the digital age, economic exploitation in education has evolved to include the unauthorized collection and monetization of students' personal data by technology companies" (UNESCO, 2025 p.65). Sadly, even at 4 years old, children need to know that some toys have ears.

Box 6.1 Parent Comms: The 'Smart Toy' Chat

Early Years teachers are perfectly positioned to casually educate parents. At your next parents' evening, gently bring up 'Smart Toys.' Remind parents that if a teddy bear or robot talks back to their four-year-old in a conversational way, it usually has a microphone connected to the cloud. Encourage them to check the privacy settings on their children's interactive toys!

I am not saying that we should throw our arms up in rage and boycott such toys, but they make a strong case for the need to teach our children early that they can enjoy the toys but not treat them as real beings.

At this point, you might be thinking, this is all well and good, but does AI really have a place in my classroom? The answer is yes. In fact, if we look back at the giants of Early Years, the godfathers of early education, we find theories that support AI literacy. We aren't rewriting the rulebook; we are simply adding an addendum.

Friedrich Fröbel, the creator of the Kindergarten, famously once said, "Play is the highest expression of human development" (Fröbel, 1826). He believed that children learn best by physical interaction with the world around them. He even introduced custom-made toys that helped children understand abstract concepts. When a child sees a Bee-Bot and programs it to move, or gives a command to a smart toy to see what happens, they are engaging in purposeful play. They are exploring an object and testing a hypothesis.

Similarly, Lev Vygotsy taught us that children learn best when they are in their ZPD or 'Zone of Proximal Development' (Vygotsky, 1978), which is the gap between those things that they can do independently and those they can do with help. Vygotsky suggests that children need a 'More knowledgeable other' to help with the process, and that person is traditionally the teacher. Today AI can also occasionally step into this role. Even if you are not using it in your classroom, interactions with voice assistants to gain knowledge will be happening all the time at home. The responses can be an immediate scaffold and help push the children from not being able to do something to achieve their goal.

Introducing digital literacy into early learning is not a betrayal of Early Years values. Hopefully it can help them evolve.

Teaching Big Ideas Through Small Hands

One of the core aspects of education at this age is allowing students to be mobile and active. We want them to climb, dig, and interact. They learn with their whole bodies, and this development is extremely important. What I propose is not replacing that essential learning with screen time; I propose a healthy synthesis between the heart and soul of education at this age, with concepts around computing and AI, which will be in the background of their entire lives.

What I am introducing to you in this section is what many call 'unplugged' computing. This is a movement in the computing world which advocates for the teaching of digital concepts through the use of drama, non-digital games, puzzles, and art. For the age group we are discussing, this approach is a gold standard in terms of bringing this learning into the classroom, but avoiding screen time.

To share some practical ideas about how 'unplugged' learning would look in the classroom, I will lean into the Reggio Emilia concept of 'provocations' to illustrate some ideas. I am not a Reggio Emilia teacher, but I like this framing, the idea that the lesson provokes thinking, not through being told the facts but through guided exploration. A 'provocation' is an activity designed to be open-ended but curated in terms of materials, to encourage curiosity, creativity, and engagement. With any of these suggestions, they are just that. Variations may need to be explored, to make sure they fit the needs of your students.

Provocation 1: The Journey Mapper

In this activity, the computing angle is decomposition and debugging: The breaking down of a process and looking at the possible errors in the situation.

The core concept: Algorithms and debugging

The book: *We're Going On a Bear Hunt* (Rosen & Oxenbury) or *The Gruffalo* (Donaldson & Scheffler)

The resources: A large sheet of paper, with a 4x4 grid drawn on it. A small toy bear and ten Post-it notes with arrows drawn on them.

The setup: Add a 'start' (home) in one corner of the sheet of paper, and a 'finish' (cave) in another. Draw a river, and mud in random squares in between,

The activity:

- Read the story together.
- A child has to create a path for the bear using the arrow Post-it notes to get from Home to the Cave avoiding the obstacles.
- They place the arrows first (writing the code).
- They then move the bear following their own arrows (running the code).
- If their arrow points into the river, for example, they have to stop and 'debug.'

The AI link: An algorithm is just like a map. If the map is wrong, the robot (the bear) gets stuck. You have to fix the code to save the bear.

Provocation 2: The Creature Sorter

The core concept: Data sets, classification, and machine learning
The book: *Knuffle Bunny* (Mo Willems)
The theory: AI learns by looking at thousands of images and finding patterns. This activity shows children that rules define what a computer 'knows.'
The resources: Two hula hoops (or chalk circles). A basket containing 20 random mixed toys (cars, blocks, dolls) and specifically 5–6 stuffed bunnies (with varied features).
The setup: Label one hoop 'Bunny' and the other 'Not a bunny.'
The activity:

- Read the book together.
- Ask the children to sort the toys in the basket, into the hoops.
- Throw in a curveball – add extra details depending on the toys you have chosen.
- Ask the children to decide which hoop it goes in and why.

AI Link: Computers learn by looking at pictures. If we only show them white bunnies, it won't know that a grey bunny is still a bunny. We have to teach it the rules.

Provocation 3: The Literal Robot

The core concept: Input/output
The book: *Press Here* by Hervé Tullet
The theory: Children project their intent onto machines, especially voice assistants. This activity shows that this is an illusion and that machines are frustratingly literal.

The resources: A barrier, like a hardback book. Two identical sets of building bricks (4–6 bricks per set).
The setup: Two children sit opposite each other and place the barrier between them. Each is given the bricks.
The activity:

- Child A acts as the programmer. They build a small tower behind the barrier. They must then describe it to Child B.
- Child B acts as the robot. They must build exactly what they hear without seeing.
- Lift the barrier to compare the 'output.'

AI link: The robot couldn't see what you were thinking; it could only hear what you said. If you don't give clear instructions, you get a messy tower. This is the concept of 'garbage in, garbage out.'

Provocation 4: The If/Then Art Studio

The core concept: Conditional logic
Book: *If You Give a Mouse a Cookie* (Laura Numeroff)
The theory: An input leads to an output.
The resources: A large piece of paper, crayons, and a large foam die. A simple stand for the 'rule card.'
The setup: The goal is to create a collaborative artwork. Write six rules on the card:

- Read the book together.
- If you roll a 1…then draw a blue circle.
- If you roll a 2…then draw a green line.
- Etc.

The activity: Children take turns rolling the die. They must follow the rule. They cannot choose what to draw; the die decides for them.

AI Link: Computers don't make choices like we do. They follow rules. If I press the button, then the light turns on.

Provocation 5: The Real or Man-Made Museum

The core concept: AI ethics and the Turing Test
The theory: Before children can understand 'deepfakes,' they must understand the difference between biological and synthetic.

Book: *The Velveteen Rabbit* (Margery Williams)
The resources: A 'museum' table with pairs of items:

- real vs. synthetic apple.
- real vs. synthetic plant.
- a photo of a teacher vs. a cartoon/AI drawing of a person.

Real or homemade magnifying glasses. Cards with either a tick (for real things) or a cross or something similar (for the synthetic things).

The setup: Place real or constructed (cardboard) magnifying glasses on the table.
Activity: Children explore objects using their senses. They place a real or man-made card next to the items they explore.
AI link: Some things look real, but they were made by a machine. Plastic apples look tasty, but you can't eat it. We have to use our senses to tell the difference.

Following these provocations, I also wanted to share two lessons I carried out with the Reception students in my current school. While writing this book, I wanted to explore some ideas for lessons with the youngest students.

Lesson 1
The first lesson was on algorithms and instructions.
The hook:

- Students were sitting on the carpet.
- I took my shoes off and then tried to put them on, but failed, with the shoes the wrong way round.
- I explained that I was a robot and didn't know how to put on shoes. I asked the students to help me.
- I asked them what a robot is, and I received the expected range of answers.
- My favourite moment was when one stated, 'robots are humans made of glass' and another chimed in with, 'no…from cardboard!'

The activity:

- I began by standing up and asking the students to direct me (the robot) from the chair to the classroom door, using only the instructions they might find on a Bee-Bot. I hammed it up a little, and took their instructions literally, walking into walls and making circles.

- This is essential to ensure that they know they need to provide better details.
- This was then followed by putting students in pairs and asking them to take it in turns to direct their partner around the room. Chaos ensued, but guided chaos!

AI link: I explained that computers, and AI, are not smart like humans. They are fast, but not smart. They only do what we tell them, exactly. If the instruction is bad, so is the output.

Lesson 2

This lesson was all about the concept that AI can create things that look real, but aren't.

The hook:

- I showed various AI-generated images: A big fluffy blue chair in the middle of a class, a see-through pair of trainers, with grass in them and a book with text from a made-up language.
- We discussed if these were real or made-up, and why. I then asked students to show me real versions, a real chair, a real shoe, a real book.

Activity:

- I shared another AI-generated image, a kitten with sunglasses and rainbow horns. Once again, I asked the students what the issue was with the picture.
- I explained that the AI doesn't actually know what a cat is. It only knows what a cat looks like because humans showed it millions of photos.
- I told them, 'we need to help the computer to learn.' We clarified what features make a cat a cat and I then asked them to draw a picture of a 'real' cat, to help train the AI.

AI link: We finished with a big question, 'Is it alive?' We discussed whether a computer can feel the sun or smell a flower. This was a moment for the students to validate their human creativity over a machine's strengths.

It Has Always Been About Agency

As I wrap up this chapter, I want to return to Jim's fears at the beginning, the idea that certain exposure to AI may result in us training children to be obedient to the internet. Hopefully, you can now see that AI literacy in early education does the exact opposite. It is all about agency. It doesn't need a re-inventing of the wheel; it needs the experts to adapt existing practices to include explicit discussion:

- When a child programs a Bee-Bot, they learn, 'I am in control.'
- When a child identifies an AI-generated image, they learn that it is ok to question the machine.
- When a child treats a smart toy with caution, they learn that they need to protect themselves from machines.

Let's wrap up by going back to Jim. He is on his knees on the classroom floor, moving a Bee-Bot across a hand-drawn grid while three four-year-olds argue passionately about whether it needs to go left or forward. He isn't teaching algorithms. He is refereeing a heated debate in which the children were completely, gloriously in charge.

He looks up at Elena, who is standing at the door, and says, "It's just floor time with an opinion."

Exactly, Jim. That's exactly what it is.

We don't need to drag four-year-olds from their play and sit them in front of screens. At this age, we don't need to teach them technical skills. We need to teach them that the magic isn't real, but their imagination is. And that they are always, always the boss of the machine.

Box 6.2 Key Takeaways from Chapter 6

Key Takeaways

Demystify the 'Black Box': Young children naturally anthropomorphise technology. If we don't explicitly teach them how machines work, they will assume AI is magic or alive. Early AI literacy is about establishing human agency – ensuring the child knows they are the 'boss of the machine.'

Screen-Free Foundations ('Unplugged' is Best): You do not need devices to teach computational thinking. Complex AI concepts like algorithms, data sets, and bias are best taught through physical, hands-on play using sorting hoops, building blocks, and storybooks.

The 'Smart' Toy Warning: In an era of AI-enabled toys and voice assistants, early digital literacy is a safeguarding issue. We must teach children the critical difference between a biological friend who listens, and a synthetic machine that records and stores data.

Fröbel's Digital Gifts: Technology should not be viewed as the enemy of early childhood play. Simple, screen-free robotics (like Bee-Bots) are the modern equivalent of Fröbel's wooden blocks – they are tactile, open-ended tools designed to help children test hypotheses and build logic.

AI in Practice: A Prompt to Try

Early Years teachers spend hours trying to link children's current obsessions to the Early Learning Goals. Let AI do the heavy lifting of brainstorming your continuous provision stations.

> *Prompt:*
> *"Act as an expert Early Years Foundation Stage (EYFS) teacher. My class of 4-year-olds is currently obsessed with [Insert Topic, e.g., dinosaurs and space]. Generate 5 play-based, screen-free 'Continuous Provision' activities based on this interest. Include one for the mud kitchen, one for the water tray, one for fine motor skills, one for the construction area, and one for role-play. For each activity, tell me the resources I need to set it up and the specific learning objective it targets."*

Professional Development: Discussion Points

Do we have any 'Smart' toys in the setting? Do we know where the data goes? Do the parents know?

Listen to how we talk about tech. Do we say *'Alexa, what is the weather?'* (personifying it) or *'Let's use the smart speaker to check the weather data'* (treating it as a tool)?

Can we identify one area of our 'Understanding the World' curriculum that is currently taught with a screen, that could be replaced with a physical 'Unplugged' activity?

Check Your Understanding

1. Why is 'Unplugged' coding recommended for Early Years?
   A) Computers are too expensive.
   B) Children learn best through physical manipulation (Piaget/Fröbel), and abstract logic is hard to visualise on a screen.
   C) It saves electricity.
2. What does Sherry Turkle note, regarding children and AI?
   A) Children are faster at typing than adults.
   B) Children form emotional bonds with 'Relational Artefacts' (robots/toys) because they simulate empathy.
   C) Children ignore robots.
3. What is the best way to teach a child that an AI isn't 'Smart'?
   A) Tell them it is stupid.
   B) Show them the 'Literal Robot' (Input/Output) game – demonstrating that if the instruction is bad, the robot fails.
   C) Don't let them use it.

Answers

1. **B.** As educational pioneers like Piaget and Papert noted, young children learn best through building and physical manipulation. 'Unplugged' activities allow children to grasp abstract computational concepts (like algorithms and debugging) by making them physical and concrete, entirely avoiding the need for screen time.
2. **B.** Sherry Turkle warns that children often view interactive tech as 'Relational Artefacts.' Because AI toys mimic human cues (like voice tone and responsiveness), children are highly prone to anthropomorphise them, forming false emotional bonds and incorrectly assuming the machine 'cares' about them.
3. **B.** The 'Literal Robot' game perfectly demonstrates that AI doesn't have common sense or human intuition. By showing that a 'robot' will only build exactly what it is told – resulting in a messy tower if instructions are poor – children learn the concept of 'garbage in, garbage out' and realise they are ultimately the ones in control of the machine.

References

Common Sense Media. (2025). *The 2025 Common Sense Census: Media use by kids zero to eight*. www.commonsensemedia.org/sites/default/files/research/report/2025-common-sense-census-web-2.pdf

Fröbel, F. W. A. (2005). *The education of man (W. N. Hailmann, Trans.).* University Press of the Pacific. (Original work published 1826).

Hashem, Y., Esnaashari, S., Onslow, K., Chakraborty, S., Poletaev, A., Francis, J., & Bright, J. (2025). *Understanding the impacts of generative AI use on children: WP1 surveys*. The Alan Turing Institute. www.turing.ac.uk/sites/default/files/2025-06/understanding_the_impacts_of_generative_ai_use_on_children_-_wp1_report.pdf

Papert, S. (1980). *Mindstorms: Children, computers, and powerful ideas.* Basic Books.

Piaget, J. (1952). *The origins of intelligence in children*. International Universities Press.

Turkle, S. (2011). *Alone together: Why we expect more from technology and less from each other*. Basic Books.

UNESCO. (2024). *AI competency framework for students.* https://unesdoc.unesco.org/ark:/48223/pf0000391105

UNESCO. (2025). *AI and education: Protecting the rights of learners.* UNESCO Publishing. https://doi.org/10.54675/ROQH4287

Vygotsky, L. S. (1978). *Mind in society: The development of higher psychological processes.* Harvard University Press.

World Health Organization. (2019). *Guidelines on physical activity, sedentary behaviour and sleep for children under 5 years of age.* https://iris.who.int/server/api/core/bitstreams/60a1cbaa-2bef-4251-9557-e52ce22112b3/content

7

KS1

Wonder, Words, and What-Ifs

It's morning break. Elena walks into the staffroom holding a piece of lined paper by the corner as if it might bite her. Jim is marking worksheets, and Chloe is trying to unjam the laminator.

Elena: We were practicing writing letters today. Look at this.

Chloe: [Yanking a plastic sheet, she reads over his shoulder] "Dear Alexa, what is your favourite colour? Do you get lonely inside the speaker? Love, Sarah." Aww, that's cute! She even drew a picture of Alexa sleeping.

Elena: [Turning around, looking serious] It's not cute, Chloe. A teddy bear doesn't talk back and tell you facts about the solar system. She genuinely thinks there is a tiny, tired person trapped inside that plastic cylinder. How am I supposed to teach a six-year-old computing when they think the computer is alive?

Jim: [Without looking up from her marking] Anthropomorphism. It's completely normal at age six, Elena. But you're right to be concerned. If we leave it as 'magic,' they become vulnerable to it later.

Elena: So what do I do? Tell her Santa isn't real, but for smart speakers?

Chloe: No. You just teach her the difference between senses and sensors. Sarah thinks Alexa has ears and feelings. You need to show her the microphone hole. You teach her that humans feel tired, but machines just run out of electricity.

Jim: So, pop the hood?

Chloe: Exactly. No magic, Jim. Just data.

DOI: 10.4324/9781003740377-9

Pulling Back the Curtain

Throughout this chapter, Key Stage 1 refers to children aged 5–7, equivalent to Kindergarten through Grade 1 in the US system, or Year 1 and Year 2 in England. Key Stage 1 is an interesting stage in Primary school. Students have moved out of the play-based infrastructure of the first two years and are now being asked to engage with more formality to both their school day and their learning. Children are traditionally expected to start solidifying core areas such as motor skills, phonics, and number sense.

These students are surrounded by AI. Unlike previous generations where the internet was the store of all information, in a static, retrievable format, these children interact with adaptive agents. From voice assistants to streaming platforms, they are passively exposed to AI and, despite this familiarity, or because of it, they harbour misconceptions about how they work (Andries & Robertson, 2023, pp. 1, 3, 14).

At this age, children may well view AI as something mysterious and all-knowing, like the great and powerful Wizard of Oz. Our goal is not to teach them how to build the wizard but rather be Toto and pull back the curtain to show all the levers. We want them to appreciate that AI isn't magic; it is a machine.

Building on the computational, command-based programming from the previous chapter, we can now move into specific AI literacy territory: Prediction and machine learning. Our students move from **Input > Process > Output** towards **Data > Pattern > Prediction**.

There are various frameworks, globally, that touch on the teaching of computing and 'AI literacy' in this age group such as SEAME (Social & Ethical Application, Model, Engine) framework (Waite & Curzon, 2022) in the UK and AI4K12 in the USA.

Designing a curriculum for 5–7 year olds requires a robust theoretical framework that accounts for their developmental stage. The AI4K12 framework has developed some excellent, granular, 'big ideas' for this age group that can be adapted to focus on tangible observations and simple differentiations:

- **Perception:** The idea that computers perceive the world using sensors, just as humans use their senses.
- **Representation & Reasoning:** To make decisions, computers need a map or model of the world.
- **Learning:** Computers can learn from data, and AI finds patterns in the data.
- **Natural Interaction:** Computers simulate human interaction but lack human understanding.
- **Societal Impact:** AI can affect lives, choices and opportunities.

In addition, just as with Early Years, the 'unplugged' approach is still the preferred and most effective method of instruction at this point, as we continue to demystify the 'magic' of AI. They are still at a developmental stage where they find it hard to comprehend abstract concepts, thus needing the ideas to be anchored in a physical reality. We also need to make sure that AI education is inextricably linked with wider digital literacy (NCCE, 2023).

Designing a curriculum suitable for 5–7 year olds should bear in mind developmental stages. Just as with Early Years, we can refer to Piaget's 'preoperational stage,' (Piaget, 1952) to identify that students at this crucial stage are able to categorise, recognise patterns, and play according to a narrative, but will struggle with concepts such as 'neural networks.'

Weaving It In, Not Bolting It On

The NCCE in the UK suggests that AI education should be inextricably linked with the wider digital literacy curriculum, while maintaining a human-centred approach.

If AI literacy feels like an 'add-on', busy KS1 teachers simply won't have the time for it. Instead we should lean on cross-curricular links, especially with the three core foci of this phase: phonics, maths, and science.

- **Science:** In science, children are working on classification, sorting things into 'living' and 'non-living.' AI is the ultimate curveball in this debate. This is a great opportunity to teach about the difference between biological and man-made.
- **Literacy:** When teaching children how to write instructions, it could be framed as 'writing an algorithm for a robot.' If the instruction is messy, the output is equally so.
- **Maths:** The foundation of AI is data sorting, which ties perfectly into KS1 Statistics. When children are creating tally charts, sorting shapes into Venn diagrams, or identifying repeating patterns (red, blue, red, blue), explicitly tell them: *'You are doing exactly what an AI does. You are looking at data and finding the pattern.'*

As mentioned above, students aged between 5 and 7 years old will struggle with abstract aspects. A foundational concept for this age group is perception. They will be well on their way to understanding their own senses and now we need to prioritise mapping these experiences to computers and sensors.

As with Early Years lessons, there is a need for sessions to have an emphasis on offline tasks. They are not merely a substitute for using screens but they also help with cognitive load, allowing the focus to be on the topic not the tool. They also encourage social interaction, something often lost when devices are involved. Finally, they help with inclusivity, negating the need to afford devices in the first place and allow students to engage in topics through physical and tactile learning methods.

What It Looks Like in the Classroom

Year 1

When planning lessons for Year 1 (aged 5) students, we need to remind ourselves where they have come from. In the UK system, they will have had at least one year of formal schooling, but in other systems, this may be the first time they have set foot in a formal classroom.

Therefore, we need to ensure that exploratory play can still happen, to reinforce points. We also need to continue the idea of promoting 'unplugged' activities over prolonged screen time. What we can do to push on, however, is to move from purely observational content to conceptual understanding.

Drawing from frameworks such as AI4K12, the Year 1 AI literacy lessons could focus on the following 'I can…' objectives:

- I can identify human senses and corresponding computer sensors.
- I can understand that computers 'see' differently to humans.
- I can understand that robots need precise commands.
- I can create a representation of a real-world space using digital tools.
- I can understand that machines 'learn' by sorting information (data).
- I can distinguish between living things and AI/robots.

As I teach digital literacy Year 1–Year 6, I have put into practice these objectives. Here are sample lessons:

Activity 1: The Sensor Safari (Biology vs. Batteries) To tackle the Senses vs. Sensors objective, we go on a 'Sensor Safari.' I give the children cardboard frames to hold up like cameras. We walk around the classroom looking at laptops, iPads, and programmable toys, hunting for the 'Sensors' (the camera lenses and microphone holes). We put green sticky notes on things that have Senses (the class hamster, the teacher) and blue sticky notes on things that have Sensors (the iPads, the interactive whiteboard). This physically reinforces that machines do not have feelings; they just have data-collecting holes.

Activity 2: The 'Human Search Engine' Game

- **The Objective:** I can understand that machines 'learn' by sorting information (data).
- **The Hook:** I began by playing the classic ice-breaker. I asked them to stand in a line. Then I asked them to get themselves in order according to their height. As this was a class of Year 1 students, they needed some guidance. Once this was achieved, we sat down and discussed what they just did – they sorted by looking at the attributes of people in their class. This is what computers do billions of times a day…
- **The Activity:** I organised students into collaborative pairs or trios. Then I distributed a mixed 'Data Bucket' to each group containing building bricks, toy animals, and vehicles.
  - *Challenge 1 (The Intuitive Sort):* 'Here is your data. Your first challenge is simple: Sort it.' Provide no further rules. Let them find their own logic. Circulate and ask each group: 'What was your rule?' (Common outcomes: Sorting by colour, species, or size).
  - *Challenge 2 (The Multi-Attribute Shift):* 'Reset your data! Now, you must sort it again, but you cannot use the same rule as before. You must find a new attribute.' This forces students to look past the most obvious characteristic (usually colour) and identify more complex properties (e.g. 'things with wheels' vs. 'things with legs').
- **The Wrap Up:** To bridge the gap between 'playing with toys' and 'understanding data structures,' I asked the class to imagine they are a computer trying to find one specific item (e.g. a green LEGO brick). *'If I asked you to find the "green lion," which of your sorting rules would help me find it the fastest? The color pile or the animal pile?'*

Year 2

In this year group, we can now assume that they have moved further away from play-based learning and are better able to tackle more abstract concepts. We can therefore dig deeper into the idea of pattern recognition, machine learning, and algorithmic bias. 'I can…' objectives could include:

- I can understand that computers learn from examples.
- I can predict what comes next in a pattern.
- I can understand how certain apps 'know' what we like.

- I can understand that there is a difference between talking to a machine and a human.
- I can identify how AI helps people.

Lesson Example: The Recommendation Robot To teach Data > Pattern > Prediction, we play a physical game.

- The Hook: Ask the class: *'When you finish watching a video on YouTube, how does it know what to play next? Is there a tiny person inside guessing what you want?'* The Activity: Put three hula hoops on the floor: Hoop 1 (Data), Hoop 2 (Pattern), Hoop 3 (Prediction).
    - *Data:* Throw five picture cards of dogs into Hoop 1.
    - *Pattern:* Ask the children to stand in Hoop 2 and shout out the 'Rule' (e.g. 'They all have four legs and fur!').
    - *Prediction:* Hold up a picture of a cat and a picture of a car. Ask the child in Hoop 3 (The Robot) to predict which one belongs in the Data hoop based on the pattern.
- The AI Link: The children physically walk through the machine learning process. We then discuss the downside: *'If the robot only ever shows you dogs, will you ever find out that you also love space?'* This is their first, age-appropriate lesson in algorithmic bias.

Taking it to the Screen: Google's Teachable Machine

Once the students understand the physical Hula Hoop game, it is time to transition to a digital tool. Google's Teachable Machine is perfect for Year 2.

- **The Activity:** Set up a laptop with a webcam. Ask the class to help you train an AI to recognise 'Happy' vs. 'Sad.'
- Have five children come up and pull a big, exaggerated smiley face into the camera to capture the **Data** for Class 1. Then, have five children pull a grumpy face to capture the data for Class 2.
- Click 'Train.' Finally, invite a new child to step in front of the camera and test the **Prediction**.
- **The AI Link:** They get to see the exact *Data > Pattern > Prediction* loop they just did with the hula hoops, but this time happening live on a screen.

Tools and Technologies

KS1 is a perfect playground for physical tools to support digital learning, but, as we know, the edtech market is flooded with all sorts of machines and software. We need to make sure that we select the tools that serve pedagogy, not the other way around. Overall, in this book, I have aimed to steer clear of specific brand names, but I feel that a few products can be mentioned at this juncture.

Robots are excellent bridges for AI literacy because they are physical products that share the child's space. I would begin with the tried and tested Bee-Bots, or Blue-Bots. These are the mainstay of the Early Years and KS1 classrooms. They may be oldies, but they are goodies. They can be used for sequencing and algorithm work, looking at programming and instructions. A step up for Y2 would be the use of tools such as Sphero Indi which can add in sensors and actuators to the mix.

There are also some great coding-based products that can help with understanding more about what goes on 'behind the curtain.' ScratchJr has been around for a while now and goes a long way to help explain block coding and If/Then logic. Code.org has modules on AI and there is also Google's Teachable Machine, a fun, web-based machine learning tool, which can be used as a teacher demonstration at this level.

Strategic Implementation

Before anything else, it is worth saying plainly: You do not need to understand how AI works to teach this chapter's content. You need to be curious, willing to say 'I don't know — let's find out together,' and comfortable sitting in the hula hoop on the floor. The lessons above are designed so that the children discover the answers themselves. Your job is to ask the questions and create the conditions for that discovery. That is something every KS1 teacher already knows how to do.

That said, building confidence across a whole school takes more than one chapter. At this level, most teachers are generalists and may feel intimidated by the complexity of AI. Building on work done in Singapore and the UK, schools can look to identify and appoint an 'AI lead' for each school or cluster. This lead would then receive training and they would run sessions in their school, designed for non-specialists.

Also, AI doesn't need to be a standalone subject. It needs to be woven into the fabric of the curriculum. Take the time to look at the objectives in all subjects and the suggested objectives linked to AI and computing above. Look at where they can be integrated and work together.

The Leadership Lens

KS1 is a sensitive time for parents when it comes to screen time; they start to worry as the formality of schooling increases, and finding the balance is difficult. Quite often device usage increases to support phonics and maths learning, and it is possible that parents would become anxious that 'AI literacy' would mean just more time spent staring at an iPad.

It would be a good practice to check in with the person who teaches the lessons, be it the class teacher or a specialist, to clarify how much time will be spent on screens during the unit. It would also be good to emphasise the need for offline learning to happen first.

Make sure that communication with parents about your digital literacy curriculum is clear, showing them that the curriculum isn't developing consumers but rather interrogators.

Rolling out AI literacy in KS1 is ambitious but achievable. It involves moving beyond the computing paradigms of the past two decades and leveraging best practices from around the world. Schools can build a curriculum that is rigorous, age-appropriate and future-proof. Remember, the goal isn't to have 7-year-old software engineers, the goal is to have AI-literate children who know that these systems are not magic. They know how they work and how to interact with them effectively.

Box 7.1 Key Takeaways from Chapter 7

Key Takeaways:

The 'Tiny Person in the Box': KS1 children naturally anthropomorphise technology. We must actively break this illusion by teaching the mechanics of the 'Black Box.'

Senses vs. Sensors: The easiest way to teach machine perception to a 5-year-old is distinguishing between human biology (eyes/ears/feelings) and machine hardware (cameras/microphones/batteries).

Data > Pattern > Prediction: Move beyond simple remote-control logic (Input/Output). Teach 7-year-olds that AI is just a fast pattern-guesser, like predicting the next number in a maths sequence.

AI in Practice: A Prompt to Try

Finding books that perfectly match the exact phonics sounds your Year 1s learned this week is exhausting. Use AI to write them.

> *"Act as an expert KS1 Phonics teacher. Write a funny, 50-word story about a cat. You must only use easily decodable CVC words (e.g., mat, sat, cat) and the specific digraphs 'ch' and 'sh'. Do not use any complex sight words."*

Professional Development: Discussion Points

Have you ever encountered a 'Wizard of Oz' moment where a student believed a device was truly alive, thinking, or had feelings? How did you handle it?

Look at your current science planning for Year 1 or 2. Where could you weave in a 10-minute discussion distinguishing biological traits (living things) from machine traits (sensors and batteries)?

Why is an 'unplugged' approach vital when teaching complex, abstract concepts like data sorting to 5–7 year olds?

Check Your Understanding

1. What is the fundamental shift in how we explain computing to KS1 students when introducing AI?
   A) From Input > Process > Output to Data > Pattern > Prediction.
   B) From writing essays to drawing pictures.
   C) From offline learning to 100% screen-based learning.
2. How does the 'Sensor Safari' activity help dispel the myth that computers are 'alive'?
   A) By teaching children how to program a robot to move.
   B) By physically showing children the difference between human senses (biology) and computer sensors (hardware like microphones and lenses).
   C) By proving that iPads need to be plugged into the wall.
3. Why does the chapter recommend integrating AI literacy into Maths, Literacy, and Science rather than teaching it as a standalone subject?
   A) Because KS1 teachers do not have the technical skills to teach it separately.
   B) Because the curriculum is already crowded, and concepts like data sorting (Maths) and living vs. non-living (Science) perfectly overlap with AI foundations.
   C) Because school Wi-Fi is often unreliable.

Answers

1. A. Traditional computing relies on rigid rules (Input → Process → Output). Generative AI, however, learns completely differently. It takes massive amounts of *Data*, finds the *Pattern*, and makes a *Prediction*. Teaching this shift is the foundational first step in

helping young children understand how modern machines 'think.'

2. B. Young children naturally anthropomorphise technology, especially when it talks back to them! The 'Sensor Safari' activity grounds them in reality by explicitly comparing biological human senses (eyes, ears) to mechanical computer sensors (camera lenses, microphones), proving the machine is just hardware, not a living creature.
3. B. The primary curriculum is already incredibly crowded. Instead of trying to squeeze in a brand new, standalone 'AI' subject, teachers can seamlessly weave AI concepts into lessons they are already teaching – such as sorting data sets in Maths, exploring character intent in Literacy, or discussing living vs. non-living things in Science.

References

Andries, V., & Robertson, J. (2023). Alexa doesn't have that many feelings: Children's understanding of AI through interactions with smart speakers in their homes. *Computers and Education: Artificial Intelligence*, 4, 1, 3, 14. https://doi.org/10.1016/j.caeai.2023.100119

National Centre for Computing Education. (2023). *Teaching computing: A guide for primary teachers.* Retrieved from https://teachcomputing.org

Piaget, J. (1952). *The origins of intelligence in children.* International Universities Press.

Waite, J., & Curzon, P. (2022). *AI education resources: What do we teach young people? The SEAME framework.* Raspberry Pi Foundation. Retrieved from https://www.raspberrypi.org/blog/ai-education-resources-what-to-teach-seame-framework/

8

KS2

Thinkers, Coders, and Ethical AI Explorers

Jim looks triumphant. He is holding a printout.

Jim: Got him. Jamie handed in a biography of Winston Churchill. It says Churchill was a breakdancing champion in the 1920s.

Chloe: *[Laughing]* No way!

Jim: The AI hallucinated. And Jamie didn't check. This is it. This is the lesson. I'm not failing him. I'm going to make the whole class fact-check it. We're going to be 'Truth Detectives.' I finally see the point, Chloe. The machine lies. And it's my job to teach them how to catch it.

Our internal fear as educators is 'How do I teach truth in a "post-truth" world?' We ask, in an era of generated content, is critical thinking the most important literacy of all?

I know what you're thinking. You are thinking that your class is at zero with AI; they have had no lessons at all. Where do I begin?

Here's a 15-minute introduction that needs no devices. Tell your class that you are going to talk to them about something called AI, but first, you need their help. Ask them to write down, on a mini whiteboard or sticky note, if they have heard of AI and what these two letters mean to them.

Collect their answers, have them read some aloud. I can guarantee that the answers are going to be varied, with some knowing what at least one of the letters stands for, others referring to well-known voice assistants and others with no idea at all. Tell the students that most of their answers make sense, but they are slightly wrong.

It is as simple as that; that's your starter. You have begun by assessing prior knowledge, you have created curiosity, and you have started the ball rolling of dispelling the 'AI is magic' myth.

DOI: 10.4324/9781003740377-10

Everything in this chapter builds from that moment. If your students haven't been taught AI literacy from Early Years, which is most likely at the time of writing, then that is not a problem. At this point I would like to clarify, the phase of school I discuss is known as Key Stage 2 in the UK; we are talking about the critical developmental window of ages 7–11 globally, from Grades 2 through 5.

Also, you don't need to teach all of what follows. You don't suddenly need to become an AI specialist. What is necessary is to acknowledge and respect that students are using AI, and some work needs to be done to help support their journey. The chapter ahead gives you a full progression, cross-curricular ideas and ready-made prompts. Take what suits you and your class right now and leave the rest for later.

Where Are We Starting From?

In an ideal world, students stepping into Key Stage 2 (ages 7–11) will have some groundwork laid in the previous years. We might hope to find a group of students prepared to question all that is put in front of them. They will have discussed what is real and what isn't, explored 'If..then' concepts and will understand that computers follow instructions and patterns. If that is where your class is, wonderful. If not, don't worry, the chapter ahead will help you build from wherever you are.

Emma Turner (2022), curriculum designer and author, has the reader of her book, *Simplicitus,* think about the 'end of phase' child, the child coming to the end of their Primary career, and what they should be leaving with in terms of knowledge, skills, and everything in between. I have used this regularly in broader, curriculum-based conversations, but we can think the same thing in the world of AI literacy.

What are the bare essentials that a student must have in their armoury when it comes to AI? What will they need to help them step into a current Secondary school world that will tempt them to use AI left right and centre?

At the moment our Secondary school and Further Education counterparts are fighting fires on all fronts linked to the use of AI. What they would appreciate, I'm sure, is being safe in the knowledge that students joining them in Grade 6/Year 7 already know how to approach the use of AI openly and responsibly, i.e. not using as glorified Google Search or as a homework writer.

In the Primary setting, students aged between 7 and 11 are arguably the most vulnerable to dangers and misconceptions surrounding AI. As mentioned in Chapter 6, surveys show that children as young as 8 years old are using GenAI (Commonsense Media, 2025). I have seen from my own experience that, by the time they leave primary school, students are already deeply involved in the online world, from social media, gaming, and use of GenAI. At the time of writing, my eldest daughter is currently navigating her final year of primary school (Year 6 in the UK, or Grade 5 internationally). Through her, I get a front-row seat to the reality of AI in the playground. She regularly relays the casual conversations her peers are having about the technology, seamlessly jumping from using chatbots for homework 'help' to purely recreational activities like generating custom songs and lyrics.

Once again, we must move past the 'digital native' narrative if mere exposure to devices leads to an understanding of the nature of the technology being used. The Year 6 (Grade 5) students can log on to play the various online games out there and message their friends, but cannot necessarily put together a simple document or navigate a cloud drive. There is still clearly a digital literacy shaped gap in schools, a glaring omission of teaching around the essentials, the skills, the 'under the hood' content, and responsible use. At best, students have the luxury of weekly, standalone lessons, right through their primary school career. At worst, and more likely than not, computing and digital literacy is seen as an optional bolt-on, taught if there is someone in the school with an interest in the subject.

In terms of consistent, clear guidelines, about AI literacy in Primary schools, we are still not there. To begin with, there is still a disparity with the rate of change in the tech world, and the adoption and training in the education sector. Around a quarter of teachers are lacking in confidence to use AI, let alone teach it. This is due to a systemic training deficit. In fact, research from the Alan Turing Institute in the UK highlights that 79% of teachers have reported that they have received no formal guidance on AI.

This gap clearly has a huge impact on equity in schools. Those schools and students with confident adopters of AI in their midst will benefit greatly, pushing on with integration into workflows and teaching. Those institutions lacking confident staff are being left behind. The 'digital divide' is widening in both access to hardware but also in terms of access to conceptual understanding.

Maps Others Have Drawn

We are seeing some frameworks appear that help guide us in our planning and rollout of AI literacy to 7–11 year olds. The first is the SEAME Framework (Waite & Curzon, 2018), mentioned in the previous chapter. Created by Raspberry Pi, and developed by DeepMind, this framework has emerged as a leading model for primary education and the domains are explained thus:

Social and Ethical (SE): This level explores the impact of AI on everyday life and its broader implications for society, introducing students to critical issues such as privacy, bias, and misinformation.

Applications (A): This level focuses on interacting with systems that use AI, helping learners recognise real-world applications and understand the difference between rule-based and data-driven approaches without needing to train the models themselves.

Models (M): This level digs into the underlying structures of AI and machine learning applications, focusing on how students can understand the processes used to train and test these models.

Engines (E): This level represents the hidden, complex mechanics that make AI models work, which for primary-aged learners is best explored through unplugged activities and visualisations.

With this age group (7–11), this is an effective framework as it allows discussions about various aspects of AI. Teachers can use different entry points. It also facilitates cross-curricular application, with only certain domains needing to be included at any one time.

As well as the SEAME Framework, we can also look at the work by the AI4K12 Initiative (AI4K12 Initiative, 2021) which provides a progression map that is useful, in particular for those teaching in the UK. It includes the following domains:

Perception – Computers perceive the world using sensors.
Representation – Agents maintain representations of the world
Learning – Computers learn from data
Interaction – Intelligent agents interact naturally with humans
Societal Impact – AI can affect society positively and negatively.

Finally, the UNESCO (2024) framework is an excellent starting place to guide learning about AI. For students aged 7–11, the emphasis on a human-centred mindset is vital to dispel the misconception of AI 'magic.' It must reinforce human agency, and the idea that AI does not think in the way that humans do.

Why This Age Group, Why Now?

As with Chapters 6 and 7, I acknowledge that there is some scepticism towards AI literacy in primary education. This is primarily due to worries about screen time and fears of issues concerning safety.

The first issue, the concern surrounding screen time, is legitimate. There are more and more schools scaling back the time they allow and expect students to be on a device during the school day. My school is one of these, and I am one of the members of staff advocating for this change. As with many things in life, it is not the act of using a device that is the problem; it is how the device is being used.

In a podcast with Ezra Klein, Jonathan Haidt, a professor who has gained notoriety globally with his work on screen time and social media, drew a direct distinction between types of screen time. He described watching a film together as genuinely valuable, "they're going to pay attention to a long movie about characters in a moral universe, so there are issues of good and bad, and norms and betrayal – it's part of their moral training, their moral formation, and they're watching it with another person. It's social" (Klein, 2024). He contrasted this sharply with solitary scrolling, which he described as 'exactly the opposite – it's solitary, it's not stories, and if they are stories, they are 15-second stories that are amoral.'

A running theme throughout this book is my promotion of 'unplugged' learning linked to AI literacy. In the oldest age category, I believe that this is still an important factor to consider, when teaching AI literacy. However I also feel that access to devices, to reiterate theory and to put together work, is essential.

The other concern, the one surrounding safety, is the exact reason AI literacy should be happening from as young as possible. The inclusion of lessons on this topic is not just to 'prepare the workforce,' but they are also a critical safeguarding intervention. The risks that primary-aged children face online are becoming more complex.

To begin with, there is the question of synthetic media and deepfakes. By synthetic media, I am referring to online content that is created using heavy use of digital tools, for example AI-generated images. Deepfakes are a form of synthetic media, using audio, videos, and images manipulated by AI to make a person say or do something they never actually did.

This technology poses a big threat to pre-teens. We only need to look at the news headlines, and we notice stories of peer-on-peer abuse involving the creation of non-consensual sexual imagery or 'nudification' using free-to-access, readily available AI tools.

In 2023, a Secondary school in New Jersey made international headlines when several students discovered that male classmates had used a free AI tool to generate fabricated naked images of them (Singer, 2023). The girls were real. The images were not. The damage, humiliation, loss of trust, and psychological impact were entirely real. The students were 14 years old. The tools were free to use and required little technical skill.

This is not an isolated incident. Similar cases have since been reported in schools across the UK and Spain.

Students must be taught that they can no longer trust what they see online. They must also learn about the rights that they have to their own biometric (face and voice) data. The PSHE Association in the UK has released specific lesson plans for the upper end of Primary school that address deepfakes as not just a technical curiosity but a violation of consent and privacy (PSHE Association, 2024).

Alongside this, we also have the issues surrounding bias, mentioned in Chapter 2, data privacy and cognitive development and critical thinking. The latter is a growing concern, with research suggesting that, without intervention, children may overestimate the abilities of AI and may end up outsourcing their thinking to chatbots. If we teach how AI learns, we can reinforce the unique nature of the human mind. The window between ages 7–11 can be seen to be a critical time period during which we can establish the boundaries between human and machine.

What Should They Know and When?

Let us now look at how we can bring AI literacy to the oldest age category in the Primary setting. In the lessons and activities I will suggest in the following section, there is an assumption that the lessons on AI, suggested in Chapters 6 and 7, have happened. This therefore means that there is a certain level of prior-knowledge needed for the coverage of the topics to be most successful.

As mentioned in Chapter 4, there is a global trend currently, to move away from purely technical instruction and towards a holistic AI model, focused on three core pillars:

Conceptual Understanding – demystifying how AI works
Applied Competence – using AI tools effectively and creatively
Ethical Reasoning – evaluating societal impact and bias

Framing AI as something woven through everyday life, rather than a topic confined to computing lessons, opens the door to teaching it across the whole school curriculum. A history lesson can explore how AI is changing how we understand the past. An English lesson can examine the stories we tell about technology. A science lesson can ask how machines learn from data. When AI becomes a lens through which children explore the world, it belongs everywhere.

This cross-curricular ambition sits at the heart of the UNESCO AI Competency Framework, which provides a strong overarching benchmark for Primary schools. Crucially, UNESCO advocates for a spiral curriculum approach for children aged 7–11. The idea is that concepts shouldn't be taught once and moved on from, but should be revisited repeatedly at increasing levels of depth and complexity.

In practice, this means working across two connected levels. The first builds on what children have already encountered in Early Years and KS1 (ages 5–7), deepening and extending those foundations rather than starting from scratch. The second introduces new concepts in the early years of KS2, then returns to them with greater sophistication by the end of Primary school.

At the point of writing, various curricula and guidelines have appeared globally, from the UK, USA, Australia, Singapore, and Finland, to name a few. They all contain their own cultural and political nuances, and I would urge you to look at them further, if you are interested. What I have tried to do is to distil the common features from all of them and suggest a year group by year group progression of ideas, beginning with Year 3 (Grade 2.)

A New Shape in Learning

In the discussion about curriculum and learning, there is always a lot of reference to Bloom's Taxonomy, shown in Figure 8.1, – the pyramid that moves from remembering at the bottom to creating at the top.

Figure 8.1 Adapted from *Bloom's Taxonomy* by Armstrong (2010). Image courtesy of the Vanderbilt University Center for Teaching (https://cft.vanderbilt.edu/guides-sub-pages/blooms-taxonomy/) used under Creative Commons Attribution licence (CC BY).

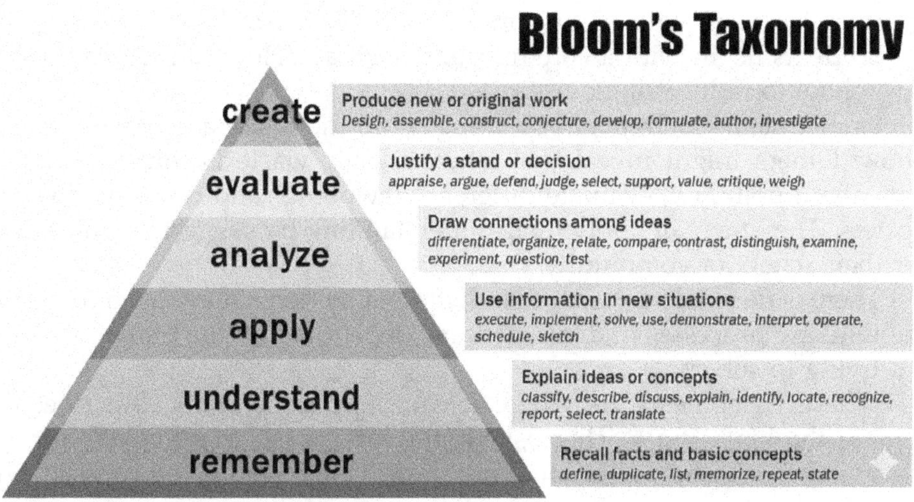

For decades, this model has helped us put together lesson structure and progression. But the arrival of AI disrupts that neat hierarchy.

If a child can write a prompt and instantly receive a polished story, poem, or explanation, then 'creation' no longer sits at the top of the pyramid, as the highest form of thinking. The output may look strong, but the thinking behind it may be shallow.

This is where Tina Austin's UnBlooms™ framework (Austin, 2025) offers a helpful reframe.

The framework doesn't ask us to reject Bloom's; it helps us to rethink it for AI-era learning. Rather than imagining learning as climbing a pyramid, or a ladder to climb, UnBlooms™ turns the process into a recursive cycle, with problem-solving at the centre. It begins with a problem, question, or challenge, and students move fluidly between different ways of thinking as they work towards understanding and solving that problem (Austin, 2025). They may need to recall prior knowledge, analyse information, evaluate ideas, and return to the earlier stages repeatedly. Learning becomes an inquiry cycle rather than a linear journey from bottom to top, and students are encouraged to reflect on their thinking, asking questions such as 'what do I already know?' or 'what would I do differently next time?' They follow a loop of:

Understand
Remember
Create
Evaluate
Analyze
Apply
(Austin, 2025)

In a classroom with AI, this might look like this:

Students begin with a core question such as, 'How can we persuade our school to reduce single-use plastic?'

One student might begin by bringing to the table facts they already know. Others might investigate where plastic waste is found, analyse data about pollution, evaluate different viewpoints, and create campaign posters. They then all apply their understanding by suggesting solutions for their school or community.

There is no single correct order. Different students may move through the thinking processes in different ways depending on the problems they are trying to solve.

Where AI comes in is where it can support learning, but doesn't replace thinking. If a teacher asked students to ask AI about the topic, e.g. 'Why is plastic pollution a problem?' they would then reflect on the response, critiquing the output for its usefulness, if it missed any key facts, did it show clear evidence, and how the content compares to their own findings.

In this way, AI is a tool for discussion, an extra source, rather than machine that gives answers. The goal of UnBlooms™ is to help students select the right type of thinking for the problems they face, while developing the ability to reflect on their own learning.

For students aged 7–11 (and beyond), this process matters enormously. At this stage, they are forming thinking habits. If we only teach them to 'spot the AI mistake,' we risk elevating critique above creativity. However if we only teach them how to create using AI, they risk outsourcing their thinking.

AI Across the Curriculum

As we move through Years 3–6, you will see how we naturally climb through the SEAME framework, starting with the hidden 'Engines' and 'Models' in lower KS2, and moving into 'Applications' and 'Social/Ethical' impacts by Year 6.

At the exact same time, every lesson is underpinned by the **UnBlooms™** mindset. You will notice that we aren't just asking students to use AI to generate a final product; we are intentionally engineering moments of friction where the machine fails or gets confused. Across all of these subjects, the goal is to force students into that recursive loop: To question, critique, and reflect.

Year 3 (Ages 7–8)

Again, the assumption is that, by this point, AI literacy will have been taught since Early Years, with topics such as algorithms, machine learning, and what is real and isn't, having already been covered.

The old baseline would have been 'AI is a robot that talks,' but we need to advance the conversation to 'AI is a prediction engine that relies on the quality of my data.'

This transition often requires us to actively de-personify the technology. Bethan Ware, a Primary Senior Leader in Wales, experienced this exact need when her students started treating the AI like a human classmate (B. Ware, response to a survey, 2025):

> *"When introducing AI tools to the class, I realised I had to strip it way back as children were saying things like 'he didn't make the right picture' [or] 'The computer isn't talking back to me.' We stripped it way back to discuss what AI actually was, a computer without thoughts and feelings.*

We recognised times that we were personifying the AI and debated whether we needed 'please' or 'thank you' at the end of a prompt."

By having these foundational debates early on, we set the stage for deeper understanding. If we have already laid the groundwork, we can jump into historically Year 6 territory. Now, in Year 3, we can focus on the need for 'fair' data to be input. Objectives could include:

- I can explain why AI needs to see many different examples to learn properly.
- I can train a simple machine learning model and predict where it might fail
- I can explain what an AI might be 'confused' if it meets someone who looks different from its training photos.

An example of a possible activity could be the following on finding patterns.

Lesson Concept: AI isn't magic; it's just really fast at finding patterns

The Story/Hook: 'I'm going to show you some alien creatures. Some are "Squibbles" and some are not. You have to guess the rule.'

Activity:

- Begin by drawing simple shapes on the board that follow a rule. For example, shapes with three eyes are Squibbles, and shapes with two eyes are not.
- Introduce a new shape. Is this a Squibble? How do you know?
- Introduce a tool like Google's Quick, Draw (free online) and allow students to explore a few rounds of the game.
- Discuss how the computer knew what the drawing was before they finished drawing. Explain that it has seen millions of drawings of the same object and found a pattern.

Year 4 (Ages 8–9)

By Year 4, the vast majority of our students are actively interacting with AI on a daily basis, even if they don't realise it. Every time they watch a recommended video on YouTube, click a suggested game on Roblox, or let Netflix auto-play the next show, an algorithm is using their data to make a prediction.

Our goal at this stage is to pull back the curtain on these 'black box' recommendations. We want them to understand that the machine isn't reading their minds; it is just reading their data.

The beauty of teaching this concept is that it doesn't require a single screen. In fact, it is often best taught completely unplugged. Ben Davies, a Primary Consultant with over two decades of experience in England, demonstrates how easily this complex computer science concept can be brought to life using nothing but the class library and some flipchart paper (B. Davies, response to survey, 2025):

> *"We had been exploring where pupils already interact with AI in their everyday lives, such as through recommendations from streaming services... The next challenge was to recommend a book for someone in the class they didn't know. We discussed what data would be helpful in making that recommendation, and how platforms like YouTube and Netflix gather such data (e.g. through ratings). Pupils then asked the person to give a thumbs up or thumbs down to a range of books in the library, and recorded the results on flipchart paper. We looked for patterns in the types of books the child liked and used this to help make a recommendation. This helped pupils understand that the recommendations they receive are a form of AI, and that data is required to enable these decisions."*

Building upon the previous work on algorithms, we can move the discussion from there being rules, to about probability. We can ensure that students understand that AI can never be 100% sure, bringing in maths understanding of probability to support the concept. Objectives can include:

- I can explain that AI gives an answer based on probability, not certainty.
- I can create a simple decision tree (flowchart) to show how a computer makes a choice.
- I can discuss why we shouldn't trust an AI to make important decisions without a human checking the confidence score.

A lesson example for this year group could be one on 'Garbage In, Garbage Out.'

The concept: If you teach AI with bad data, it learns bad habits (GIGO)
The Hook: 'We are going to train a robot to recognise the "best fruit".'
The activity:

- Use Google's Teachable Machine (free, browser-based) and make sure you have fruit for students to use.
- Create two categories: 'good' fruit and 'bad' fruit.

- Ask the class to only hold up apples for 'good' fruit and only hold up bananas for 'bad' fruit. Train the model.
- Test the process. Have students hold a third fruit. This will prompt the model to classify the fruit as 'bad,' or it will be confused, as it doesn't look like an apple.

At the end of the session, before you reveal anything, ask the class to vote: 'Put your hand up if you think the machine made a mistake.' Most hands will go up. Then ask: 'Put your hand up if you think WE made a mistake.' Pause and let the room sit in confusion.

Then you can ask three more questions, in sequence.

'Did the machine do what it was asked to do?'
'Did we show it the whole truth?'
'Whose fault is the wrong answer?'

Students will hopefully realise that the machine was perfectly obedient, but it doesn't know what it doesn't know. It can only work with what we give it. The bias wasn't in the machine; it was in the room.

Year 5 (Ages 9–10)

Now that the core 'under the hood' work has been taught and built upon in the previous years, we can pay respect to our older students' improving emotional maturity and understanding of the world, by exploring bias, fairness, and social impact. By Year 5, the curriculum focus shifts from simply using the tools to actively critiquing how they are built. If AI is a prediction engine, what exactly is it predicting *from*? This is the year we introduce the concept of 'training data' and the thorny ethical issues of copyright, consent, and bias.

At this age, children possess a fierce sense of fairness. If you give them the space to debate the ethics of AI, they will routinely surprise you with their depth of thought. Claire Walmsley saw this happen during a lesson where she asked her students to sort data sources into 'OK to use' and 'Not OK to use' for training an AI:

> *"There were many brilliant moments of discussion but a few have stuck with me. The first was the debate around using celebrity photos for training data versus regular people. Many of [the] children quite strongly disagreed with the use of regular people's photos being used in case their face appeared on someone's output. However, they were less concerned with celebrities... We then debated whether celebrities like*

Taylor Swift had less right to privacy... Another child who has spent a lot of the discussion quietly listening to others raised her hand and essentially said that AI is neither good nor bad and that we should be able to train it [on] as much data as possible... She argued, quite articulately, that it was people who needed to be trained and educated to be kinder and more ethical in their use. It was quite a profound moment on a Wednesday afternoon."

Lessons can look at algorithmic bias in the real world. Discussions can answer the question, 'Just because we can build it, should we?' Objectives could cover:

- I can define 'algorithmic bias' and give real-world examples.
- I can explain the environmental cost of AI.
- I can audit a search result or video feed, aware that I am only seeing things the computer thinks I agree with.
- I can debate whether it is fair to use AI to judge art or writing competitions.

For this year group, the lesson example could focus on bringing in GenAI tools. It is important to ensure that those used are school-approved and have strong guardrails.

The concept: To get what you want from AI, you need precise language and vocabulary.

The Hook: 'I have a picture in my head. I'm going to describe it to this AI image generator. Let's see if it can create it.' Begin with something too simplistic to create a great image.

The Activity:

- Show the class a specific, detailed image that was created prior to the lesson, using an AI image generator.
- Challenge students, in pairs, to write a text prompt that gets an AI image generator to create something as close to the target image as possible. Use a child-friendly AI model for this.
- The students will realise that they will need to add adjectives, style words, lighting descriptions, and other finer details.
- Discuss with students, compare their results. Who was closest? Why?

The 'Aha!' moment: Students realise that the AI is the tool, like a paintbrush. The quality of the output depends on the person holding the brush or typing the words.

Year 6 (ages 10–11)

In the final year of Primary school, we can make sure that our 'end of phase child' is leaving with an understanding of data protection, deepfakes, and intellectual property. We can emphasise the need to understand who owns our data, and what happens when we create content using GenAI. Objectives could cover:

- I can explain the concept of 'intellectual property' regarding AI-generated art and text.
- I can read a simple 'privacy policy' to understand what data an app is taking from me.
- I can check an image effectively to spot signs of Deepfake.
- I can argue for or against facial recognition in public spaces.

The suggested activity for the final year group, the eldest students in the school, encourages them to be 'truth detectives.' Before they make the transition to Secondary school or middle school, they need to be equipped with the ability to spot deepfakes, bias, and misinformation.

The concept: Seeing is no longer believing; source verification is key.

The hook: Show them a photorealistic image of someone who never existed. Have students vote on whether they think it is real or not. Then tell them the truth.

'That person has never been born. They have no mother. They have never spoken a word. The AI built their face from millions of photographs of real people – including, possibly, photographs of people in this room.'

The activity:

- Show students a series of AI faces using one of the various sites that has been created to illustrate the point about deepfakes.
- Teach students about the 'tells' of current AI images (this will become harder over time.) Tells could include too many limbs, background text being gibberish, and the texture of skin being unrealistic.
- To mitigate the ever-improving AI image generation, also make sure that there is a discussion about checking the source of the image. Ask, 'Who posted it?' and 'Is it from a reputable site'?

The 'Aha!' moment: Students will realise they can't trust their eyes' they also need to trust research skills. Finish the session by asking one, final question, 'If you received a photo that upset you, of yourself, or a friend, what would you do first?'

Box 8.1 Teacher Tip: Gamify the Hallucinations!

Teacher Tip: Gamify the Hallucinations!

Don't hide AI mistakes from your older KS2 students; celebrate them! Turn fact-checking into a game of 'Spot the Hallucination.' Generate a text about a topic you are studying and intentionally leave the AI's subtle mistakes in. Offer a reward to the 'Truth Detective' who can find and prove the AI's error using a real book or primary source.

Progression

Hopefully the content above helps you at least get a feel for the type of lesson that can be carried out in standalone situations, surrounding AI. I will discuss cross-curricular options in the next section, but before I do, I encourage you to refer to Table 8.1, which shows a potential progression map for this age group.

AI in All Subjects

For many teachers, dedicated digital literacy lessons simply aren't a realistic option. Timetables are full, and curriculum pressure is real. But this needn't be a barrier. Integrating AI literacy into existing subjects isn't just a practical workaround; it's actually good pedagogy. When children encounter AI concepts in history, science, English, and art, not just in computing, those ideas stop feeling like a specialist topic and start feeling like a normal part of how the world works. That's precisely the outcome we're aiming for.

In this section, I aim to suggest some feasible, low-screen time options which allow for the teaching of existing objectives but with an AI twist. At this point, I would like to reiterate the importance of human-centred use of AI, referring back to the H-AI-H mentioned in Chapter 4. In any of the suggestions about how students can use AI, I am encouraging this to be done at the final stages of a process, with ideation and structural organisation firmly rooted in offline and analogue activities. We need to ensure that we are still respecting the different areas of cognitive science associated with brain development at these ages.

Table 8.1 KS2 AI Literacy Progression Map (Ages 7–11)

Domain	Year 3 (Age 7–8) (The Basics)	Year 4 (Age 8–9) (The Mechanics)	Year 5 (Age 9–10) (The Creator)	Year 6 (Age 10–11) (The Critic)
Concept	I can explain that AI learns from examples (data), not just rules.	I can explain that AI makes a ***guess*** (prediction) based on what it has seen before.	I can explain that AI does not 'know' anything; it is just matching patterns.	I can explain how an algorithm (like YouTube) decides what to show me next.
Ethics & Safety	I can say why it is important to be kind to voice assistants (Siri/ Alexa).	I can explain why an AI might be 'biased' if it only sees one type of picture.	I can discuss who owns a picture if an AI makes it.	I can identify deepfakes and explain why I should double-check surprising news.
Practical Skill	I can use a simple tool (like QuickDraw) to help an AI recognise my doodles.	I can train a simple model (e.g. Teachable Machine) to recognise rock, paper, scissors.	I can use a generative AI tool to help me brainstorm ideas for a story.	I can 'audit' an AI response to see if it is true or hallucinated.

Teacher-Facing

From a teacher-facing point of view, AI is something that can be used to reduce time spent on low-impact administrative tasks. It can also be used to create bespoke resources to help cater for the needs of students. Linked to the ideas shared in Chapter 3, below are some ideas for AI use in classes with 7–11 year olds. Before you use anything, however, take a look at this '60-second teacher checklist.'

Box 8.2 The 60-Second Teacher Checklist

The 60-Second Teacher Checklist

1. **The Fact-Check (The 'Hallucination' Filter)**
   - **Does it sound plausible but wrong?** AI is a confident 'liar.' It might invent a Viking King named Steve because it sounds right in a sentence.
   - **The Check:** Scan for names, dates, and specific scientific facts. If you aren't 100% sure, a quick 10-second Google search is your best friend.
2. **The 'Kid-Speak' Check (The Readability Filter)**
   - **Is it actually age-appropriate?** AI often defaults to corporate academic speech. It might use words like *utilize* when your Year 4s need the word *use.*
   - **The Check:** Read one paragraph aloud. If you find yourself stumbling over fancy words that will make ten hands go up in the air at once, simplify them.
3. **The Tone & Bias Check (The Inclusion Filter)**
   - **Does it reinforce stereotypes?** If you ask for a story about a scientist, does the AI always make them a man? If you ask for a story about a family, is it always a nuclear family?
   - **The Check:** Intentionally seek diversity. If the AI output feels a bit standard, ask it to: *'Rewrite this with a more diverse range of characters.'*
4. **The 'No-Fly Zone' Check (The Safety Filter)**
   - **Are there hidden Easter eggs?** Occasionally, AI can pull in odd references or slightly edgy humour that isn't quite right for a 7-year-old.
   - **The Check:** Read the entire output. Don't just skim the first and last bits. Make sure no adult concepts have snuck into the middle of your word bank.

5. **The 'So What?' Check (The Impact Filter)**
   - **Does this actually help them learn?** Sometimes a resource looks pretty but is actually 'low floor, low ceiling.'
   - **The Check:** Ask yourself: *'Does this resource help the child think for themselves, or is it just doing the work for them?'* A word bank is a tool; a pre-written essay is a shortcut.

Science lessons – Solving the 'too hard to read' problem.
Teachers often spend hours searching for texts that match topics and reading levels. You might have a great diagram of a heart, but the textbook explanation is too dense for those students who struggle to read.

To help with this, you could ask for differentiated levelled texts.

Prompt:

"Write a 300-word explanation of the circulatory system for Year 6 students. Include keywords: ventricle, atrium, oxygenated. Add a glossary at the end."

Humanities – Building vocabulary
To support the 'thinking first' phase, AI can be used to generate resources for offline lessons. While this might sound contradictory, remember that you, as the teacher, have final say in any output you receive. In a humanities lesson, you can create a list of vocabulary for a topic, to help support initial lessons.

Prompt:

"Create a word bank of descriptive verbs and adjectives for a Year 4 lesson on Ancient Egypt, organised by theme (the River Nile, gods and pharaohs, daily life)"

English – The instant model text
You can generate model texts to demonstrate specific skills. An essential part of many English lessons, this can be a powerful tool. You could even ask AI for a good example and a bad example.

Prompt:

"Write two versions of a paragraph about a storm. Version A: Perfect grammar with a semi-colon and personification. Version B: Identical, but remove all punctuation and use 'nice' instead of descriptive adjectives. Let's compare them."

Maths – The world problem machine

AI is brilliant at working to a theme. It can take any dry calculation and turn into a story in seconds. You may have taught the method for column addition, well, but the class is not enthused by the standard textbook examples.

Prompt:

> *"Create five word problems for 8-year-olds involving column addition of 2 digit numbers by 2 digit numbers. Theme them around a space mission to Mars."*

P.E. – The skills coach

Even a practical subject such as P.E. can benefit from AI use. You might be teaching hockey, football or athletics. There are 30 children and only you. You could put together a simple list of success criteria to put on a clipboard for student leaders to use.

Prompt:

> *"Break down the technique for a standing long jump into four simple teaching points for a 7-year-old. Use child friendly language e.g. swing your arms like a pendulum."*

Art – The inspiration engine

You could be studying a famous artist, Georgia O'Keeffe, Roy Lichtenstein, or Wassily Kandinsky. You would like the students to create some of their own work in the style of the artist, but they are struggling to begin. AI can be used to spark interest and imagination. You could use it to generate visual prompts or create questions to help the students look closer at their work.

Prompt

> *"List 5 specific things a Year 4 student should look for when sketching a close-up of a flower e.g. the way a petal curls"*

Music – The lyricist

AI is a really good tool to use in music lessons. One situation could be in composition. Students could be tasked with creating a song on a particular theme, but they might be stuck on the lyrics. You may not be a songwriter, and you need a quick example to show them.

Prompt

"Write a four-line rhyming chorus about Viking longships. It needs to be easy to chant and include the words, 'sail' 'dragon' and 'fjord'."

A similar process could also be used with AI music generators, which are becoming more and more able at recreating music of different genres at the touch of a button.

With all of these suggestions, I would be remiss if I didn't reiterate the need for discussion around creativity and intellectual property with students. We need to feel able to showcase the use of AI in our workflow, but we also need to remind students that we do so with an understanding of who owns what.

Student Facing

The Ground Rules

I will repeat, because it bears repeating, GenAI tools should only be used with students in controlled situations. Firstly, I would hold off handing them over to students younger than 9 years old. There is nothing scientific to this other than the fact that the older students in the primary system may be better equipped to approach AI use in a more cautious and deliberate fashion. Secondly, I urge you to always ask 'Why?' before anything else. If the use of AI does not dramatically enhance the learning experience, compared to traditional methods, then rethink your choice to use it.

We must also be aware of the dangers surrounding what is called 'De-skilling' (Risko & Gilbert, 2016). The theory is that, before we hand AI tools over to students, we must confront the theory that human users of automated systems begin to lose the 'situational awareness' and experience required to solve problems. In the adult world, this could look like a pilot forgetting how to fly a plane manually because they have become too reliant on autopilot.

If a Year 5 student uses AI spellcheck tools and grammar aids, every time they write something, they will get a perfect result but will not experience the cognitive struggle required to learn why certain rules exist. To prevent this, teachers need to be deliberate about when we allow the AI help. Going back to the calculator analogy, we do not give a calculator to a 6 year old when they are learning bonds, because they need to build a mental model first. We do give calculators to 11 year olds working on statistics because calculation is not the main objective.

We can ensure that this deliberate use happens by being clear with students about when they can use AI and when they can't. For example, when the objective of the lesson is to learn a skill, AI cannot be used. The student must do the heavy lifting. However, if the objective is application or creativity, AI can be invited in as a collaborator, helping with ideation and checking, as long as the student remains the expert in charge.

Supporting Readers

Reading is the primary mechanism for acquiring knowledge, but we know that reading levels vary dramatically. Alongside the levelled texts and vocabulary word banks created by the teacher, students can also access previously hard-to-read content through TTS or text-to-speech tools. AI-powered versions of these tools can mimic human expression and intonation, adding to the authenticity of the experience. There are also tools such as immersive readers, which can break down sentences and words into syllables and can provide visual definitions of key vocabulary. What would traditionally need to be done in a different room, with a teaching assistant, can now be done in the classroom, with a pair of headphones. This encourages independence and also removes the stigma attached to needing help.

One of the other core components of reading is the discussion around content. The whole-class guided reading model works well for those with few needs but can leave some students behind, unable to keep up, or contribute. This would traditionally point to the need of a 1:1 tutor, but a student could turn to AI, live in class, instead. A student reading *Goodnight Mister Tom* could ask the AI, 'Why is William so afraid?' The AI could be prompted not to give the answer but to guide the student to find the answer themselves, 'Think back to how his mother treated him in London. Can you find a quote showing his fear?'

Enhancing the Writing Process

Writing is a very human endeavour. Research associated with the process of handwriting shows that something distinct happens when pen is put to paper. Therefore, all my suggestions here are detailing how AI can enhance the end of the writing process, assuming the planning has happened offline.

Once the initial offline planning has happened, using Post-its, oral retelling, and note-taking, there is the possibility for students to move to the screen. The first scenario could be something that aids those who find the physical act of writing difficult. This has historically stopped the story-writing process before it has started. A child could have a fantastic imagination and story ideas, but can't get the text down on paper. This is where speech-to-text tools could be used. AI transcription could allow students to dictate their drafts, potentially maintaining the complexity of sentence structure which might otherwise have been lost.

In some special cases, a teacher might even allow a student to input a bullet point plan to AI and ask it to expand the content into a rough draft. The student would then need to rewrite and improve. This removes the blank page fear experienced by some.

Additionally, AI can be used as an editor and a 'critical friend.' Our eldest students are required to demonstrate a mastery of complex punctuation and grammar, but they can use AI to help point out simple typos and syntax issues. They can also take advice about their grammatical and vocabulary choices from AI, using the tool as a thesaurus or proofreader.

Finally, when publishing, students can bring AI tools to help add polish. Using approved text-to-image generators could help generate illustrations for stories. This would probably not be a one-off prompt and would lead to iteration and the student imposing their creative views on the AI. Students could also use AI to suggest the format of a product like a newspaper or brochure.

In conclusion, the integration of AI, across all subjects with students aged 7–11, is more than feasible. When used well, this use offers a profound opportunity to enhance the access to learning and the quality of final outcomes. For the teacher, it is not a replacement but a relief mechanism and quite possibly reviving a love of the craft.

For a student, if anchored in pedagogy that respects the importance of the human input, they can leave our phase physically or metaphorically with a strong ability to use AI properly in the next step of their academic career.

Leadership Lens

If you are reading this as a headteacher, deputy, or phase leader, this section is specifically for you. Everything else in this chapter equips your teachers. This part is about making sure their efforts are not undermined the moment they leave the room.

The single biggest barrier to effective AI literacy in Primary schools is not technology, budget, or time. It is inconsistency. When one teacher permits AI-assisted writing, and another treats it as cheating, students learn one thing very quickly – that the rules depend on who is watching. That is not AI literacy. It is confusion disguised as progress.

The largest part you can play in integrating AI into your teachers' workflow is to allow them to experiment, exploring the possibilities. The other aspect is facilitating the discussion about when AI is permitted across the school. Sit down with phase or subject leaders and define the different stages of AI use in a project or piece of work or assignment.

We are now at a point where we cannot leave it up to individual teachers to decide what constitutes AI integrity. Without a solid, unified approach and policy, there will be inconsistencies which will lead to more harm than good.

What does an inconsistent approach actually look like in practice? It looks like a Year 5 student who has been taught to use AI as a thinking partner in one classroom, being told in another that they have cheated for doing exactly that. It looks like a Year 6 teacher spending time building critical AI literacy, only for it to be quietly ignored because there is no policy requiring it to be valued. It looks like a safeguarding gap – where one staff member understands the risks of deepfakes and another has never heard the term.

A unified school policy does not need to be long or complex. It needs to answer three questions clearly, and answer them the same way for every member of staff:

- When is AI permitted in student work, and at what stage of the process?
- How do we define AI integrity — and how does that differ from academic dishonesty?
- Who is responsible for updating our approach as technology changes?

Without answers to those three questions agreed across the whole staff, you do not have a policy. You have a collection of individual opinions – and the students will find every gap between them.

Box 8.3 Key Takeaways from Chapter 8

Key Takeaways

From Consumers to 'Truth Detectives': AI is a pattern matcher, not a truth teller. Our primary goal in KS2 is to teach students that Large Language Models simply predict the next word rather than actually 'knowing' facts. Critical thinking and source verification are now the most important literacies of all.

The 'Digital Native' is a Dangerous Myth: A child's ability to navigate Roblox or a tablet interface does not equate to an understanding of algorithmic bias, deepfakes, or data privacy.

We cannot assume tech fluency equals tech literacy; explicitly teaching the mechanics and ethics of AI is our gap to fill.

Rethink the Learning Pyramid (The UnBlooms™ Cycle): Because AI can instantly generate a finished product, we must shift from a linear learning pyramid to a recursive loop. Teach students to *Generate* (offline first!), *Question, Critique, Refine,* and *Reflect*. The struggle of learning happens in the editing, not just the creating.

The Human Is Always the Editor-in-Chief: Whether a teacher is generating a differentiated science text or a student is using AI as a sounding board for a history project, the human must always have the final say. Embed this principle across all subjects so AI literacy becomes a normal part of how the world works, not just a standalone computing lesson.

AI in Practice: A Prompt to Try

You have a spare 10 minutes at the end of the day, and the class is restless.

Prompt:

> *"I want to play a game called 'Two Truths and a Lie' with my class of 9-year-olds about [Insert Topic, e.g., The Romans]. Generate three statements: two factual, and one subtle hallucination that sounds real but is wrong."*

Challenge the class to spot the AI's lie.

Professional Development: Discussion Points

If a student uses AI to generate an essay plan, but writes the essay themselves, is that cheating or smart planning? Where do we draw the line in our school?

Have you tried asking AI to 'roast' a lesson plan? (e.g. 'Act as a bored 10-year-old and tell me why this lesson on fractions is boring').

Look at the UnBlooms™ cycle. If AI can instantly generate a 'perfect' final product, how do we need to change our marking and feedback policies so we are rewarding the *process* of refining and reflecting, rather than just grading the final shiny piece of work?

Check Your Understanding

1. When explaining how Generative AI works to a Year 3 (7–8 year old) class, which explanation aligns best with the 'prediction engine' concept?
   A) 'The AI is like a super-smart robot brain that knows everything in the world.'
   B) 'The AI is like a search engine; it looks up the correct answer from a library of facts.'
   C) 'The AI is a pattern-spotter; it predicts the next word in a sentence based on millions of examples it has seen before.'
   D) 'The AI is magic; we don't really know how it works, but it is always right.'
2. Why does the chapter argue we must move past the 'Digital Native' narrative when teaching KS2 students?
   A) Because students today spend less time on screens than previous generations.
   B) Because the term is offensive to older generations of teachers.
   C) Because assuming a child who can play Roblox also understands data privacy and file management is a dangerous misconception.
   D) Because digital literacy is no longer required in modern curricula.
3. According to the '60-Second Teacher Checklist,' what is the primary risk of using AI to generate educational resources without a 'Human-in-the-Loop'?

   A) The AI might produce a resource that is too short for the lesson.
   B) The AI might 'hallucinate' facts (like inventing a breakdancing Prime Minister) or reinforce subtle biases.
   C) The AI will take the teacher's job and make lesson planning obsolete.
   D) The AI cannot format text correctly for a worksheet.

Answers

1. C. As discussed in the Year 3 section, moving students from 'it's a robot' to 'it's a prediction engine' is key. It doesn't 'know' facts (B) or 'think' (A); it matches patterns.

2. C. Exposure = Understanding. The text highlights that while students are fluent consumers of games/media, they often lack the 'under the hood' understanding of how these tools actually work.
3. B. The AI might 'hallucinate' facts (like inventing a breakdancing Prime Minister) or reinforce subtle biases.

References

AI4K12 Initiative. (2021). *Five big ideas in AI.* Retrieved from ai4k12.org

Armstrong, P. (2010). *Bloom's Taxonomy.* Vanderbilt University Center for Teaching. https://cft.vanderbilt.edu/guides-sub-pages/blooms-taxonomy/

Austin, T. (2025). *UnBlooms™™: Rethinking learning in the age of AI.* Zenodo. https://zenodo.org/records/17298679

Common Sense Media. (2025). *AI and our youngest learners: How children ages 0–8 are using AI tools.* Common Sense Media.

Davies, B. (2025). *Response to author survey.* Unpublished raw data.

Haidt, J. (2024). *Interview with Ezra Klein. The Ezra Klein Show.* New York Times Podcasts.

Mani, F., as reported in: Singer, N. (2023, November 4). *High schooler calls for AI regulations after manipulated pornographic images shared online.* CNN. Retrieved from cnn.com

PSHE Association. (2024). *Digital deception: Understanding deepfakes and manipulated images.* PSHE Association. Retrieved from pshe-association.org.uk

Risko, E. F., & Gilbert, S. J. (2016). Cognitive offloading. *Trends in Cognitive Sciences, 20*(9), 676–688.

Turner, E. (2022). *Simplicitus: The joined-up approach to primary teaching.* Independent Thinking Press.

UNESCO. (2024). *AI competency framework for students.* United Nations Educational, Scientific and Cultural Organization. Retrieved from unesco.org

Waite, J., & Curzon, P. (2018). *The SEAME framework.* Raspberry Pi Foundation. Retrieved from raspberrypi.org

Ware, B. (2025). *Response to author survey.* Unpublished raw data.

9

Inclusion and AI

Every Child, Every Voice, Ethically Supported

It's Friday lunchtime in the staffroom. A stack of topic books is teetering on Jim's desk, open at a page all about The Romans.

Jim: [Rubbing his temples, staring at a workbook] It's heart-breaking, honestly. I know Leo knows this. We spent twenty minutes talking about aqueducts yesterday. He explained gravity flow, engineering, everything. But look at this.

Chloe: [Peering over] Two sentences?

Jim: 'Romans built roads. Water goes down.' That's it. That's all he could get down in forty minutes. His handwriting speed is the bottleneck. It's like he has a symphony in his head and a broken harmonica to play it with.

Elena: [Pouring tea] Cognitive load, Jim. He's spending so much working memory just holding the pencil and forming the letters, there's no bandwidth left for the history.

Chloe: So, let's remove the pencil. Have you tried that new 'Speech-to-Structure' AI tool I sent round?

Jim: [Skeptical] Dictation? We've had that for years. It never picks up his accent, and he still rambles.

Chloe: No, not just dictation. This isn't about transcribing; it's about translating thoughts. Watch. *[Chloe pulls out her tablet. She opens an AI voice app.]*

Chloe: Pretend you're Leo. Ramble at it. Just tell me everything about aqueducts, don't worry about grammar.

Jim: [Sighs, then adopts a 'Leo' voice] Um, well, the Romans were clever because they knew water can't go uphill, right? So they made these big bridges with arches, and they had to be slanted just a tiny bit, so the water flowed to the city... and I think they used lead pipes which wasn't good but... yeah, gravity.

DOI: 10.4324/9781003740377-11

Chloe: [Taps 'Refine for Year 4 Literacy'. The screen buffers for a second.]
Elena: Read the output, Jim.
Jim: [Reading screen] *The Romans were expert engineers who used gravity to move water. They built large arched bridges called aqueducts that were slightly angled so water could flow downhill into the cities.*
Jim: [Silence. He looks back at the two sentences in the workbook.] That's what he *knows*.
Elena: Exactly. For a child like Leo, the blank page is a glass ceiling. The GenAI didn't 'think' for him, he provided the knowledge. The AI just acted as the scaffold. It's not cheating, Jim. It's a wheelchair ramp for his ideas.
Jim: I've been marking him on his handwriting, not his history.
Chloe: And now we can mark him on his mind.

The shift from passive presence to active engagement is no longer an academic ideal; it is a government mandate. In the recent UK government white paper, *Every Child Achieving and Thriving* (February, 2026), there is a call for an education system where all children, especially those with additional needs, are 'active participants in their learning – debating, questioning, challenging…not passive recipients of information.' As we saw with Leo in the opening scenario, traditional barriers like handwriting or decoding can push clever minds into passive roles. GenAI and assistive tools can act as the bridge, allowing us to mandate this advice by removing physical barriers to intellectual participation.

The Classroom Reality

Inclusion is part of every Primary school's core values, either mentioned explicitly or subtly integrated in some way. It is one of the fundamental pillars of our education system. It is out of the question that a mainstream state-funded or private institution in today's world is not focused on being inclusive in some way.

At this point I want to pinpoint what I mean by inclusion to add clarity to the rest of the chapter. All our students walk through our doors with something different and quite often unique as part of their personality or makeup? They could have just arrived from a different country or culture, they could be from a single-parent household or, as I have experienced, a four-parent household (that's a story for another day.) They could be Buddhist, Christian, Muslim, or Jewish. They could have issues with their sight or with their mobility. The list goes on.

An inclusive school is one that accepts those differences and tries to pitch its academic provision and its infrastructure at a point where all its students are seen and supported. The UNESCO Salamanca statement (1994) enshrines this approach when it says, "We believe and proclaim that every child has a fundamental right to education...every child has unique characteristics, interests, abilities and learning needs...education systems should be designed...to take into account the wide diversity of these characteristics and needs."

Despite this declaration, the scale of the challenge remains immense; recent data suggests that an estimated 240 million children live with disabilities, and approximately half of them are out of school entirely (Hamdan et al., 2025). Therefore, there is an urgency to address these issues.

The use of AT or Assistive Technology is nothing new, but the introduction of widely available GenAI tools can help schools and teachers achieve their inclusion goals.

When we look at how AI can aid inclusion in Primary education, we can place its use into three categories:

Assistive and Rehabilitative AI

These are AI tools that are designed to help bypass specific barriers to learning. For example, AI-powered Text-To-Speech (TTS) or Speech-To-Text (STT) products can assist students with dyslexia or motor impairments and computer vision tools can help visually impaired students see the world. These assistive technologies can be greatly enhanced by machine learning, for example, texts can be automatically adjusted by AI to meet the reader's needs.

Adaptive and Personalised Learning Systems

This is a big area and highlights the idea of AI 'tutors,' 1:1 platforms that can use machine learning to analyse student performance and make adjustments, in real time, accordingly. For students who struggle with 'one size fits all' approaches to learning, these tools provide a personalised pathway. There are various platforms that can diagnose reading fluency issues or maths insecurities. There are a lot of promises in this domain, especially the idea of replicating the benefits of a private tutor at scale.

Generative AI

The most recent and disruptive use case of AI is the reason why I am writing this book. GenAI allows all users to create text, image, and video from scratch on various topics. This can help with inclusion as it can help scaffold resources in the classroom. Teachers can use GenAI to generate different versions of a core text, translate materials into other languages, and create images to support learning points and many more ideas.

The classroom reality of GenAI is that it can be used to augment human capacity. When used correctly, teachers can use GenAI to help them reach the students who would historically have been marginalised, for various reasons. On the student-facing side, the tools can be used for accessibility, allowing every student to participate in the same conversations and activities. On the teacher-facing side, the tools can be used to relieve the administrative burden of resource creation and can free up the time to spend in conversations with students.

Now that I have introduced the tools being used, I want to share how GenAI can tie in with pedagogical practices we have studied and use widely.

UDL (Universal Design for Learning)

Think about the last time you prepared a lesson for a class with five different reading levels, a child who processes information better through images, and another who needs to move to think. UDL (CAST, 2018) asks us to plan for that reality from the start, building in multiple means of representation, expression and engagement. In practice, this has always meant hours of preparation. A teacher differentiating a single science lesson might need a simplified text, a visual diagram, a vocabulary list, and a speaking frame, four separate resources for one lesson. Jim, who spent last Sunday doing exactly this by hand, would recognise that calculation immediately. With GenAI, that same teacher can generate all four versions of that resource in under five minutes, keeping the same learning objective at the heart of each one. UDL stops being the thing you aim for when you have time, and starts being the thing you actually do.

Vygotsky's Zone of Proximal Development

We've all set work that was either too easy or too hard, and watched the room either switch off or shut down. Finding that 'just right' level, what Vygotsky called the Zone of Proximal Development (Vygotsky, 1978), is one of teaching's hardest daily tasks. AI tutors can do this automatically, adjusting difficulty in real time as a student responds. They can't replace the moment you notice a child's eyes fill with tears, but they can handle the pitch.

However, the Zone of Proximal Development or ZPD ties in well with AI. One of the main points that Vygotsky makes is that learning happens best when teachers find the sweet spot, the point where the work is challenging but not too challenging. The holy grail is the 'just right' piece of work where there is challenge but not frustration. From a human standpoint, this can often be harder than it sounds. From an AI standpoint, this is where it comes into its own.

AI tutors can personalise and pitch tasks at just the right level, at this sweet spot, with ease. They can also adapt as they go. It is worth mentioning at this point that AI tutors can do this very well, but what they can't do is provide the emotional support a teacher can. It is crucial to still maintain the 'human in the loop' at all times.

The SAMR Model

Most of us have been there, using an iPad essentially as a very expensive notepad. Puentedura's SAMR model (2006) gives us a useful ladder for thinking about this. At the bottom, technology simply substitutes for a traditional tool; a child types their story instead of writing it. As you climb, it augments, then modifies, and finally redefines what's possible, creating learning experiences that simply couldn't exist without it. A child who is non-verbal recording a multimedia book report. A newcomer student collaborating in real time with a peer, across a language barrier, on a shared document. Historically, reaching the top of that ladder took years of confidence-building and technical expertise, and research suggests that without deliberate design, technology use tends to cluster at the substitution and augmentation levels, not through lack of ambition but through lack of time and resource (Romrell et al., 2014).

AI changes that timeline dramatically. The jump from substitution to redefinition is no longer a years-long climb; it can happen in a single lesson. Take Leo from our opening scene. A child who couldn't produce two sentences is now being assessed on his actual knowledge. That's not substitution, that's redefinition.

The Promise – Access and Engagement

The three categories above represent a genuine toolkit for inclusion. But here is the honest caveat that sits underneath all of it. A tool is only as good as the hands it is placed in and the infrastructure surrounding those hands. The OECD (2024) warns that without adequate teacher training and institutional support, AI risks deepening existing educational disparities rather than closing them.

The schools that need these tools most are frequently the least equipped to implement them well. In other words, AI in the hands of a well-supported teacher in a well-resourced school will thrive. The same tool, given to an overwhelmed teacher in an underfunded school without training or infrastructure, can compound the very inequalities it promised to solve. This is not a reason to avoid AI. It is a reason to be deliberate about how we introduce it. The rest of this chapter is about doing exactly that.

The Teacher Toolkit

IEPs (but Be Careful)

IEPs (Individual Education Plans) or equivalent are extremely important, but can be a perfect example of one of those time-consuming pieces of paperwork. Writing them can add stress and act as an obstacle in the way to doing more important parts of your job. The UK government white paper I referred to at the beginning of the chapter puts the IEP or the ISP (having been rebranded) at the heart of inclusive education. However, they are the perfect example of time-consuming paperwork. The new guidance puts more pressure on the already busy teacher, but AI can relieve that pressure, with a task like this, very easily.

To begin with, you can use an AI chatbot to turn your quick and possibly messy observational notes into something organised and cohesive. You can then have AI help you with wording and formatting of an IEP document, refining of grammar, and clarity of the goals. If you have a pre-existing school template, you can upload this to your conversation, which allows you to fine-tune the content you are going to write in there.

Here is a real example, using our protagonist, Elena.

It is the end of the day, and an exhausted Elena has collated a collection of hastily scribbled notes on a child who is of particular concern. She types in the following prompt:

> *"Student A is 7. He is reading at a 5-year-old level. He knows his phonics but guesses words based on the first letter instead of blending them. He gets frustrated when reading aloud and tries to hide the book"*

She then adds the persona and instructions to AI,

> *"Act as an expert Special Educational Needs Coordinator. Turn these notes into three SMART IEP targets. For each target, provide two practical classroom strategies I can use to support him."*

The AI produces a set of perfectly formatted goals. Elena does not just copy and paste the output; she now reads the targets and decides whether they are realistic and suitable for the child in question. She is not the special needs coordinator, so she would also pass the recommendations on to the relevant person. What has happened is that Elena has consolidated her notes and has created a set of potentially actionable targets. The last step of her checking the output maintains human oversight and keeps her as the expert in the room, and is the most important.

There are, however, caveats to IEP work using AI. There are several legal and ethical pillars, used globally that should be referred to and observed. You may be reading in a country outside of the scope of these regulations, but I still urge you to keep them in mind. In Europe, there is both the GPDR, on general data protection, and the EU AI Act, focused more on a risk-based approach to AI use. In the USA, there is FERPA and, globally, UNESCO also has guidelines on these areas.

To begin with, the use of AI for any educational purpose is classed as 'High-Risk' (European Parliament, 2024). This is not because the AI tool is inherently dangerous; it is because we are dealing with data belonging to minors. Here are five rules to help you understand how to use AI safely, when working on an IEP.

1. Never use a child's real name, school name, or exact medical diagnosis. Call them 'Student A' as above or use a pseudonym. Instead of using a specific disorder, describe the symptoms.
2. Keep the process human-centred. AI doesn't know about the finer details linked to a student, such as recent family events or daily routine.
3. Do not use AI to determine a child's emotional state. There are tools for this, and they are improving, but this should remain a purely human process.
4. Do not use AI to write recommendations and then use them without checking them first. AI is not the expert, you are. What may seem feasible could be detrimental.
5. Parents hold the rights to their child's educational records. You cannot share their content with external vendors or unapproved tools.

Box 9.1 'Remember'

Remember – AI can sometimes 'hallucinate' (make up) specific medical terms or milestones. Always cross-reference the AI's 'SMART targets' with your local curriculum standards or clinical advice. The AI is your ghostwriter, but you are the Editor-in-Chief.

Language

As a parent with bilingual children and a teacher who has spent most of their career in international schools, I have seen how language barriers can affect learning and integration into the social fabric of a school.

Multilingual learners are not just apparent in international schools either. In the USA, 5.3 million students (National Education Association [NEA], 2025) have more than one language, with 55% of educators claiming to have at least one multilingual learner in their classroom. In England, over 20% of all students speak English as an additional language (Lindorff et al., 2025)

Within this high percentage of multilingual learners, there are students who enter a school with no understanding of the main language of instruction. Traditionally known as 'newcomers,' these students are often segregated through 'pull-out' interventions, thus removing the students from valuable curriculum and social time. It is not surprising that this is the go-to solution, as teachers find the need for differentiation through instruction and activity, a burden that is difficult to achieve manually.

The whole idea of inclusion is that all learners, regardless of their native language and other 'differences,' should receive equitable access to high-quality teaching in the main classroom. AI can help make this a reality.

On the teacher's side of things, here are some examples of how to use AI to support multilingual learners.

- You can take a complex science article about 'Photosynthesis' and ask an AI tool to 'Rewrite this for a 7-year-old at a beginning English level.' It keeps the facts but fixes the words so the child isn't just staring at a page they can't read.
- You can tell an AI, 'Give me 5 sentence starters and a bilingual glossary for a lesson on the Vikings.' It's done in seconds.
- You can use AI image generation to create visual representations of topics and texts.
- You can send a newsletter home, and AI can translate it into ten different home languages perfectly, so the parents actually feel like part of the school community.

From the student side of things, this is where the most exciting things can happen.

In Real-Time

- Students can use a personal device on their desk that displays translated subtitles of your instruction. The downside to this is the extended screentime.
- You can project side-by-side captions on your whiteboard. Using AI to help with the translation, this removes the stigma of a child needing a special device and adds an element of normality to multilingualism.
- Students can use two-way translation tools on a device during collaborative work. This allows for a real conversation, and a newcomer can make friends and participate from day 1.
- A newcomer student can wear a specialised earpiece that listens to the spoken instruction and instantly translates the content into their native language. In reality, this is one to think very carefully about in a Primary setting. Earpieces can be lost, damaged, or covered in something sticky, very quickly.

Independently

- The use of an AI 'buddy' to practice language skills can be effective as they are non-judgmental, tireless, and patient.
- If a student makes a grammatical error, an AI can pinpoint why it happened. It can then explain the rule in an age-appropriate way.
- For independent reading, students can consume the exact same grade-level content as their peers, but can use AI to simplify the sentence structure and the vocabulary to match the current reading level.
- When working on independent assignments, AI tutors can be given parameters that have them work like a supportive 'Socratic' coach, offering subtle hints and breaking down complex rules. This would be something to be used by the oldest students in Primary school.

To provide you with a quick understanding of how AI could be used with language

learners, please refer to the content in Table 9.1.

To see what this looks like in practice, we only need to look at the work of Michael Lubelfeld, a School Superintendent in the US, who successfully implemented this exact approach for his younger multilingual students. By restricting the AI tools, he ensured the focus remained entirely on safe language acquisition (M. Lubelfeld, response to survey, 2025):

Table 9.1 An overview of AI assistive tools for language learners.

The Tool	How it helps the child	How it helps you (the teacher)
Live translation	They understand the 'gist' of the lesson instantly.	You don't have to concentrate on differentiating your content in as much detail.
Text simplifiers	They read the same topic as their peers, just with more manageable vocabulary.	No more staying up rewriting worksheets manually.
AI Chat Tutors	A non-judgmental place to practice speaking without embarrassment.	Allows you time to focus on other groups.

> *"The 'Walled Garden' model was designed for the 4th-grade cohort... serving a high population of Multilingual Learners (MLs). The primary objective was safe exploration. Just as a physical walled garden protects young plants from harsh winds while allowing them to access sunlight, this digital environment protects students from the toxicity, bias, and hallucinations of open AI models, while allowing them to benefit from the advantages of generative feedback. The pedagogical focus was on literacy and narrative construction, using AI as a scaffold for language acquisition."*

This 'walled garden' approach is the perfect blueprint for primary inclusion. It gives students the tireless support of an AI language buddy to build their literacy, while the school maintains a firm, safe boundary around the technology.

Pitfalls

As with any use of AI tools, there are some pitfalls to be cautious of, before jumping in wholesale with rolling out AI for language learners.

Firstly, there is the danger that AI will become a 'crutch.' When they have unlimited access to translation tools, it is a risk that they will always use the tool to find the answer, bypassing the productive struggle required to actually learn. To deal with this, teachers must make sure that the tools are set up to offer hints, rather than give away answers and, most importantly, they still require the students to practice the messy, human work of decoding and speaking.

It is also worth mentioning that there will be bias towards those with unique accents. Most AI models are trained on native speakers of a language, and therefore, the speech recognition software struggles. Being flagged for poor pronunciation can lead to frustration and low self-esteem. To mitigate this, it is important that there is constant human oversight.

Finally there is, once again, the issue of data privacy. To work effectively, the AI must collect a massive amount of potentially sensitive data from students. This can include voice samples and emotional responses. There is an ethical risk with third-party companies using this data to target the vulnerable, 'newcomer' student.

Equity

To begin this weighty topic, I want to return us to Elena, our middle of the road AI user. She uses AI to help with a 'newcomer' family, to great effect.

It's 3:45 pm on Friday. Amara's mother is standing at the school gates, slightly distanced from the other parents. She is looking intently at a letter her daughter has handed her. She has only been in the country for four months. She smiles when Elena approaches, but Elena can tell that she doesn't understand what she has in her hands. The letter is about next week's trip, and there is a permission slip attached. Without it, Amara cannot go. Elena dashes back inside, takes a photo of a spare copy of the letter, and uploads it to AI. She asks for a translated version of the letter, into Urdu, Amara's home language. She prints it and hands it over. Amara's mother reads it, looks up, and says something Elena doesn't understand, but she doesn't need to.

Equity in education has been historically hard to achieve, due to resource and time-constrained classrooms. But GenAI has the potential to serve as a profound structural leveller in Primary schools.

Before I continue, there can be a common confusion between the words 'equality' and 'equity' in reference to education. 'Equality' refers to a standardised approach, ensuring every student receives the exact same resources, curriculum, and instruction. 'Equity,' on the other hand, refers to a responsive approach that respects socioeconomic inequalities, cultural barriers, and systemic biases. It demands that resources and instruction be differentiated so that all students have a fair opportunity to achieve academic mastery.

Here are some thoughts on how GenAI has the potential to improve equity.

Expert Tutoring for All

Bloom's influential 1984 research suggested that one-on-one human tutoring provides the best results (Bloom, 1984). But this privilege has always been one enjoyed by affluent families. The ability to pay for tutoring has always given certain children an educational advantage, thus compounding the equity divide. AI can disrupt this narrative by providing rigorous, scalable tutors for all. The potential for these tools to close the equity divide is backed by emerging data. Studies show that AI-enhanced educational platforms can boost student performance by up to 30% and enhance engagement by over 60% (Hamdan et al., 2025). Despite the AI tutor not being human, interactions can be effective. The ability to use Socratic dialogue (prompting but not giving the answer) and scaffolding can guide students and enable long-term knowledge acquisition. AI tutors can provide expert support to struggling students while simultaneously pushing high achievers to meet their full potential.

We may read about both individualised learning and personalised learning in connection with AI tutors. There is a distinction between these approaches: Individualised learning involves students progressing through pre-structured, standardised curriculum at varying speeds. In this model, the system fine-tunes the difficulty of problems based on a student's readiness. This approach might help classroom management, but it only really adjusts the pacing of a predetermined system.

In contrast, personalised learning is tailored to the different needs and interests of the student. In a well-tuned GenAI setup, all aspects of the learning process can vary all at the same time. This is beneficial to students as the AI can adapt according to responses and allows repetitive or seemingly simplistic questions, breaking down emotional barriers to learning.

Preservation of Underresourced Languages

Tying into the section on using AI for language learning, GenAI can tackle the educational challenge of the lack of materials available in underresourced languages. An example of this is with the Generative AI for Education (Tapo et al.,2025) toolchain and workflow that has been used in Mali, with the local Bambara language, to counteract the bias in LLMs towards Global North content and to build literacy. The process involved local authors using LLMs for creation of story drafts which were then translated using translation tools and finally refined by human translators and linguists. Enhanced by visuals generated using text-to-image models, this AI-assisted approach allowed researchers to create a library of 174 illustrated children's books, in Bambara, in the space of 6 months. The subsequent use of these books in pilot programs resulted in a 67% reduction in the number of children unable to read in Bambara.

The research has proved that GenAI can rapidly scale production of native-language educational materials, provided there is a rigorous, bias-aware, human-centred process.

Empowering Neurodivergent Learners

Historically, schools have treated disabled students like they are broken and need to be fixed, to fit in with everyone else. They are forced to follow the same rigid rules and lessons as everyone else, even if it doesn't work for them. AI changes this. Instead of trying to change the student, AI changes the environment. It acts like a digital Swiss Army knife that can instantly reshape a lesson to fit the student's needs, focusing on making the world more accessible rather than making the student act 'normal.' Here are some examples:

- Dyslexia and cognitive load – Students with dyslexia struggle with immense cognitive load, and this limits their mental resources. AI can be used to summarise texts, simplify sentences, and can match up text and images.
- Social-Emotional learning – For students with Autism Spectrum Disorder, GenAI chatbots provide endlessly patient, entirely non-judgemental conversation partners. This can provide an outlet and, as with language learners, a safe space to practice communication and empathy without the fear of peer judgment and frustration.

Please remember that use of chatbots must be closely monitored by an adults, to ensure the AI doesn't 'hallucinate' inappropriate social advice of encourage isolation.

Reclaiming Time for Human Connection

To achieve equity in education, one of the core components is the deep, meaningful connections made between teachers and students. With GenAI removing the heavy workload that causes teacher burnout, teachers can gain back the time previously unavailable and use it to maintain the relationships with their students.

When I am talking about reclaiming time, I am not, sadly, talking about sitting an extra 5 minutes in the staffroom, drinking coffee. I am referring to the smaller components of lessons that can build equity. We didn't become teachers to be experts in data handling and writing emails, we are here for the 'lightbulb moments.' Let me share some of these components.

- More time to 'check-in' – Having used GenAI to generate levelled texts before the lesson, you can spend your time listening to readers 1:1 instead of having to re-explain the difficult vocabulary to one of the groups.
- The bridge conversation – You can use an AI translation tool to create key science terms in a student's home language. This means you don't have to spend 10 minutes trying to communicate through

gestures. Instead, you can go through the words together and build an instant bond.

- Improved emotional bandwidth – You used AI to help alleviate the 'Sunday Scaries' by asking it to automate your weekly newsletter and admin emails. This means that you walk into school on Monday morning with more 'emotional bandwidth' and therefore engage better with your students' needs.

If you do nothing else with AI in your daily workflow, this is the most important. We don't have to use it to look 'tech-savvy,' but we can use it so we can be more present for our young charges. Every minute saved by using AI is a minute you can spend looking a child in the eye. This is the ultimate equity.

Socioeconomic Achievement Gap

AI holds immense potential as a structural leveller in schools but also presents the danger of deepening the 'digital divide' further.

Schools with a demographic of students from low-income families have historically struggled with academic levels due to chronic absenteeism, behaviour, and teacher turnover rates. If employed thoughtfully, AI can provide learning experiences previously reserved for students on accelerated courses, in wealthier catchment areas.

The new iteration of the 'digital divide' however is no longer restricted to hardware or internet connection, though these are still persistent issues in underfunded areas of the world. Instead there is now a divide surrounding AI literacy and the nature of how the AI is used by the student.

Emerging evidence suggests that a student's socioeconomic background influences how they engage with AI tools. The College Board (2025) found sizeable differences in AI use by socioeconomic status at the secondary level, with better-resourced schools more likely to have guiding policies in place – meaning that without deliberate intervention, AI risks reinforcing existing advantage rather than disrupting it.

In the Global South, AI has the potential to reduce the 'digital divide' by:

- Preserving Native Language Literacy – As referred to above, the most effective way of building foundational literacy is by teaching children in their mother tongue. AI can be leveraged to do this.

- Scaling Tutoring in resource-constrained areas – AI can provide cost-effective, personalised instructions in regions with teacher shortages and oversubscribed schools.
- The Rise of 'Small AI' – Researchers are focusing on rolling out smaller AI models, optimised to work on mobile devices, locally, thus reducing the need for high-speed internet and heavy data transfers. This would allow AI to be used extensively in rural or developing regions.

While these are strong ideas, there are, of course, hurdles to overcome and potential reasons that AI could exacerbate the 'digital divide.'

- Infrastructure and funding – AI deployment needs a strong digital infrastructure, but some areas only have internet penetration of around 37%. Also, there is no access to venture capital for local AI startups.
- Data poverty and bias – Populations in the Global South are underrepresented in the dominant AI models. Results are regularly inaccurate and don't reflect local culture and customs.
- Digital colonialism – There is a fear that AI is just another form of 'digital colonialism' with the resources of countries in the Global South being traded for imported, proprietary software from Western companies.
- Techno-solutionism – The final fear is that there is a flawed assumption that AI will solve all the woes in schools. AI used as a quick fix, without addressing core socio-economic inequalities will cause educational resources going to the wrong places, resulting in no improvement of learning outcomes.

Scaling It Up

You may be a Jim; you have just read what I have written above and said to yourself, this sounds like another one of those 'revolutionary' tools which would work wonders for one child, with access to the best technology available. It wouldn't, however, work with a class of 30 children, six IEPs, and various undocumented learning needs.

I understand where you are coming from, but I would say that scaling AI use up for a whole class of students isn't about handing over logins and hoping for the best. It's about systemic support: Using the AI to do the hard work so you can actually be a teacher.

Here are some thoughts about how to achieve an equitable classroom, with limited resources, framed through Jim's frustrations.

1. 'I don't have enough devices' – If you only have five tablets in the class, don't try to make the whole class use AI at once. Instead, use it as a learning station. In group work, you can target one set of students while you can allow access to a specific AI tutor, for another set.
2. 'I don't have time to prompt for 30 children' – Scaling up doesn't mean more screen time. You can use AI to create differentiated activities to print, in 5 minutes.
3. 'The tech will fail and ruin the lesson' – Use GenAI to generate printed resources before the lesson.
4. 'How on earth am I supposed to meet the needs of five different reading groups, three IEPs, and two ELL students at the same time without cloning myself?' – Think of AI as a digital teaching assistant that doesn't need a coffee break. It can buy you some breathing room so you aren't stuck at the photocopier when the class is waiting for you.
5. 'I am a teacher, not a help desk. I can't help Sally with her phonics because I'm busy unblocking a pop-up window on Toby's screen.' – To keep AI use manageable, use 'low-friction' tools. You don't want to have to deal with 30 students asking what their password is. If it takes more than three clicks for a student to get going, keep it out of the primary classroom.

A Prompt Library for SENCOs

A school SENCO (Special Educational Needs Coordinator) should be likened to an air traffic controller of a school. They are always inundated with deadlines, requests from teachers, emails from parents, and the content of their support lessons.

If you are a SENCO or know one, the collection of prompts shown in Table 9.2 is designed to be high-impact but low-friction, actionable, and quick to use.

Table 9.2 A prompt library for special needs coordinators.

Category	The Goal	The Prompt
Policy to Practice	Convert policy to practice	*'I have a 4-page clinical report for a student with Dyspraxia and Auditory Processing Disorder. Based on this text, create a bulleted "Cheat Sheet" for their classroom teacher. Include: 3 environmental triggers to avoid, 5 specific seating/tool accommodations, and 2 ways to give instructions that won't overwhelm them. Use plain classroom language.'*
	Polishing IEP goals	*'Here is a high-level IEP goal: "The student will improve social interaction skills." Break this down into 4 "Small Steps" (SMART targets) suitable for a 6-year-old, focusing on turn-taking during Lego play.'*
The Environment Architect	Supporting in-class accommodations	*'Suggest a "Sensory Protection Plan" for a primary school student with sensory-sensitive Autism for a science experiment involving 30 children and the vinegar/bicarbonate of soda reaction. The student struggles with [specific trigger, e.g. strong smells and loud sudden noises]. Provide options for safe participation, sensory-reducing equipment, and "escape" protocols. Focus on inclusive strategies that maintain the student's agency. Include a "pre-teaching" suggestion. What can the teacher show the student 5 minutes before the lesson to lower their anxiety?'*
Advocacy and Communication	Writing difficult emails to parents.	*'I am a school SENCO. Draft an empathetic and professional email template for a parent explaining a transition from a 1:1 support model to a "Group-Support and Independence" model. The email should focus on the benefits of building student autonomy and peer interaction. Include a warm invitation for an in-person meeting. Do not include any student-specific names or unique identifiers.'*
	Evidence gathering for a funding application	*'I am a SENCO drafting a funding application. I have written five professional observation notes (completely anonymized) regarding a student's speech development. Use these notes as a data source to help me structure a draft report that compares these specific milestones against standard age-related expectations for [Insert Age]. Focus on professional tone and clarity. I will review, verify, and finalize all conclusions.'*

Leadership Lens

All the above puts a spotlight on the monumental challenge that is making sure a school is inclusive. The pressure on staff and school leaders is nothing new, but now there is a potential solution, if employed correctly. AI can lighten workload and bring formerly passive students back into mainstream learning.

As a leader, you can do several things.

- If you are in the UK, adopt AI for the new ISPs – SENCOs and teaching staff need to be trained to use secure, approved AI text-generators to draft these documents.
- Before a single IEP/ISP has been drafted, make sure the tools are vetted, thoroughly make sure that any data is private and not used to train public models.
- Encourage staff to use AI to generate secondary, jargon-free reports for parents. True inclusion means the parents also understand the plan and are active partners.
- When looking at school tech budgets, prioritise the purchase of AI tools that offer real-time translation and speech-to-structure capabilities over flashy, generic learning apps. Frame these purchases as 'inclusion' resources, not 'computing' resources.

Box 9.2 Key Takeaways from Chapter 9

Key Takeaways

The Blank Page is a Glass Ceiling: For students with transcription difficulties or cognitive load barriers, the physical act of writing can mask their true intelligence. AI tools act as a wheelchair ramp for their ideas, allowing teachers to mark their minds, not their handwriting.

The Three Tiers of Inclusive AI: AI aids inclusion by being *Assistive* (bypassing physical/sensory barriers), *Adaptive* (personalized tutoring at the perfect Zone of Proximal Development), and *Generative* (scaffolding resources and differentiating text instantly).

IEPs/ISPs Can Be Ghostwritten: Time-consuming SEND paperwork can be streamlined using AI, leaving teachers with more energy to actually teach. However, strict data privacy must be maintained – never input real names, schools, or exact medical diagnoses into an LLM.

Breaking the Language Barrier: Generative AI and live translation tools allow multilingual 'newcomer' students to be active participants in the mainstream classroom from day one, reducing the need for isolating 'pull-out' interventions.

The Ultimate Equity is Time: AI should not be used to replace the teacher with a screen. Instead, by automating resource creation and administrative heavy lifting, AI gives teachers back the time and emotional bandwidth needed to build the 1:1 human connections that truly drive inclusive education.

AI in Practice: A Prompt to Try

You are teaching a whole-class topic, but your students span multiple reading ages, including an EAL (English as an Additional Language) newcomer.

Copy and paste this into your AI tool:

"Act as an expert inclusive Primary Teacher. I am going to paste a standard textbook paragraph about [Insert Topic, e.g., the Water Cycle] below. Please rewrite this text into three distinct versions so my whole class can access the same knowledge:

1. ***Target Level:** Keep the core vocabulary but make the tone engaging for an 8-year-old.*
2. ***Accessible Level:** Simplify the sentence structures and reduce the cognitive load for a struggling reader, but maintain the core scientific facts.*
3. ***Newcomer Level:** Provide 5 bullet points using highly simplified English, paired with a bilingual glossary in [Insert Language, e.g., Polish]. Here is the text: [Paste Text]"*

Professional Development: Discussion Points

Look back at Leo in the opening scenario. If a student uses an AI speech-to-structure tool to organize their verbal knowledge into a written paragraph, how do we assess it? At what point does scaffolding cross the line into the AI doing the work for them?

The new *Every Child Achieving and Thriving* white paper demands that parents are active partners. Have we ever considered sending home two versions of an IEP/ISP – one clinical version for the file, and an AI-generated, jargon-free (or translated) version for the parents?

Research suggests that wealthier students use AI as a collaborative 'thought partner,' while lower-income students often use it as a shortcut 'answer generator.' How can we actively teach collaborative AI literacy in our school to close this gap?

Check Your Understanding

1. What is the primary benefit of using a 'speech-to-structure' AI tool for a student like Leo?
   A) It provides him with historical facts he didn't learn in class.
   B) It removes the cognitive load of handwriting and transcription, allowing his actual knowledge to be assessed fairly.
   C) It teaches him how to improve his handwriting speed.
   D) It translates his English into another language.
2. According to the EU AI Act and global data protection guidelines, what is the most important rule when using Generative AI to help draft an IEP (or ISP)?
   A) Always include the child's full name and exact medical diagnosis so the AI can be as accurate as possible.
   B) Share the AI-generated report directly with external vendors for further clinical analysis.
   C) Use the AI to determine the child's emotional state instead of relying on human observations.
   D) Never use a child's real name, school name, or exact medical diagnosis; use a pseudonym (e.g. 'Student A') and describe the symptoms instead
3. How does the chapter define the *new* iteration of the 'digital divide' regarding AI?
   A) It is solely about which schools can afford the most expensive tablets and high-speed internet.
   B) It is the gap between teachers who use AI and teachers who refuse to use it.
   C) It is the difference in AI literacy and usage; wealthier students tend to use AI collaboratively, while lower-income students often over-rely on it as an answer generator.
   D) It is the divide between students who learn coding and those who do not.

Answers

1. B. It acts as a 'wheelchair ramp' for his ideas, separating his historical knowledge from his physical ability to write it down.
2. D. Entering personally identifiable and sensitive medical data into a public LLM is a major safeguarding and privacy violation.
3. C. The new divide isn't just about access to hardware; it is about having the pedagogical support to use the tool as a critical thinker rather than a passive consumer.

References

Bloom, B. S. (1984). The 2 sigma problem: The search for methods of group instruction as effective as one-to-one tutoring. *Educational Researcher, 13*(6), 4–16. https://doi.org/10.3102/0013189X013006004

CAST. (2018). *Universal design for learning guidelines version 2.2*. http://udlguidelines.cast.org

College Board. (2025). *Variation in high school student, parent, and teacher attitudes toward generative AI*. College Board Research. https://research.collegeboard.org/media/pdf/AI%20Research%20Brief%202_vf.pdf

Department for Education. (2026). *Every child achieving and thriving*. HM Government. www.gov.uk/government/publications/every-child-achieving-and-thriving

European Parliament. (2024). *Regulation (EU) 2024/1689 of the European Parliament and of the Council laying down harmonised rules on artificial intelligence (Artificial Intelligence Act)*. Official Journal of the European Union. https://eur-lex.europa.eu/legal-content/EN/TXT/?uri=CELEX:32024R1689

Hamdan, S., Al-Abdullatif, A., Alqahtani, M., & Alshehri, M. (2025). Inclusive education with AI: Supporting special needs and tackling language barriers. *AI and Ethics*, 5, 5729–5757. https://doi.org/10.1007/s43681-025-00824-3

Lindorff, A., Strand, S., & Au, I. (2025, February). *English as an Additional Language (EAL) and educational achievement in England: An analysis of publicly available data*. The Bell Foundation; Unbounded Philanthropy; University of Oxford.

Lubelfeld, M. (2025). *Response to author survey*. Unpublished raw data.

National Education Association. (2025). *Using AI tools to enhance language learning for multilingual learners: Resources for schools and educators*. www.nea.org/sites/default/files/2025-10/ai-for-multilingual-learners_resources-for-schools-and-educators_final.pdf

OECD. (2024). *The potential impact of artificial intelligence on equity and inclusion in education*. OECD Publishing. www.oecd.org/en/publications/the-potential-impact-of-artificial-intelligence-on-equity-and-inclusion-in-education_15df715b-en.html

Puentedura, R. R. (2006). *Transformation, technology, and education [Blog post]*. http://hippasus.com/resources/tte/

Romrell, D., Kidder, L. C., & Wood, E. (2014). The SAMR model as a framework for evaluating mLearning. *Journal of Asynchronous Learning Networks, 18*(2), 1–15. https://files.eric.ed.gov/fulltext/EJ1036281.pdf

Tapo, A. A., Coulibaly, N., Diallo, S., Diarra, S., Homan, C. M., Keita, M. K., Leventhal, M., Messaoud-Galusi, S., & Mounkoro, I. (2025).

GAIfE: Using GenAI to improve literacy in low-resourced settings. *Findings of the Association for Computational Linguistics: NAACL 2025*, 7929–7944.
UNESCO. (1994). *The Salamanca statement and framework for action on special needs education*. UNESCO. https://unesdoc.unesco.org/ark:/48223/pf0000098427
Vygotsky, L. S. (1978). *Mind in society: The development of higher psychological processes*. Harvard University Press.

Part 3

Broadening Perspectives and Building an AI-Ready Future

10

The Human Bit

Championing What AI Can't Do

It's Friday afternoon, 3.20 pm. Jim's classroom smells like damp coats, and Chloe and Elena are helping him tidy up a soggy 'Roman Villa' display that fell down during wet play.

Jim: You know what? If an AI wants my job, it can have this bit. This and the 45 minute refereeing an argument about a Lego tire, while trying to explain auxiliary verbs to a child who has just discovered that they have a new wobbly tooth!

Chloe: I don't think that AI is quite ready for that, or the next 'Great Glue Stick Shortage.'

Elena: Exactly! I spent my planning time using AI to reword a science text for Leo, and it was brilliant. It saved me lots of time. Then I walked, all prepared into my next lesson only to come across Maya in floods of tears because she missed her Mum. The AI didn't factor that in!

Jim: This is my point. I spent yesterday morning at the gate welcoming our students. It wasn't productive from a workload point of view but the interactions left me, and hopefully some of the students, in a positive mood for the rest of the day.

Chloe: All these examples are what we call 'Human in the loop' Jim. AI did all the paperwork so that Elena could do the 'Maya-work' and you could enjoy the beginning to the day.

Jim: I just worry that we are getting so excited about the 'efficiency' and are losing sight of the fact that children aren't machines to be optimised. You can't automate a relationship.

DOI: 10.4324/9781003740377-13

The Love Affair Is Over

Outside of the pro-AI bubbles, promoting all sorts of different AI models, agents, and tools, the human view on the so-called Age of AI is mixed. Our love affair with Big Tech is definitely over. Fifteen years ago, we were told that social media would be a force for good, bringing communities together. While we can find positive stories, this, on the whole, is untrue, with social media doing the opposite in many situations. It isn't surprising, therefore, that we haven't all thrown ourselves into a world with AI, in the way that some people would want us to. It is arriving in schools with a lot of noise, and it makes sense to ask: Is this any different?

One of the biggest arguments against the use of AI brought to the table is the idea that it will gradually drain the essence of humanity, removing our purpose and breaking down our relationships. The Center for Humane Technology, the nonprofit behind the Netflix documentary *The Social Dilemma* and *The AI Doc*, has warned that AI risks eroding the very relationships and cognitive capacities that make us human (Center for Humane Technology, 2026). One of the big questions facing teachers is 'Will AI replace me?' It's a fair question, and not one to dismiss. We are already seeing whole teams replaced by automated systems in other industries. Teaching feels different, and we'll come to why, but the anxiety is real and deserves to be taken seriously, not talked away.

As Elena and Jim showed us at the beginning, the attractive feature of AI in the workplace is that it is an automation expert. It can take on mundane, repetitive tasks with ease. AI use in education is growing as educators and administrators use it to aid curriculum design, policy writing, and lesson planning. The question is what happens to the time it frees up, and whether we use it wisely.

It is also important to remember that there is a lot in teaching that AI cannot do. Teaching is, in some ways, a very human job. Yes, AI can write a scheme of work for Year 2's science topic on insects in a matter of seconds. But can it stand on duty in the cold and wet, dealing with arguments, bumps and scrapes, and that one child who wants to tell you their life story for the 15th time? Can it direct a chaotic Early Years Nativity performance? The answer is, no.

As businesses around the world bring in AI agents, still focusing on user engagement and productivity, we in the classroom owe it to our students to educate them so they can change the narrative. When they step into the world after full-time education, they do not need to sell their soul to the 'extraction' market. They can use AI to help them, but they can also keep themselves, the human, at the centre of the process.

As an author of a book on AI, I am definitely an advocate for its use. My life has been dramatically changed by the patterns I use daily. That said, I work in an environment that is built on human relationships. A core value of all the schools I have worked in has been 'community,' and I have been lucky enough to be part of some fantastic school communities. We must work hard to preserve what makes us human above all.

Why You Are Irreplaceable

The greatest risk isn't that teachers use AI too much. It's that our students learn to stop thinking all together. That is the line we cannot afford to cross.

A large contradiction at this point in time is that on the one hand, we are pushing the use of AI and asking people to learn how to use it and to integrate into their workflows, but on the other hand, we are trying to scale back screen time and make sure that we remain, as Chloe said at the beginning, 'humans in the loop.' This phrase, now commonplace in AI discussions, refers to the idea that, for now, AI works best with human help, and you want to be that helpful human (Mollick, 2024). It is a huge temptation to hand over the reins to AI, delegating every task to it. However, AI doesn't understand what it's saying. GenAI produces responses based on patterns in data, which means it can sound completely confident while being completely wrong.

Nobody knows exactly what the world will look like in ten years. Some naively believe that humans will still have a role to play, despite us leaving AI to do its thing, and others call for a slowing down of AI developments to ensure that we still remain relevant. What we do know is that the people who thrive are not the ones handing everything to AI. They are the ones who know when to use it and when to put it down. It is not a skill that our children will pick up by accident; we have to teach it in our classrooms.

The international schools group Nord Anglia Education and Boston College (2026) recently released a report titled *Teaching the skills AI can't replace*. This timely research looks at how metacognition prepares students for a future dominated by AI. The findings suggest that while technology can provide instant answers, schools must explicitly teach children how to reflect, navigate uncertainty, and problem-solve in the absence of digital assistance.

The risk of over-reliance on these instant answers can weaken a child's ability to deal with challenges, make decisions, and persevere when things don't go their way. When a child can get an instant answer to any question, why would they sit with the discomfort of not knowing? Therefore, our challenge in primary education is not whether students should avoid technology, but ensuring that they still learn how to think for themselves. Over-reliance on AI affects who our children become. Resilience, patience, and the ability to think for themselves are not academic skills; they are life skills, and they are built in the learning struggle.

In its *Future of Jobs Report 2025*, the World Economic Forum predicted that nearly 40% of today's core skills will change by 2030. Those that won't will be analytical thinking, creativity, adaptability, and lifelong learning. Primary education must prioritise these areas that an algorithm cannot replicate. We need to have a next generation of confident adults who can make informed decisions, without shortcuts.

To understand what this looks like in practice, we only need to listen to the educators who are navigating this shift daily. As Allandra Russell, an educator based in The Bahamas, beautifully noted when reflecting on the limits of this technology (A. Russell, survey response, 2026):

> *"For me, the human bit shows up in the everyday moments. It's when I tell a student, 'You're bright, you're talented,' and I see the smile spread across their face. Or when a child comes up and asks, 'Ms. Russell, did I do a good job?' and I can respond with encouragement that builds their confidence. That kind of validation, that human connection, is something no AI can replicate. School is where we build not just skills, but self-belief, and that will stay with them forever.'*

Your Turn

You now have AI working for you. The question is how you make sure it stays that way, in your classroom, with your students, on your terms. What follows are four practical approaches that will help you keep the human at the centre of everything you do. None of them requires a budget, a policy document, or permission from above. Just you, your classroom, and a clear sense of what matters.

Metacognition

In her book *Thinking with AI*, Amelia King (2025) draws a crucial distinction that every teacher needs to hear: Cognitive offloading, using AI to handle tasks so your brain is free for more important work, is sometimes a good thing. Cognitive replacement, where AI does the thinking entirely, is always a problem. That line, between offloading and replacing, is exactly what we are trying to protect in our classrooms.

Children will inevitably challenge us on this boundary. When they realise what these tools can do, they will naturally question why they have to do the hard work. Allandra Russell found out firsthand during a writing lesson that you have to be ready with a rock-solid, logical analogy when a student questions the point of the struggle (A. Russell, survey response, 2026):

"During a writing lesson, I asked students to draft an essay... One student asked, 'Why learn how to write if I can just use AI?' That question opened the door to an important ethical conversation. I explained that while it's okay to use AI, it should never replace their own creativity. We talked about what would happen if they didn't have access to the tool one day; just like having a calculator doesn't mean you shouldn't know that 1 + 1 = 2. The discussion helped them see AI as a support, not a substitute, for their own thinking.'

The calculator analogy is the ultimate defence against cognitive replacement. We use calculators to handle the heavy lifting, but if we don't understand basic number bonds, the calculator is useless.

To ensure we stay on the right side of this line, Amelia King's combination of the UK Educational Endowment Fund's research on task structure and Roger Azevedo's more granular thinking helps us see how a lesson could be deliberately designed to keep the human brain in charge throughout.

The Planning Phase – Completed offline to begin with, with a pen and pencil, students formulate a plan of attack by working out their prior knowledge and their next steps. This will help them know to what detail they will need AI support in later steps.

The Monitoring Phase – The devices come out, but the thinking doesn't stop. Students interrogate the AI's response rather than accepting it. Is it accurate? Is it clear? Is it actually answering what we asked? This is where children learn that AI is a starting point, not a finishing line.

The Evaluating Phase – The devices are away. Students now self-assess to pinpoint what they have learned, rather than what they have just seen or heard. Asking questions about how AI has helped them, or hasn't, builds the ability to be discerning about the quality of the information they have gathered. It also helps them understand when to trust AI and when to be more critical.

So, what would this look like in a Primary school? Here's a hypothetical situation involving our AI sceptic, Jim.

Jim is teaching about habitats and, in particular, Snow Leopards.

1. **The Planning Phase**
    - Jim tells the class to leave the tablets in the charging cart. He hands out mini-whiteboards and pens.
    - He tells the students, "We are designing a snow leopard habitat. Before we go anywhere near a device for our research, what

do we already know? What are three specific things we need to use AI to help us find?"

- Students understand that they know how snow leopards live in the cold and eat meat. They identify, 'We need to ask the AI what specific meat they eat in the mountains.'

This process means that the students have formulated a plan of attack without AI dictating the lesson. The children are in control.

2. **The Monitoring Phase**
   - The tablets come out. A student asks the AI what snow leopards eat, and AI gives a long, complex paragraph using difficult vocabulary.
   - Jim stops the class. He explains that they cannot just take the first output. They have to critique it.
   - Jim models how to push back to the AI, 'I am 8 years old, explain your research at my level.'
   - Students now know they don't have to accept the first answer. They are monitoring the AI's output. If they don't get what they want, they adjust their strategy.
3. **The Evaluating Phase**
   - The habitats are drawn, the devices are put away, Jim brings the class back together for a debrief.
   - He starts a conversation, forcing students to reflect on the process. 'Pinpoint one thing you learned today that surprised you.' 'Did the AI get confused or give you useless information?'

By asking students to evaluate the helpfulness of AI, Jim has built critical discernment. He has shown that AI is powerful, yet flawed and needs a human to guide it. By the end of the lesson, Jim hasn't just taught his class about snow leopards. He has taught them that AI is powerful, flawed, and needs a human mind to guide it. That is the lesson underneath the lesson.

Championing Physicality

You already know this, but it is worth saying out loud: children are physical by nature. They are not meant to sit still. They are meant to touch, break, and make things. In their younger years, in particular, they explore with their senses. Primary school life can be extremely chaotic and messy, and it should stay this way.

AI is inherently the opposite. It is 2D, it is neat and tidy and deals with text, pixels and audio. The efficiency of devices and AI will tempt us to keep our children glued to screens because it makes our lives easier, and a lot cleaner. This is a mistake. A child generating an AI response is making far less mess than a child building a Roman catapult, but the child building is learning something the other isn't.

What we can do, if we are to combine the digital and physical worlds, is to implement the 3D rule.

Picture this, AI can be used to do the labour-intensive, time-consuming work like writing a script for a play about Victorian Britain, or compiling the instructions for a science experiment. The students, however, keep it physical. They act out the play with props that they have made themselves, and they carry out the experiment, following the written instructions. This approach stops the teacher from having to spend 3 hours writing the script and leaves the fun part to the students.

That is the 3D rule in the action. The messier, the better.

Protecting Social 'Friction'

Sometimes, the endlessly patient and non-judgmental AI chatbot can be very useful (see Chapter 9). But in other situations, we must avoid it. Humans are the opposite of patient and non-judgmental and Primary school students need to experience the daily 'friction' that comes with their relationships. They must know the art of negotiation, tact, and compromise. With an AI, they will not be able to learn these skills.

An idea to help with this is to enforce tech-free 'collaboration zones.' When it's time to work in groups or teams, make sure that there are moments when they can use a device, and others when they must speak, plan, and organise face to face. Make sure they look each other in the eye, debate, get frustrated and experience all the other realities of working with other people.

Box 10.1 Pedagogy Pause: Protect the Social Friction

Pedagogy Pause: Protect the Social Friction

AI chatbots are endlessly patient, never get annoyed, and never interrupt. Human beings are the exact opposite. Do not let AI replace the messy reality of collaborative group work. Children need to argue over who gets the red marker. They need to learn how to compromise. Protect the social friction in your classroom – it is where the real learning happens.

AI can teach students knowledge, but it cannot teach them how to handle the human situations they will find themselves in on a daily basis. The child who only ever gets instant, frictionless answers will struggle the moment life pushes back. Life always pushes back.

Process over Product

Here is the uncomfortable truth that AI has forced into the open: If the final written product is all you are assessing, you can no longer be sure who produced it.

In his LinkedIn Pulse article *Future Skills Schools Cannot See*, Phillip Alcock (2026), co-founder of PBL Future Labs, identifies something that should stop every teacher in their tracks. In a recent audit of a leading project-based learning school, assessment across every year group was almost entirely product-focused, whether students had made the thing, completed the chart, or delivered the presentation. Whether they had grown as communicators or thinkers over six weeks was nowhere to be found, because there was no system for capturing it. The product proved the task was completed. It proved nothing about whether growth occurred in the process. In a separate piece for ET Magazine, Alcock (2025) describes watching his own students produce sophisticated, interdisciplinary thinking during a creative AI-assisted project, thinking that never would have appeared on a conventional assessment. The process was extraordinary. The product was just the surface.

So what do we do about it? The most powerful tool is the simplest one: conversation. Sit with a child and ask them to walk you through their thinking. Ask them why they made a choice. Ask them what they would do differently. Ask them the questions their worksheets don't answer. You can fake the written work. You cannot fake a conversation.

This is not about catching children out. It is about finding out what is actually there – the curiosity, the reasoning, the understanding that AI cannot replicate and a rubric cannot capture. That is what only you can see. That is what only you can find.

Box 10.1 Key Takeaways from Chapter 10

Key Takeaways

- **The AI is the Assistant; The Human is the Boss:** We must explicitly teach students that AI is a tool to be managed and critiqued, not an oracle to be blindly trusted.

- **Adopt an 'Offline First' Approach:** The most important part of any AI-assisted task happens before the screen is turned on. Use a 'Pen-to-Prompt Pipeline' to ensure students have formulated their own ideas and questions before seeking AI input.
- **Protect the '3D' and the 'Messy':** Childhood is physical and social. Champion the human element by ensuring AI is used to handle 2D admin, freeing up time for hands-on building, messy science, and real-world peer negotiation.
- **Assess the Process, Not the Product:** If an AI can generate a perfect essay in seconds, the written product is no longer a reliable measure of learning. Shift towards assessing *how* a child arrived at their answer through conversation and oral defence.

AI in Practice: A Prompt to Try

With this prompt, you can use AI to help you plan your offline tasks (the irony is not lost on me.)

> *"I am teaching a primary school lesson on* ***[Insert Topic]*** *to a class of* ***[Insert Age]****-year-olds. I want to use an 'Offline First' approach. Please give me 3 ideas for a 15-minute, highly interactive, screen-free group activity to start the lesson. The activity must require the children to:*
>
> 1. *Get out of their seats or use their hands.*
> 2. *Experience some 'social friction' (e.g., they have to negotiate, share limited resources, or debate an idea).*
> 3. *Formulate their own questions about the topic before they are allowed to do any digital research. Keep the setup simple and use standard classroom supplies (paper, whiteboards, blocks, etc.)."*

Professional Development: Discussion Points

Think about a standard research project your year group does. Where is the exact line between cognitive offloading (using GenAI to handle the heavy lifting, like providing a simplified text) and cognitive replacement (allowing the student to outsource their thinking entirely)? How do we communicate this boundary to the children?

Look at your current assessment rubrics for this term. As Phillip Alcock notes, how many of them rely entirely on a written final product? Choose one upcoming assessment and brainstorm how you could shift the focus to the *process through* 1:1 conversation or an oral defence. What would you need to change in your classroom management to make that possible for 30 children?

We know that AI bots are endlessly patient and non-judgmental, but human beings are not. Looking at your weekly timetable, where are you intentionally protecting 'social friction'? Are there defined, tech-free collaboration zones where students are forced to disagree, negotiate, and compromise face-to-face?

Be honest: Are you feeling more like a Jim (protective of the human messiness, worried about losing the essence of teaching) or a Chloe (excited, ready to try new efficiency tools) right now? What is one specific reassurance the 'Jims' in your school need from leadership to feel safe trying the 'Offline First' method?

Check Your Understanding

1. According to the chapter's approach to Metacognition, what is the primary purpose of the 'Planning Phase' being completed offline before touching a device?
   A) To save the school's Wi-Fi bandwidth during busy morning periods.
   B) To ensure students formulate their own plan of attack and identify their prior knowledge before the AI dictates the lesson.
   C) To punish students who forgot to charge their tablets.
2. Based on Amelia King's research mentioned in the chapter, what is the critical difference between 'cognitive offloading' and 'cognitive replacement'?
   A) Offloading is using AI to handle tasks so your brain is free for more important work, whereas replacement is a problem where AI does the thinking entirely.
   B) Offloading is when a teacher uses AI for lesson planning, and replacement is when a student uses it for homework.
   C) Offloading means saving your AI chats to the cloud, while replacement means buying a newer device.
3. Why does the chapter argue that teachers must shift their assessment focus from the 'product' to the 'process' using conversation?
   A) Because verbal assessments take less time to grade than written worksheets.
   B) Because children are losing their fine motor skills and handwriting abilities.

C) Because if GenAI can instantly generate a perfect written product, the product itself no longer proves who did the thinking.

Answers

1. B. By starting with mini-whiteboards and pens (like Jim's Snow Leopard lesson), students establish what they already know and what specific questions they need the AI to answer, keeping the human brain in control.
2. A. The chapter emphasises that we want to protect the line between offloading mundane tasks (good) and allowing the machine to replace the student's cognitive struggle (bad).
3. C. As Phillip Alcock notes, the written product can now be faked in seconds. Teachers must rely on conversations – asking students to walk through their thinking and explain their choices – to see if actual learning occurred.

References

Alcock, P. (2025). *Project-Based Learning 2.0: The evolution (not revolution) of AI in education.* ET Magazine. https://et-mag.com/project-based-learning-2-0-the-evolution-not-revolution-of-ai-in-education/

Alcock, P. (2026). *Future skills schools cannot see.* LinkedIn Pulse. www.linkedin.com/pulse/future-skills-schools-cannot-see-phillip-alcock-gto8e/

Center for Humane Technology. (2026). *What's at stake: Preserving what makes us deeply human in the age of AI.* https://centerforhumanetechnology.substack.com/p/whats-at-stake-preserving-what-makes

King, A. (2025). *Thinking with AI.* Thinking EdTech. ISBN: 978-1919203805.

Mollick, E. (2024). *Co-intelligence: Living and working with AI.* Portfolio/Penguin.

Nord Anglia Education & Boston College. (2026). *Teaching the skills AI can't replace.* www.nordangliaeducation.com/metacognition/teaching-the-skills-ai-cant-replace

Russell, A. (2026). *Response to author survey.* Unpublished raw data.

11

For the Future

Parents and the School Community's AI Journey

Elena is holding a printout of an email from a parent. Subject line: 'ROBOT TEACHERS??'

Elena: Mr. Henderson is furious. He thinks we're using AI to 'brainwash' his kids and that we're too lazy to teach.

Chloe: He's scared. He reads the headlines and they do nothing to help us manage the hype.

Jim: So invite him in. Don't email back. Bring him in. Show him the 'Truth Detective' lesson. Show him Tom's graphic novel. Show him that we are driving the bus, not the robot. Parents don't trust the tech, but they trust us. If we hide it, they panic. If we show them, they partner.

Elena: Great idea, I will do it now.

As educators broaching new, controversial topics, we are faced with the internal fear that our community will turn on us. Parents are, rightfully, asking questions all the time. When it comes to AI, they want to know if we are paying attention to the headlines and how we build trust when the tools we use are 'black boxes.'

Reading the Room

You may be sitting here as an experienced educator, confused by all the edtech offerings on the market and, in particular, the AI tools. They are overwhelming, a myriad of logins, personalised pathways, and gamified extrinsic rewards.

If you are feeling overwhelmed, put yourself in the shoes of your students' parents for a moment. To understand the root of their fear,

DOI: 10.4324/9781003740377-14

we must acknowledge how AI is often perceived by those outside the classroom. Claire Walmsley, a primary Computing Specialist in England, captures this dynamic perfectly when reflecting on the adults in her school community (C.Walmsley, survey response, 2025):

> *"Working with staff [and adults] has highlighted that lack of understanding about how AI models work contributes significantly to their fear and uncertainty around AI. To most, it's like magic and they just accept this mystical aura. And whilst that can seem charming, it can have unintended consequences. Just like anthropomorphising AI (attributing human-like qualities) this lack of understanding can lead people to both overestimate and underestimate AI's capabilities."*

When parents view AI as magic, they naturally overestimate its threat (like Mr Henderson's fear of the 'robot teacher') or underestimate its data risks. Drawing on survey data and my experience in schools, most parents fall into one of three categories. I have named these:

The Functional Novice: The parent who has dabbled with a tool or two but is not aware enough to mitigate the fear of cheating and risks. They are anxious, and their anxiety tends to appear in your inbox.

The Informed Pragmatist: The parent who uses AI in their daily workflow. They know enough to have experienced limitations, and they are cautiously optimistic. These are the ones who can be your cheerleaders but need convincing first.

The Concerned Sceptic: The parent who has read every alarming headline and formed a firm view. They're not technophobic, they're paying attention. If you can bring them round, they become your most powerful allies, because the community already trusts them.

Knowing which parent you're talking to changes everything about how you communicate.

When thinking about parental concerns, and AI, it is important to take a world view. What might be the case for one culture could be different for another. As an international school leader, I always have this at the back of my mind, in everything that I do.

The parent standing at your school gate in Singapore is not the same as the one in Stockholm, São Paulo, or Slough. Context shapes everything: The cultural relationship with academic pressure, the level of trust in institutions, and the access to technology at home. When it comes to AI in schools, certain anxieties cross borders with remarkable consistency.

The Ipsos Education Monitor 2025, which surveyed over 23,700 adults across 30 countries, found that the effects of AI and social media ranked among the top concerns for parents globally (Ipsos, 2025). In every single country surveyed, a majority wanted social media banned for children under 14. The distrust of digital technology in children's hands is not a Western phenomenon.

Within that global anxiety, research suggests parents tend to cluster around recognisable concerns, regardless of where they live:

Cheating – 68% of parents in the US believe AI-assisted cheating is at least somewhat common in schools (Learner.com, 2025).

Data Privacy – A third of US parents strongly agree they are concerned about data privacy risks for their child. In the UK, the Ada Lovelace Institute found data security and unauthorised use of data to be among the public's primary concerns about AI (Barna, 2024; Ada Lovelace Institute, 2025).

Critical Thinking – 61% of parents agree that greater AI use will harm students' critical thinking skills (RAND, 2025).

Human Connection – 56% of parents expressed concern about the potential for a lack of human interaction as AI becomes more embedded in children's lives (Morning Consult/Samsung, 2024).

Creativity Loss – 71% believe AI tools may reduce creativity and original thinking (Mobicip, 2025).

But how parents express and prioritise these concerns varies enormously. A 2025 peer-reviewed review of international research found that parents in Nordic countries, where play-based learning is deeply valued, often reject AI tools they perceive as overly didactic or test-focused. Meanwhile, parents in East Asian contexts, where academic competition is more culturally embedded, may be more open to AI as a learning accelerator. Religious and conservative communities in various contexts raise ethical concerns that go beyond data privacy into questions of values and moral development.

What this means practically is that there is no single script for talking to parents about AI. The concerns are largely the same; the emotional register, the cultural framing, and the level of institutional trust are not. A parent in Finland who already trusts the school system implicitly needs a different conversation than a parent in a context where that trust has to be earned, or where it has already been broken by a bad experience with technology.

This is why the approach that follows is built around listening first.

Parents have been conditioned to question all things digital, and we should let them. If we want to build a community of critical users, we need our parents, raising the students, to become more discerning. They are pushing back against the 'Tech Bros.' and questioning the necessity of consumer rhetoric. On the other hand, their fear and anger comes to the fore, in the school setting.

The cautionary tale here is recent and close to home for many educators. In New York City, parents began raising the alarm when they discovered their kindergarten and first-grade children were using voice-recording software embedded in a new AI-assisted literacy curriculum, with no clear communication that this was happening and no obvious way to opt out (Gould, 2026).

One Brooklyn parent, a digital archivist, asked to have her daughter removed from the activity. Her child now sits in the corner doing a separate task while her classmates use the app. At meetings held by Panel for Educational Policy, a governing body of New York Public Schools, parents pushed back, not, as one mother was careful to say, because they were 'technophobes,' but because, in her words, there seemed to be 'an absence of a tech plan.' The lesson is not that AI in literacy tools is wrong. The lesson is stark and simple: If you introduce AI as a stealthy black box, without transparency or consent, you will lose your community's trust, and you may not get it back.

It is clear that we need to be on the front line, helping our parents navigate this overwhelming digital world. If we achieve this, we strengthen the communication loop and this, in turn, will make sure that there is a consistent message being given to students. To invoke the ancient phrase, the village still raises the child; it just needs to know how to use the new tools.

The aim of this chapter is to empower you, the teachers, to change the narrative. You can use transparency as a strategy, opening channels with parents to dispel the myths and turn the AI 'cheating tool' into a 'Family tutor.' We want parents to keep track of what their children are doing but also they should feel able to understand the new world they are facing.

If you don't work on and build parent confidence, you create a silo. Between 9 am and 3 pm, students enter a world of responsible use and guidance, but when the bell goes, that mindset stays in school. We can't let the WhatsApp groups dictate the content and the mood.

There is a risk of a new digital divide appearing. On the one hand, parents currently feel out of their depth, with tools moving faster than any of us can comfortably track. As adults, this is an uncomfortable feeling. On the other hand, the students are moving forwards, experimenting and bringing AI into everything they do. As we educate their children, we need to make sure that we are also reminding the parents that it can be fun to be students once again.

From Newsletter to Partnership

We can't engage parents through dry newsletters. If my experience of schools is anything to go by, readership of weekly communications is woefully low.

Instead we need to get practical, bringing parents back to the classroom to learn. Schools should be putting on AI literacy modules for parents in person or online and should be teaching the same as we are teaching the students. Teachers aren't the only slice of society who like a good takeaway. Busy parents love practical and achievable tips. Give them some of the theory, but also send them home with things to try straight away.

Here is my recommended pathway to parent engagement. I can't guarantee this is going to work every time, but I think this is a strong, structured approach. I would approach things in three phases, with one practical pitstop on the way.

Phase 1

Begin with a temperature check.

Before we start talking, allow parents to share their true thoughts and feelings in survey form. I love a good survey, in many different ways, as they provide real data and give you an understanding of how lots of people feel all at once. If you curate the questions well, you will be able to cut through the noise and get started at the right place.

The survey could be very simple. Beginning with five easy questions, you can get a feel for the room. Here are some to try:

- How confident do you feel about AI? (1–5 scale)
- Have you personally used any AI tools (like ChatGPT, Siri, or autocorrect)?
- What's your biggest question or concern about AI and children?
- Would you attend an evening session about AI at school? (Yes/Maybe/No)
- What is your preferred format: In-person evening / Online webinar / Video I can watch anytime

The data from this can then shape everything that comes next. Identify your Informed Pragmatists and your Concerned Sceptics early.

Your Informed Pragmatists, the parents already using AI in their daily lives, are your potential cheerleaders. Reach out to them personally and ask whether they would be willing to share a two-minute real-world testimonial at any information events. Peer-to-peer always carries a different weight than a teacher standing at the front of a room.

Your Concerned Sceptics need a different approach. Don't wait for them to raise their hand in a meeting; they probably won't. Instead, look for the parent who forwarded the alarming article to the class WhatsApp group, or who asked a pointed question at the last parents' evening. Reach out to them quietly and directly before any group event. If you can bring a sceptic into the conversation early, rather than letting them build a case in the car park, you dramatically increase your chances of turning opposition into partnership.

Normalise AI

At the same time as you gauge feeling, make discussions about AI part of the fabric of the school. Be transparent about how AI is being used in the classroom and the wider school community. Announce that you will be sharing your learning with parents too. That single sentence does more for trust than a dozen policy documents.

Address Concerns Proactively

Your parent body, whatever the context, will have concerns. Addressing these head-on goes a long way in building the trusting relationship you need to move forward. Parents don't expect you to have every answer, but they want to be reassured that the school is paying attention and preparing their children as best it can for an uncertain future. A simple FAQ, sent home before any event, can pre-empt the questions you know are coming. For example:

- How will you stop children using AI to cheat?
- Will AI interfere with my child learning to read, write, and think for themselves?
- What about data privacy – who owns my child's data and where does it go?
- Is it even legal for my child to use these tools?
- Will AI replace teachers?
- How do I know what's allowed and what isn't?

Phase 2

Now you have built a culture of discussion about AI, you can bring in the activities. Organise a parent session, in person if possible, that tackles the big issues and the core knowledge. The aim is to make parents feel more comfortable: To allay fears and to start building AI proactivity. You could run an initial 90-minute 'AI Discovery Night' to which both parents and students could be invited.

Remember Mr Henderson from the beginning of the chapter; the parent who was furious, convinced that the school was using robots to brainwash his children? Elena invited him in. He sat next to his daughter at a table in the school hall, and together they asked an AI chatbot questions about their dog's breed. The AI got two things wrong. His daughter spotted both errors before he did. He laughed. That was the moment. It didn't require a PowerPoint presentation or a policy document. It required 15 minutes, a laptop, and his child sitting next to him.

This is the spirit of the AI Discovery Night. You could include the following content.

AI in action – Show parents something genuinely impressive, then immediately show them something AI gets embarrassingly wrong. Both matter equally. The first builds curiosity; the second builds critical thinking and, crucially, reassurance that the machine is not infallible.

Parent-child AI tasks – This is the heart of the evening. Pairs ask an AI a question about a topic the child knows well: Their football team's history, their favourite book, their home country. They then work together to fact-check and critique the output. The child becomes the expert. The parent becomes the learner. The dynamic in the room shifts noticeably when this happens.

Discussion cards on the big topics – Short, focused prompts on cheating, data privacy, creativity, and screen time that small groups can work through together. The conversations that happen between parents at these tables are often more valuable than anything a teacher says from the front.

Outlining the school's approach – End with clarity. What is allowed, what isn't, and why. Parents leave knowing the school has a plan.

The goal of this style of event is to build on the idea of AI transparency. One of the biggest barriers to parent support will be lack of understanding. If you are able to address worries, try out tools and also have some fun (very important) you will see a shift in attitude. Not in everyone, but in enough.

Box 11.1 Practical Pit Stop on AI homework

Practical Pit Stop – The AI homework policy

Parents will ask about the use of AI with homework. A clear approach to incorporate into your existing policy could be in the form of a traffic light system:

Red: No AI allowed. Use this for tasks where the process of independent thinking is the whole point. The struggle is the learning

Yellow: AI for brainstorming or outlining only. The student must show their thinking (human interaction must be visible).

Green: AI used fully as a tutor or editor. The student works with AI as a thinking partner, but the assessment includes a critique. The child remains the pilot.

Sharing this framework with parents before questions arise does two things: It demonstrates that the school has thought carefully about responsible use, and it gives parents a simple vocabulary for conversations at home.

Phase 3

The AI Discovery Night was an event. This phase is a habit.

The risk after any successful parent engagement is that the momentum quietly disappears, absorbed back into the rhythm of the school year, buried under the next parents' evening or sports day. The goal of Phase 3 is to make sure that doesn't happen. Not through grand gestures, but through small, consistent signals that the conversation is still open.

The simplest tool is also one of the oldest. A question box, physical or digital, somewhere visible but low-pressure, invites parents to submit queries as they occur to them, rather than waiting for a formal meeting. A parent who reads something alarming on a Sunday night is much more likely to drop a note in a box on Monday morning than to book an appointment. Address the questions that come in through your newsletter, and do it regularly. Over time, the questions themselves become a resource – a live map of what your community is thinking.

Beyond that, the most powerful thing you can do is send parents home with things to try. Not reading material. Not policy documents. Things to actually do, at the kitchen table, with their children. Here is a simple week-by-week prompt sequence you could share:

Week 1: What's something a computer can do that seems really clever? How do you think it learned to do that?
Week 2: Watch a video together and spot the AI recommendations. Why does the app think you'd like those?
Week 3: Try asking Siri or Alexa a tricky question together. Did it answer well? What did it get wrong?
Week 4: When should we trust AI, and when should we ask a person instead?

These questions do something quietly important. They position the parent not as the homework police, but as a fellow investigator. They make it acceptable, even enjoyable, not to have all the answers. They reinforce at home exactly the critical thinking habits you are building in school.

Think back to Mr Henderson. He didn't leave the Discovery Night converted to AI evangelism. He left with a question his daughter had asked him in the car that he couldn't answer. He sent Elena a message the next morning to ask where he could find out more. That is the goal, not certainty, but curiosity.

The AI Co-pilot in Parenting

Often, in this book, I refer to AI in an academic sense. However, it can be leveraged to support the emotional and relational side of parenting. Kunal Dalal, in his book *Our Incredible, Fragile Moment,* refers to 'The Three-Corner Model' and asks us to picture a triangle. At one corner is the child, at one is the parent and at the other, AI. If we bring a third point to a usually linear and sometimes complicated route, we can use AI as "a transparent, neutral space where both of you can express yourselves" (Dalal, 2024).

This thought process isn't about AI replacing the parent. Just as with our discussions about our roles as teachers in a world of AI, we can mirror this in a discussion about parenting. Primary school children ask some of the hardest questions humans ever face: About death, fairness, and why the world works the way it does. When a child asks something that leaves their parents genuinely stumped, the parents should feel allowed to say, "I actually don't know the answer to that, let's ask AI and figure it out together." By doing this, parents are modelling healthy use of AI through iteration and asking good questions. They are also showing their children that it is okay to ask for help.

As teachers, we can introduce parents to this mindset. We can shift the narrative away from the parent who feels they must have all the answers, and towards the parent who is curious alongside their child. By giving parents permission to say "I don't know, let's find out," we are encouraging intellectual humility, and this in turn reinforces the human-centred philosophy we teach in school. The goal isn't knowing everything. It is knowing how to ask better questions.

Parent Field Guide

To help parents navigate using AI at home, I have compiled some simple dos and don'ts which could be made into a single-page flyer to be sent home.

DO:

- explore AI together (it's less scary when you learn alongside your child).
- ask "How do you know that's true?" when your child shares AI-generated information.
- use AI as a starting point, not an ending point.
- brainstorm solutions to specific problems.
- model healthy scepticism.

DON'T:

- assume all AI use is cheating (context matters).
- forbid all AI (this often backfires). Forbidding tech often creates the 'forbidden fruit' effect, where children use it in secret.
- panic if your child has used AI; use it as a conversation starter.
- expect your child to know the rules if no one has explained them.

Box 11.2 Key Takeaways from Chapter 11

Key Takeaways

- **Transparency builds trust while secrecy breeds fear.** Parents are fearful of the negative sides of AI use, such as cheating, data privacy, and loss of critical thinking. If schools hide what they do, the fear increases. If schools show what they are doing and that teachers are 'driving the bus,' then parents become partners

- **Understand the audience to bridge the divide.** Educators must prevent a digital divide where students practice responsible use at school but enter a different mindset at home, empowering parents to understand the new world they are facing.
- **Move beyond newsletters to practical engagement.** A structured, phased approach will move past the dry newsletter to hands-on sessions demonstrating the benefits of AI tools being used in schools.
- **Empower families with specific advice.** Provide parents with clear guidance, a list of 'dos and don'ts,' that helps them approach AI use critically and allows them to enter valuable conversations with their children. The goal is to shift the narrative from AI being a cheating tool to it being something that can support conversations at home.

AI in Practice: A Prompt to Try

"Act as an empathetic and innovative educator who specialises in family engagement. I need to create a one-page resource for parents titled 'AI is a Family Tutor, Not a Replacement.'
Please generate three specific, 10-minute activities parents can do with their children at home to demystify AI. The activities must address the following concepts:

1. ***The Dinner Table Cheat Code:** Create an activity where the parent uses AI to generate 'curveball' conversation starters based on their child's specific interests.*
2. ***The Truth Detective:** Create a task where the parent and child ask the AI a question about a topic the child knows well, and then work together to 'grade' the AI's answer for accuracy, identifying hallucinations or mistakes.*
3. ***The Creative Spark:** Create a collaborative storytelling or image-generation prompt where the human provides the imagination and the AI provides the polish, ensuring the child remains the 'pilot.'*

For each activity, include a specific 'Parent Script' – a sentence the parent can say to their child to frame the activity positively (e.g. 'Let's see if we can outsmart the robot')."

Professional Development: Discussion Points

Considering that parents are concerned about tools being hidden in a 'black box,' are our current communications transparent enough to prove we are 'driving the bus?'

How can we support the parent majority, the 'functional novices' who are anxious and willing to learn rather than speaking to just the tech-savvy?

What specific examples can we show parents to move them from sceptics to regular users within their family?

Check Your Understanding

1. Why did the New York school system face significant parent backlash when introducing AI reading tools?
   A) Parents were worried the tools would make their children too advanced for the curriculum.
   B) The tools were introduced as a 'black box' without transparency, leading parents to feel their children's biometric data was being harvested without consent.
   C) The AI tools were too expensive and impacted the school's budget for physical books.
2. In Kunal Dalal's 'Three-Corner Model,' what is the primary role of AI in the relationship between parent and child?
   A) To act as a 'Homework Police' to ensure the child isn't cheating.
   B) To replace the parent as the primary source of knowledge for complex questions.
   C) To provide a neutral, transparent space that encourages dialogue and allows the parent to model intellectual humility.
3. According to the chapter's 'Reading the Room' framework, what is the most effective strategy for engaging a 'Concerned Sceptic' parent?
   A) Wait for them to ask their tough questions during a large, public school meeting so you can address everyone at once.
   B) Reach out to them quietly and directly before any group event to bring them into the conversation early.
   C) Send them a dense policy document proving that their fears about AI are scientifically unfounded.

Answers

1. B. Transparency is the currency of trust. Even with the best intentions, introducing tech 'subtly' almost always triggers a defensive community response.
2. C. By moving from a linear (Parent → Child) to a triangular relationship, the pressure is taken off the parent to know everything, turning the task into a shared 'Truth Detective' mission.
3. B. The chapter advises against letting sceptics 'build a case in the car park.' By identifying them early (e.g. the parent forwarding alarming articles to the WhatsApp group) and reaching out directly, you dramatically increase the chances of turning opposition into a partnership.

References

Barna Group. (2024). *Parents worry about AI but know little about it*. www.barna.com/research/parents-ai/

Dalal, K. (2024). *Our incredible, fragile moment (The A.I. parent)* (2nd ed.). Kunal Dalal.

Doss, C. J., Bozick, R., Schwartz, H. L., Chu, L., Rainey, L. R., Woo, A., Reich, J., & Dukes, J. (2025). *AI use in schools is quickly increasing but guidance lags behind: Findings from the RAND survey panels*. RAND Corporation. https://doi.org/10.7249/RRA4180-1

Gould, J. (2026, February 1). *New AI rules for NYC schools coming this month as tech upends classrooms*. Gothamist. https://gothamist.com/news/new-ai-rules-for-nyc-schools-coming-this-month-as-tech-upends-classrooms

Ipsos. (2025, August). *Ipsos education monitor 2025: A 30-country Ipsos global advisor survey*. www.ipsos.com/sites/default/files/ct/news/documents/2025-08/Education_Monitor_2025%20(1).pdf

Learner.com. (2025). *'Hey Siri, will AI change my kid's future?' What parents really think*. www.learner.com/blog/ai-education-survey

Mobicip. (2025). *What US parents really think about AI and its influence on kids*. www.mobicip.com/blog/what-us-parents-really-think-about-ai-its-influence-on-kids

Morning Consult. (2024, September 18). *Future-proofing education: How AI is shaping learning for Gen Alpha & Gen Z[Survey commissioned by Samsung Solve for Tomorrow]*. Samsung Electronics America.

https://news.samsung.com/us/88-percent-us-parents-gen-alpha-gen-z-students-say-ai-crucial-to-childs-future-success-samsung-solve-for-tomorrow/

Perkins Coie & UKG (Ada Lovelace Institute & Alan Turing Institute). (2025). *How do people feel about AI? A nationally representative survey of public attitudes to artificial intelligence in Britain*. https://attitudestoai.uk/findings-2025

12

Schools of Tomorrow

Rebuilding Education with AI and Humanity

For this chapter, our three protagonists find themselves visiting a pilot school of the future, one where there are no corridors, closed doors, and rows of chairs.

Jim: [Checking his watch] It's 10:30, Elena. Where's the bell? It's break time. They've been working on that... whatever that is... for two hours.

Elena: There are no bells, Jim. Bells are for factories. They signal that 'Learning Unit A' is finished and it's time to move the conveyor belt to 'Learning Unit B'. Here, they stop when the mission is at a pause point, or when their bodies tell them they need a rest.

Jim: [Gesturing to a group below] But look at that table. You've got a Year 6 girl working with... that lad can't be more than Year 2. How do you differentiate that? She's doing algebra; he's probably still on phonics.

Chloe: [Checking the digital display on the wall] They aren't doing 'Maths' or 'English', Jim. Look at the mission board. They're designing a 'Sustainable Habitat for Mars.' The older girl is calculating the oxygen exchange rates. The younger boy is designing the sensory garden for mental health. They are working on the same problem, but at their own cognitive depth.

Jim: So who's teaching them? I see a hundred kids and... maybe four adults? And none of them are standing at the front.

Elena: They aren't teachers anymore, Jim. They're 'Learning Guides'. Look at that guy in the corner – the one with the tablet.

Jim: He's just watching them.

Elena: He's observing. The AI is handling the knowledge side of things. If the girl needs to know the formula for volume, the

DOI: 10.4324/9781003740377-15

AI gives it to her instantly. It marks her calculation in real-time. The Guide isn't there to deliver facts. He's there to spot the human blocks and ask questions. Is she frustrated? Is the little boy feeling left out? Is the group collaborating or arguing?

Chloe: It's the ultimate synthesis. The AI handles the 'Knowledge' and 'Comprehension' layers of Bloom's Taxonomy. That frees the human Guide to focus purely on 'Synthesis' and 'Evaluation'. The robot teaches the content; the human teaches wisdom.

Jim: [Watching the boy laugh as the older girl high-fives him] So... no rows. No silence. No 'eyes on me'.

Elena: No. Because the industrial model was designed to produce compliant factory workers who could sit still for eight hours. This model? It's designed to produce creative problem solvers who can work with machines without being replaced by them. It prioritizes wellbeing, notice how calm it is?

Jim: It is calm. Unnervingly calm. But what happens when they leave? The real world has deadlines. It has bosses.

Chloe: Jim, look around. This is the real world now. Project-based, collaborative, tech-integrated. The only place that still looks like a 19th-century factory... is our school.

Jim: [Sighs, watching the Guide sit down on a beanbag next to a struggling student] I suppose I wouldn't miss the marking. Or the bell giving me a headache.

Elena: We aren't scrapping the learning, Jim. We're just scrapping the conveyor belt.

The conversation above hasn't happened yet, but it could. Perhaps sooner than we think. In the previous 11 chapters, I have talked about schools and AI of the present day. This chapter is different; this is about what comes next.

What is a 'School of Tomorrow' in an age increasingly shaped by AI? How might we rebuild education with both AI and humans flourishing at its core? Throughout the book, I have tackled the AI of now, present day. Hopefully my advice and thoughts are future-proof enough to still be applicable for many years to come, but this chapter is dedicated to hypothesising about the future of schools, both near and far.

The Shifting Landscape of Education

I recently sat down and watched Wall-E with my children (Stanton, 2008). It had been a long time since I had last seen it, and a lot of the message in the film struck a chord. If you haven't seen it, the short version is this: Humanity has abandoned a ruined Earth and is drifting through space on a cruise ship, waited on entirely by machines. Nobody walks. Nobody thinks. Nobody even looks up from their screen. The machines do everything, and in return, the humans have slowly stopped being human. We follow the last active robot on Earth, Wall-E, as he lives out his daily routine, collecting rubbish, crushing it into cubes, and building waste 'skyscrapers.' One day, this changes as a probe named EVE comes to Earth, and Wall-E falls head over heels for her. This leads to him returning with her to the human cruise ship, and chaos ensues.

What is interesting about this plot is that the human overeliance on the machines in the space ship has led to them being overweight (they don't need to walk) and also unable to think for themselves. There are two moments that stand out to me. Firstly, Wall-E accidentally distracts a lady from the screen in front of her, and she notices the outside world for the first time. This leads to her meeting another human and striking up a relationship. The second moment is when the Captain of the ship realises that the 'Auto-pilot' has been manipulating him and his predecessors, and he fights back. He regains his autonomy and makes decisions himself.

As educators, these aren't just feel-good movie moments. They are our job description. We are the ones who pull children away from the screen. We are the ones who teach them that the autopilot isn't always to be trusted.

In 2008, the future depicted in the movie was still somewhat fantasy. Only those in the niche world of AI and robotics at that time would have had some idea about whether this future would be real. Fast forward nearly 20 years, and a lot more of the scenario seems possible. The advent of smartphones, tablets, social media, VR, and AI means that it is more than feasible that humans could end the way of those in Wall-E, if we don't react now.

I am not the only one to see these comparisons. Matt Karabinos, Emerging Technology and Project Specialist in Pennsylvania, wrote this, in response to a survey question of mine, about the future of AI (M. Karabinos, survey response, 2026):

> *"I gave my students the example of a Wall-E future where AI can do all our work, money doesn't matter anymore, and we can do what we enjoy and want. They pushed back and said what about hanging out with friends in person? What about playing together? What about going outside? Their responses made me realize our students value connection more than we might think. It's on us to show them how to do it, with or without technology."*

AI has changed the game. Holes are appearing in the traditional educational models. Some educators and policymakers are desperately trying to cling on to the past, with a 'better the devil you know' mentality. Conversely, innovators are pushing on, selling an alternative, 'new' version of education. Which mentality will prevail? I see the future of education going one of three ways. These ways tie in with the general prognosis concerning AI development outlined by authors such as Richard Susskind, Max Tegmark, and Ray Kurzweil – whose books are listed at the end of this chapter for those who want to go deeper.

Three Potential Futures

1. The Traditional

The least likely option of the three, but worth discussing because it is driven by a very real, very human exhaustion. One possible future is that we all have enough of AI and cut it off in its prime. This would lead to educationalists treating its appearance as a flash in the pan, another fad in the edtech world. AI slowly disappears from all the urgent posts, and schools go back to the status quo: Chalk and talk, knowledge-based education.

This may sound regressive to some, but there is a growing movement, focused on all areas of technology, that make this future one to bear in mind. As mentioned previously, social psychologist Jonathan Haidt, author of *The Anxious Generation*, has been a leading light in the push for 'smartphone-free' schools, arguing that play-based childhoods should be ringfenced. His philosophy also extends to AI. In an interview with 'USA Today,' Haidt stated 'AI is going to take all the pathways of harm from social media and multiply them' going on to make the point that just because a technology seemingly is here to say, every child has to have access to it 24/7 (Hale, 2025).

In this future, schools move in the opposite direction to the rest of the world. Instead of incorporating screens into everything we do, schools become an offline sanctuary, away from algorithms. For the rural teacher with limited tech and patchy internet, or the inner-city educator exhausted by being surrounded by extractionist media, this may actually sound quite an appealing approach. All the way through this book, I have championed 'unplugged' approaches as much as I have use of AI.

2. The Hybrid

This eventuality has already arrived and, if we are honest, it is where most of us are currently living. There is an assumption that we can absorb AI literacy and the use of AI tools into our pre-existing curricula and processes. Many discussions surround the idea that we will keep our lesson formats, school days, and structures essentially the same as they have always been, but we will try to shoehorn AI into the process. Leaders treat AI as another buzzword, flavour of the month. They acknowledge it, they appoint an AI lead, they dutifully carry out some staff INSET days, and then they forget about it, allowing teachers to use it or not, depending on their views.

The problem with this future is that it creates what Ethan Mollick, Professor at the Wharton School, calls the 'homework apocalypse' (Mollick, 2023). The loop goes like this: A teacher uses AI to generate a differentiated worksheet on the solar system, sends it home, and the student uses AI to complete it. Nobody learned anything. The teacher is exhausted. The student is bored, and everyone pretends otherwise.

Importantly this model has semi-functioned in the past years when AI has remained a chatbot, a smart dictionary we could dip in and out of. The advent of widespread agentic AI shatters this illusion. Agentic AI doesn't slot into the traditional model of schooling. It can perform multiple tasks independently at speed. This breaks the bounds of the classroom we are all used to, and it means that eventually, some part of this model is going to break.

3. **Education Revolution**

The third road is the hardest and the most exciting. It starts with an honest admission, school as we know it was never designed for this. In this future, leaders stop trying to fit the new reality into the old container. Out of the window go desks, didactic teaching, traditional grading, and age-restricted grade levels. In come flexible thematic working spaces in which students are not held back but are encouraged to follow their own learning patterns. Teachers are still present, but they are no longer gatekeepers of knowledge; they are facilitators who bring in their experience and pedagogical expertise to help students get the most out of their exploration.

Sal Khan, founder of Khan Academy, puts it simply in his book *Brave New Words*: Give every child an infinitely patient AI tutor for the knowledge side of learning, and you don't replace the teacher, you finally free them to do what they actually came into the profession to do (Khan, 2024). Dan Fitzpatrick makes the same argument in *Infinite Education*, framing it as a shift from the factory conveyor belt to something genuinely limitless, a model where the ceiling on a child's learning is no longer set by the pace of the slowest student in the room, or the exhaustion of their teacher on a Friday afternoon (Fitzpatrick, 2025).

So what might this new room look like? I have spent some time thinking about this, and fittingly, I have spent a lot of that time, discussing it with AI.

The Catalyst: From Chatbots to Agents

To understand where schools are heading, it helps to understand where AI itself is heading. As we explored earlier in this book, we are moving rapidly from a world of chatbots, tools that answer questions, to a world of agent systems that act on them. A chatbot can suggest a lesson idea. An agent can check the school calendar, draft the parent letter, schedule the meeting, and send it, all without being asked twice.

According to Google DeepMind's research, we are moving toward what they call 'delegation networks' (Tomasev et al., 2026), entire systems run autonomously by AI agents working in concert. In a school context, this means the administrative backbone of the institution could, in theory, run itself. Registers, reports, timetables, parent communications, automated, end-to-end.

For leaders, this shifts the role from being 'in the loop' to being 'on the loop,' overseeing rather than doing, and that raises a question that gets more urgent by the day: If the machines are handling the infrastructure, what exactly are the humans for?

Signals from the Horizon

It is very easy to see talk of the 'school of the future' and dismiss it as fanciful and far-fetched idealism. In reality, the shift mentioned earlier, the teacher moving from the gatekeeper of knowledge to the guide, is already happening. Across the world, there are examples of schools appearing that are looking to redesign the school day, and education, around the premise I discussed in Chapter 5. They are bringing in the machines to do the heavy lifting of knowledge transmission and are focusing on the messy, collaborative, human-centred learning. I will discuss some examples in this section, but I will say that these are not endorsements of a particular brand or model. I am discussing them to explain what is already out there.

The first and arguably most famous example is Alpha School in Austin, Texas. A fast-growing brand, they operate on a model they call 'Two-Hour Learning.' For the first two hours of the day, students work on core academics, such as English and maths, using an AI-driven tutor. The tutor provides adapted work and content, depending on the child's ability. The rest of the school day is handed back to the humans, allowing students to pursue passion projects and hobbies. The adults in the room are not called teachers; they are called 'Guides.' Their role is to provide hands-on workshops and to teach life skills, such as financial literacy.

In Europe, we see schools with inquiry-based models with institutions such as Ellinogermaniki Agogi, demonstrating how AI can power deep STEM learning. AI is used to process data and run simulations, allowing students to engage in higher-order, scientific debate. Similarly, across Denmark, schools are pivoting towards something called 'audit-based' literacy, where the educator's role is to lead critical reflection of AI-generated content.

Asia also has examples, with schools in Vietnam and Singapore harnessing AI for social-impact research and embodying 'explore-then-instruct' pedagogy, allowing students to use AI tutors and gamified simulations. By automating the drill and practice part of the curriculum, teachers are finding small but significant windows of time to return to human-centric projects and community problem-solving.

Acknowledging the existence of these schools and ideas does not mean suggesting that every primary school should, or could replicate all that they do. However, we should not ignore them. These schools act as proof that the concepts I have discussed are actionable. They prove that we can synthesise technology and human input successfully. The challenge for the rest of us is not to buy into a particular program, but to borrow the mindset. If a machine can handle the rote mechanics of a lesson, how can we reclaim the time for other pursuits?

My Primary School of the Future

When I find myself wrestling with a big question these days, I've developed a habit, I take it to AI. Not for the answer, but for the conversation. So when I started imagining what a primary school of the future might actually look like, that's exactly what I did. I had fledgling ideas of my own. I wanted to see what happened when I pressure-tested them.

I started thinking about what the primary school of the future would look like, both on a curriculum level and physically. What would need to change? What would need to be added? How could we create a space that works for students in this new normal? – a world of agentic AI, projects, and collaborative learning. I had some initial thoughts in my head, but I went to AI for some suggestions.

I began by asking,

> *"What did education look like before the mass changes of the industrial era – what organic and natural approaches to learning could be revisited in the education systems of the future?"*

I felt that education prior to the creation of the system we are all used to may have held some clues and suggestions that might help form the future landscape in some way. Interestingly, with a few back and forths, it was established that a lot of education prior to the industrial revolution happened to someone, while they were living their lives, rather than it being something that someone did in a classroom.

Before schools and classrooms, people learned through observation and conversation. For example, the trades such as carpentry and blacksmithing were learned through apprenticeships, learning on the job. Knowledge wasn't held in books; it was held in community conscience, in stories passed down from generation to generation by word of mouth. In Classical cultures, learning was dialectic and argumentative. In the world of Socrates, students didn't sit and listen passively; they engaged in the contact sport of debate.

Bearing this all in mind, I then went on to push AI to discuss the future, acknowledging that education wasn't all rosy and wasn't available to all.

> *"'Iron out all the inefficient and painful parts of historical education such as class and elitism, but explore these ideas in a potential new curriculum and how the logistical side of things could look."*

The output was intriguing and also absolutely feasible, in line with a lot of my thinking. Using AI in this way to help add clarity to the fog of ideas was brilliant. Together, in discussion, we agreed that we can remove the dangers and difficult aspects of education systems of the past but preserve the truly human aspects: The idea of mentorship, learning by doing, and the need for human interaction. Unlike the Wall-E future, where technology slowly hollows out what it means to be human, in this version, we could reclaim all the good bits of how humans have learned for millennia, and enhance them with the technology we have created.

This is where the conversation began to gain traction, and the idea was good enough to be named. Drawing from the Greek word for truth, for 'un-hiding', I've called this the Aletheia Model.

Content-Centric to Human-Centric

The first thing that came up in the discussion was the need to break down the barriers, the invisible walls currently in place. In particular, the factory-style systems such as year groups, 50-minute lessons, and subject silos.

In their stead, we could move from cohorts to 'learning pods' – multi-age units of students guided by one lead educator (with a newly defined role). These pods would be fluid and organised by developmental readiness and shared interests. Vygotsky's work on social learning and the zone of proximal development, the idea that children learn best by working just beyond their current ability, guided by someone slightly ahead of them, supports this model far more than it supports the current one (Vygotsky, 1978).

Instead of following specific subjects, the pods would learn through missions. Essentially project-based learning, the curriculum would be based around a series of complex, long-term missions that require all the elements of maths, English, science, and humanities.

The curriculum itself could follow a dual-helix approach with two strands running parallel through every mission.

The first helix is unapologetically human. Empathy. Ethics. Creativity. The ability to sit with a difficult problem and not immediately reach for an answer. These are the capacities that no algorithm can replicate, and they are precisely what our current system tends to squeeze out in favour of things that can be tested on a Friday afternoon.

The second helix is about learning to live and work alongside AI, not in a computer science sense, but in a deeply practical, human one. It has three strands. First, learning to communicate with AI effectively, which, at its core, means learning to articulate your own thinking clearly, out loud, in your own words. Second, becoming a digital detective, developing the habit of questioning what AI produces, sniffing out bias, checking sources, pushing back. Third, using AI as a personal tutor, letting it handle the knowledge acquisition, the drilling, the explaining, so that the human in the room can focus on what comes next.

Two helices. One always pulling toward what makes us human. The other ensuring we can navigate the world we've actually built.

Despite these changes, one thing that I would be remiss in omitting is literacy. Literacy would not necessarily bend to the new model. It would still have a strong position, not pushed to the side as a skill that can be acquired and pushed aside. In a world being suffocated by AI-written content, the ability to read and write critically and clearly, putting an original thought on paper, is not one to be dismissed. Literacy is something that upholds human integrity and cognitive control.

The Role of the Teacher

In this new setup, what is the teacher's role? It certainly isn't standing at the front of the room, the gatekeeper of all knowledge, the strict disciplinarian.

In an educational model where knowledge isn't power, the teacher is still hugely important, but their position within the room and the institution changes. They are part of the human learning side of the helix curriculum. AI named them *Chief Human Officer,* but the corporate ring of it felt wrong, and very LinkedIn. Instead I moved towards terminology that emphasises that the role of the adult is to steer students in the right direction. Therefore, a title such as *Human Guide* would work better.

This title matters because it captures a shift. The Human Guides would not be content experts but process experts, providing questions, not answers. They would be the primary guardians of well-being, working hard on making sure students' human relationships are strong and commonplace. In project-based lessons, they would be the architect of the missions, using processes like those mentioned in Chapter 5, to create complex and sufficiently open-ended challenges that would push students to discover through various means rather than just asking AI.

The New Assessment

In this new model, there would be no place for standardised testing. That is the ultimate industrial-age tool as it measures what AI does best and what humans do worst, i.e. rote recall under pressure.

In the Aletheia Model, assessment could be 100% open AI, with students being encouraged or expected to use AI on every task. This is how the world of work, however that may look, will expect. The question would never be, 'Did you use AI?', it would always be, 'What did you do with it?'

The measure of success wouldn't be a grade, but a portfolio. Portfolios are nothing new in some circles, but they could be used across the board. They would include evidence of learning in different ways, such as a proposal for a new playground, a script for a podcast, or a working prototype for a water filter they have designed. There would be a final showcase of the work, but as mentioned throughout the book, the emphasis of assessment wouldn't be on the output alone; it would also be on the skills, human attributes, and use of AI during the process.

That said, for the major projects, the capstone, or main event at the end, would be a presentation of the project and also a defence of the project. Similar to the process of 'learning showcase,' students would be required to explain and defend their process. They would outline their AI use, a trail of prompts good and bad, how they refined them, and examples of where the AI output was weak and human values were used to create the final product. A combination of assessment during and at the end would build a comprehensive picture which couldn't be faked, because it is unmistakably human.

The Physical Space

With all these changes happening, it is clear that the traditional school building would not be fit for purpose. Once again, heading back to the conversation, I asked AI simply,

"Now suggest how a school campus would look, based on the Aletheia model, if one is needed at all."

I included the last part to allow for a suggestion that a campus and school buildings might not even be needed. It is a serious question, not a provocative one. If we can gain knowledge anywhere, any time, is there a need for a static location for learning to happen? I think the arguments against are very strong, but one thing trumps them all, the need for human gathering. Humans can absorb facts from anywhere, but they can't engage with other people, debate, feel supported, and feel pain and happiness behind a screen. Instead of the school being a centre where learning happens, it becomes a location where the parts of learning that matter the most, the human parts, happen.

Once again AI reflected my own feelings on this. It conceded that all knowledge acquisition could be achieved anywhere, with an AI tutor, but that the essential human core to the setup would still require proximity, friction, and shared personal space with other people. To this end, it suggested that a campus of some sort be essential, as a space for high-fidelity human interaction.

However, at this point, we began to explore the idea that the space would look nothing like a current school: Less like a factory or office but more a mash-up of creative studios, university quads, community centres, and R&D labs. The 'Aletheia Campus' would include the following:

A core space – Where the learning pods would convene. They would be modular spaces, with wall space for writing down and sharing ideas, quiet spaces for small group work, and also a kitchenette area that would help the space feel more like a home. This area would be the 'mission control' for the long-term projects and the primary location to explore social-emotional learning.

Specialist space – Outside of these units, there would be specialist spaces such as labs and studios where large-scale physical creation could happen. Similar to the current Makerspace model, there would be access to digital tools such as 3D printers, VR and also manual, crafting materials for carpentry, pottery, sewing, and painting. This is where students can bring theory into practice.

Human space – The third component to the campus would be the spaces that emphasise the human core. There could be a circular space, similar to the amphitheatre and forums of old, designed to encourage debate and the location of the process defences mentioned earlier. There would also be a technology-free, well-being space where students could recharge, reflect, and counsel each other. There would be areas for social development, such as green space, wooded areas, and creative hubs such as theatre, libraries, and music studios. Spaces that remind everyone inside them that education is not preparation for life. It is life.

Early Years Paradise

A word for Early Years teachers, because this section is for you specifically, and because the Aletheia model might actually feel most natural in your setting of all. The learning environment for our youngest children wouldn't look dramatically different from those of today. The messy, play-led spaces and themed zones would still be hugely important in the new model of teaching and learning. What could be the case is that there would be a separation of two worlds within one. From a student perspective, the technology in the room remains the wood blocks, water trays, and paints.

What changes is invisible to the children. While a four-year-old is absorbed in building a tower or negotiating who gets the red spade, AI works quietly in the background: Observing, noting, and tracking the developmental moments that even the most attentive human eye can miss. It updates learning journeys. It maps the portfolio. It flags the child who has been playing alone for three days running.

This, of course, raises serious ethical questions about observation, data, and consent, questions that will need careful answers before any of this becomes reality. But the promise is significant: If AI can handle the clipboard, the Human Guide can put the clipboard down. They can get on the floor. They can play. They can be fully, completely present, which is, when you strip everything else away, exactly what a four-year-old needs most.

The Heart of the Community

Then there is the most radical idea of all, the one that reframes not just what a school looks like but what it is for.

The Aletheia campus has no gates. There isn't an administrative bottleneck at the front door, no checkpoint between the school and the street. The grounds are part of the curriculum, community gardens, sustainable food production, and solar panels that the students helped design and can explain to you. The wider community moves through the space. Local craftspeople, elders, experts, parents, they are not visitors. They are part of the learning.

If we are serious about returning to the apprenticeship model, about learning that happens in the world rather than away from it, then the school cannot be a walled garden. It has to be the heart of the village. Open, rooted, alive.

Some of this might sound idealistic, and at this moment in time, it is. If I had unlimited funds and political power, I would bulldoze the factory model tomorrow. For the moment, however, the reality is that most of us will wake up tomorrow and walk back into a traditional school building, governed by bells, silos, and standardised tests.

That said, nothing that I have mentioned above is out of our capabilities. A lot of what I have suggested doesn't need a dramatic leap in technological capabilities. It just requires some people to take the leap, and try it out. We might not be able to break down the physical boundaries of our education, but we can start chipping away at the pedagogical walls. We can design missions, not worksheets. We can use AI to lighten our workload so that we can spend more time with our students.

The school of tomorrow is not just a place we might build some time in the future. This is a choice we can start making in our classrooms today. If we are going to help ourselves and our students navigate the AI Generation, we have to put a halt to trying to 'out-compute' the machines and begin nurturing what makes us human.

Box 12.1 Key Takeaways from Chapter 12

Key Takeaways

- **The 'Factory Model' is Breaking:** We are at a crossroads. We can either retreat to tech-free sanctuaries, endure an exhausting 'hybrid' arms race where kids just use AI to do the AI-generated homework, or completely revolutionise our schools. The rise of autonomous AI 'agents' means the old conveyor belt of rigid timetables simply won't survive.
- **From Knowledge Gatekeepers to Human Guides:** If an AI can patiently deliver the perfect fractions lesson or explain a phonics rule, our role isn't diminished – it is elevated. We finally get the time to focus on what we actually came into the profession to do: Mentor, coach resilience, and manage the beautiful, messy social dynamics of growing children.
- **The End of the Standardised Test:** If a machine can pass the test in three seconds, the test is measuring the wrong thing. Future assessment won't be about silent rote recall; it will be about children proudly explaining their creative process, sharing their trail of AI prompts, and defending their messy, physical prototypes in front of their peers.

- **Tech-Rich Doesn't Mean Screen-Heavy:** For our youngest learners, the 'School of Tomorrow' will remain incredibly analogue – full of wooden blocks, mud kitchens, and paint. The AI will operate invisibly in the background, taking over the clipboard observations and endless admin, so Early Years teachers can actually just play and be present.
- **The Revolution Starts with Mindset, Not Architecture:** We don't need unlimited funds or a futuristic, wall-less campus to start changing things. We can start tomorrow morning in our traditional classrooms by designing collaborative 'missions' instead of isolated worksheets, and fiercely protecting the human connection at the heart of our teaching.

AI in Practice: A Prompt to Try

For this chapter, my suggested prompt is less about productivity in the classroom and more about using AI to spitball ideas. Considering all the hypothetical content I have discussed above, why not chat with an LLM about possible futures of schooling:

> *"You are an experienced educator and school leader, having worked as a leader in different settings and completed a PHD in school leadership. You are knowledgeable about PBL and the world of AI, having read works by [Insert authors]. Suggest a possible future roadmap for education, so that schools are better equipped to educate students in critical thinking, problem solving, self reflection."*

If you do use this prompt, please feel free to share it with me. I would love to hear from you.

Professional Development: Discussion Points

The content of this chapter is not about current pedagogy; it's about how the future of education could look. The following discussion questions will need time afforded to them, to dig deep into how you and your colleagues view the next steps. Allow a good chunk of time for group discussion, or even send them out before any arranged meeting, so that colleagues can put together their thoughts with more structure:

If we treat the brain like a muscle, what is the one 'difficult' task (like essay planning or mental maths) that you will insist your students still do 'the hard way,' simply because the struggle makes them stronger?

If AI eventually takes over the heavy lifting of lesson planning and marking, how will you use that freed-up time? What is the one 'Human Superpower' (like mentoring, listening, or debating) that you want to make the centre of your new role?

As the world becomes faster and more digital, what is the one 'slow,' 'messy,' or 'analogue' experience in your classroom that you will fiercely protect as a strictly AI-Free Zone?

Check Your Understanding

This chapter doesn't ask you to memorise facts; it asks you to examine assumptions. Take five minutes, ideally with a pen and paper rather than a screen, to respond honestly to the following:

Think about the classroom you walked into this week. Which elements of it belong to the factory model, the bells, the rows, the subject silos, the silent test? Now think about the moments in that same classroom that felt genuinely human, a conversation that surprised you, a child who made a connection you didn't expect, a moment of real collaboration.

Those human moments didn't happen because of the system. They happened despite it.

What is one thing you could protect, prioritise, or change, starting tomorrow, that would give those moments more room to breathe?

References

Fitzpatrick, D. (2025). *Infinite education: The four-step strategy for leading change in the age of artificial intelligence*. TeacherGoals Publishing.

Hale, R. (2025, October 16). *Jonathan Haidt is an icon in the parenting world. He says there's a new problem looming*. USA Today. www.usatoday.com/story/life/health-wellness/2025/10/16/jonathan-haidt-anxious-generation-ai-tech-new-advice/86610638007/

Karabinos, M. (2026). *Response to author survey*. Unpublished raw data.

Khan, S. (2024). *Brave new words: How AI will revolutionize education (and why that's a good thing)*. Viking.

Mollick, E. (2023, July 1). *The Homework Apocalypse*. One Useful Thing. www.oneusefulthing.org/p/the-homework-apocalypse

Stanton, A. (Director). (2008). *Wall-E* [Film]. Pixar Animation Studios; Walt Disney Pictures.

Tomasev, N., et al. (2026, February 12). Intelligent AI delegation. arXiv. https://arxiv.org/abs/2602.11865
Vygotsky, L. S. (1978). *Mind in society: The development of higher psychological processes*. Harvard University Press.

Further Reading

Kurzweil, R. (2024). *The singularity is nearer: When we merge with AI*. Viking.
Susskind, R. (2025). *How to think about AI: A guide for the perplexed*. Oxford University Press.
Tegmark, M. (2017). *Life 3.0: Being human in the age of artificial intelligence*. Knopf.

Epilogue: From Panic to Purpose

As we come to the end of this journey, let us join our three teachers once more. It is Friday afternoon, 4 pm. The school is empty, quiet, and the only sound that can be heard is the floor buffer humming in the hall. In the staffroom, the kettle has just boiled.

Elena is packing her bag, ready to go home. She has already finished her weekly parent emails, drafted by AI in three minutes, and she is looking forward to a weekend of brisk, cold walks with her family and time spent lounging with a well-earned drink in hand. Chloe is sat on the sofa, scrolling through a list of AI-generated lesson hooks for Monday's science lesson. Jim? He is putting his coat on. For once, he isn't struggling with a stack of exercise books to mark. He isn't stressed about writing a differentiated text for struggling readers, because that is already printed and ready, on his desk. He is leaving on time.

Jim: Right I'm off. If the robots take over this weekend, tell them they are leading the assembly on Monday.

Chloe: Have a good weekend, Jim

Elena: Wait, you're leaving now? I thought you had that display to finish?

Jim: I have turned it into a project. The kids are building it themselves on Monday morning. AI planned the curriculum links, but I'm leaving the fun and mess to the children. See you both next week.

Jim leaves the room, not as a teacher who has been replaced by AI, but as a teacher who has used a machine to reclaim his weekend, his energy, and his profession.

When you opened this book, you may have felt a bit like Jim did. The headlines were hard to miss; the age of the human teacher is over, the 'homework apocalypse' has arrived. The message was clear; students are going to stop thinking. It is completely normal to be defensive when faced with something that threatens all that we hold dear about schooling and our roles as teachers.

Over these chapters, we have pulled back the curtain. We have stopped treating AI as a magic, abstract entity, the elephant in the room, and just another piece of edtech to add to the list of failed innovations. We have realised that AI isn't a sentient brain coming for our jobs; it is a probabilistic engine. It doesn't 'know' facts; it just spots patterns.

As we progressed, we discussed how we didn't need to rip up and throw away our degrees, or abandon the pedagogy that has underpinned our teaching methods for decades. We discovered that if an AI tool can write a perfect essay in seconds, then we need to turn our assessment on its head, looking at process not product. We are teaching students to be Truth Detectives. We are the Editors-in-Chief.

Most importantly, we have reframed AI from being a threat to an equity lever. We can see how it can be a 'wheelchair ramp' for a child whose brilliant ideas are trapped by poor reading or handwriting. Live translation can turn a terrified child, fresh off the plane, feel immediately part of the class and the lesson. Their parents can turn up at the school gate as a confident partner in their child's education.

As we look to the future, whether that is a wall-free, learning community such as the Aletheia campus, or just a standard primary school classroom next Tuesday, one truth remains absolute. The more automated the world becomes, the more valuable the un-automatable, human skills become.

AI is amazing. It is life-changing and can provide 'wow' moments on a regular basis. We can create funny images and brand new songs or turn our homework policies into a rap. But the algorithm cannot comfort a child who misses their mum. It cannot manage the delicate, essential social friction of a group project falling apart. It cannot look a struggling student in the eye and say, 'I know this is hard, but I believe in you.'

If you take nothing else away from this book, remember that you are the most important thing in the classroom. Feel empowered to start the revolution, introduce your students and colleagues to 'you 2.0.' You have the same values, personality, and dress sense, but you have outsourced the 2D, heavy lifting to AI, allowing you to buy back time and emotional bandwidth. Take that time and renewed energy, get back down on the carpet and do the messy, strictly 3D work of teaching.

Glossary

1. The AI Fundamentals: From Inputs to Outputs

- **Artificial Intelligence (AI):** Machine-based systems designed to simulate human-like cognitive functions (e.g. pattern recognition, prediction).
- **Generative AI (GenAI):** A subset of AI that uses probabilistic modelling to create *new* content (text, image, audio) rather than just retrieving existing data.
- **Large Language Model (LLM):** The engine behind tools like ChatGPT; trained on massive datasets to predict the next likely word in a sequence.
- **Algorithm:** A set of rules or instructions followed by a computer to solve a problem.
- **Training Data:** The 'textbook' for the AI; the vast datasets (scraped from the web) used to teach the model patterns.
- **Data Scraping:** The automated harvesting of internet content to build training sets – raising significant questions about **Human Authorship** and copyright.
- **Machine Learning (ML):** The process by which systems improve their performance on a task by identifying patterns in data without being explicitly programmed for every outcome.
- **Transformer:** The architectural breakthrough in AI that allows models to weight the importance of different parts of an input (the 'Attention' mechanism).
- **Hallucination (Confident Nonsense):** When an AI generates factually incorrect information but presents it with absolute linguistic authority.
- **Prompt / Prompt Engineering:** The specific instructions (the 'Input') given to an AI. Professional practice often uses the **PREP Framework** (Position, Request, Expanse, Parameters).

2. Cognitive Science & Learning Theory

How AI interacts with the biological reality of the classroom.

- **Cognitive Offloading:** Delegating 'low-level' mental tasks (e.g. summarising) to a tool to free up 'bandwidth' for higher-order thinking.

- **Cognitive Replacement:** The risk of a student bypassing the 'mental struggle' entirely, leading to **De-skilling.**
- **Desirable Difficulty:** A concept from Robert Bjork; the 'friction' required during learning to ensure long-term retention. AI risks removing this friction.
- **Neuroplasticity:** The brain's ability to rewire itself. In primary education, we must ensure AI interactions don't negatively 'wire' a child's **Cognitive Patience.**
- **Deep Reading:** The ability to engage with complex, long-form text. The 'skimming' nature of AI interactions can erode this.
- **Bloom's Taxonomy:** A hierarchy of learning objectives. We use this to distinguish between AI handling 'Remembering/Understanding' while humans focus on 'Evaluating/Creating.'
- **Metacognition:** 'Thinking about thinking.' Vital for students to monitor their own reliance on AI tools.
- **Social Friction:** (Add to Section II) The messy, essential challenges of human interaction (negotiating, disagreeing) that endlessly patient AI cannot replicate.
- **Zone of Proximal Development (ZPD):** The 'sweet spot' of learning. AI can act as a scaffold to keep a student within their ZPD.

3. Ethical Foundations: Bias, Privacy, & Representation

- **Algorithmic Bias:** When an AI produces prejudiced results because its training data reflects societal inequalities (e.g. gender or racial stereotyping).
- **The Coded Gaze:** A term coined by Dr. Joy Buolamwini describing how the priorities and blind spots of developers are baked into software. For example, her research found that commercial facial recognition AI had a maximum error rate of just **0.8%** for lighter-skinned men, but an error rate of up to **34.7%** for darker-skinned women, proving that algorithms can mathematically scale racial and gender discrimination.
- **Anthropomorphism:** The tendency to attribute human traits (feelings, friendship) to AI. A significant risk for children who may see a chatbot as a 'friend.'
- **Digital Fair Trade:** Considering the ethical conditions of the 'invisible' workforce (**Data Labelers**) who 'clean' AI data in the Global South.

- **Anonymisation:** Removing **Personally Identifiable Information (PII)** before using AI tools to comply with **GDPR** or **FERPA**.
- **EU AI Act:** The world's first comprehensive legal framework for AI, classifying educational AI as 'High-Risk.'

4. Pedagogical Frameworks & Strategies

- **The 4As Model:** A workflow for student AI use: **Ask** (the prompt), **Adapt** (the output), **Author** (the human layer), **Analyse** (the critique).
- **H-AI-H (The Sandwich Model): Human** Inquiry → **AI** Generation → **Human** Reflection.
- **TPACK:** The intersection of **T**echnological, **P**edagogical, **A**nd **C**ontent **K**nowledge.
- **Unplugged Learning:** Teaching AI concepts (like algorithms or **Sensors vs. Senses**) through physical movement, role-play, and paper-based tasks.
- **Oracy:** The focus on spoken language and debate as a way to 'AI-proof' assessment and ensure **Human Agency**.
- **Process over Product:** Shifting assessment to focus on *how* a child learned rather than just the final (potentially AI-generated) essay.
- **The Aletheia Model:** The proposed human-centred vision of future schooling built around multi-age learning pods, mission-based curricula, and portfolio assessment, rather than age-restricted factory-model cohorts.

5. Safeguarding & Digital Citizenship

- **Synthetic Media (Deepfakes):** AI-generated images or audio that look/sound real. This leads to **Synthetic Abuse** (e.g. **Nudify apps**).
- **CSAM:** Child Sexual Abuse Material. A primary concern for **DSLs** (Designated Safeguarding Leads) when dealing with AI-generated content.
- **Attention Economy:** The business model of tech companies designed to keep children 'hooked' to screens via algorithms.
- **Digital Nutrition:** Teaching children to balance their 'digital diet' – distinguishing between 'junk' consumption and 'nutritious' creation.
- **KCSIE:** 'Keeping Children Safe in Education' – the statutory UK guidance that now must account for AI-driven risks.

6. The Technical-Educational Bridge

- **Deterministic vs. Probabilistic:** A calculator is *deterministic* (5+5 is always 10). AI is *probabilistic* (it guesses the most likely next word).
- **Human-in-the-Loop:** A requirement that a qualified human vets and takes responsibility for any AI output before it reaches a student.
- **Wrapper Sites:** Simple websites that 'wrap' around a complex model like GPT-4 to make it look child-friendly, but often lack robust safety filters.
- **Theory of Mind:** The psychological stage where a child realises others have different thoughts. AI can confuse this if children think the machine 'thinks.'
- **Spiral Curriculum:** A curriculum that returns to themes (like AI Ethics) with increasing complexity across **EYFS, KS1, and KS2**.

Index

Note: Page locators in **bold** and *italics* represents tables and figures, respectively.

www.ingramcontent.com/pod-product-compliance
Lightning Source LLC
LaVergne TN
LVHW060416030926
846999LV00034B/454
* 9 7 8 1 0 4 1 2 4 1 4 9 2 *